COMPREHENSION EXERCISES FOR SELECTIVE SCHOOLS TESTS AND SCHOLARSHIP EXAMINATIONS.

Contents Part A

LARGE PAINTINGS AND LARGER ARTISTS

EXERCISE 1

Since 1997, the two artists, Vitaly Komar and Alexander Melamid, have been teaching elephants to paint with their trunks, and The Museum of Contemporary Art in Sydney is proud to be able to bring you an exhibition of their work. Yes it's true, elephants are able to create colourful abstract artworks that are promoted and distributed by the Asian Elephant Art and Conservation Project. The aim of the project instigators is to raise awareness of the plight of the Asian elephant whose numbers are steadily declining in countries such as Thailand, India and Indonesia. Destruction of habitat, civil unrest and a ban on teak logging in many countries, together with government indifference has put many of the elephants and their mahouts out of work. The situation is perilous and funds are urgently needed for elephant conservation.

At the conclusion of the exhibition at the Museum, paintings by the elephants will be available for sale in an on-line auction accessible through the World Wide Fund for Nature (WWF) website, with the money going to elephant conservation across the Asia-Pacific region.

Included in the exhibition area will be a resource room providing information and background on the careers of Komar and Melamid, as well as never-before-seen footage of Asian elephants learning to paint and interviews with supporters of the project, courtesy of the sponsor, Animal Planet.

1 The kind of painting that the elephants have been able to learn produces
- **A** realistic landscapes.
- **B** colourful but formless paintings.
- **C** photographic masterpieces.
- **D** artworks similar to kindergarten children.

2 The numbers of elephants have been steadily declining because of
- **A** the cessation of teak logging.
- **B** destruction of wild living areas.
- **C** lack of government action.
- **D** All of the above.

3 It is hoped the paintings will raise much-needed funds by means of
- **A** sale of paintings at the Museum.
- **B** the production of a video.
- **C** combining with the firm, Animal Planet.
- **D** sale over the internet.

4 Visitors to the exhibition will be treated to
- **A** a spectacular demonstration.
- **B** a rare insight into the training methods employed.
- **C** an informative lecture by the artists.
- **D** a free tour of the exhibition.

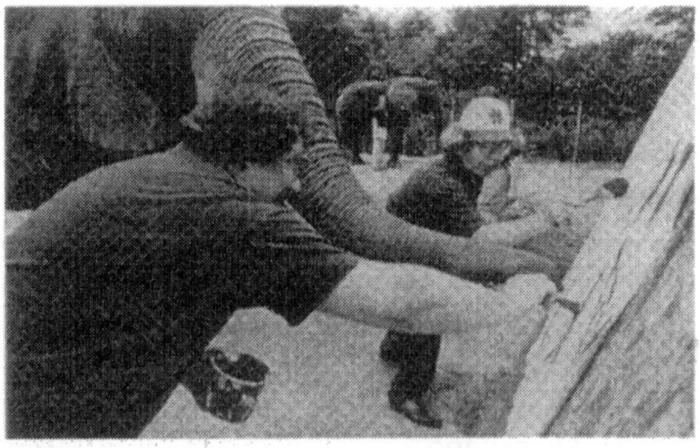

The artists at work

5 In Sydney the exhibition is sponsored by
- **A** Animal Planet.
- **B** the Museum of Contemporary Art.
- **C** Komar and Melamid.
- **D** the WWF.

6 The word 'plight' means
- **A** need for conservation.
- **B** sorry condition.
- **C** uselessness.
- **D** home.

7 From the passage , a mahout is likely to be
- **A** a variety of wood.
- **B** a forest worker.
- **C** an elephant controller.
- **D** a forest conservationist.

LARGE HOLES FROM SMALL DIGGERS

EXERCISE 2

I am a solitary animal, about 15 cm long with a dark velvety coat, long pink snout, whiskers, small weak eyes, sharp teeth, and huge turned out front feet. I'm a mole, that's me. Oh, and I have a tail that I use to guide me when I'm underground, which is where I spend most of my time.

I spend about half of my day looking for food, mainly worms though I am partial to the odd cricket and beetle (black ones are best). If I am lucky and my tunnels are located in a good worm area, all I have to do is collect them as they drop in. Forest glades and soft grassy paddocks are best and if there are too many for me to eat, why, I just nip off their heads and store them in a side tunnel for later.

Talking of tunnels, I'm a good tunneller. My tunnels are shallow and quite long with many side tunnels. I have to dig the side tunnels so I can get rid of the dirt from the main tunnels. I push the dirt up these smaller tunnels to the surface to make small hills. (Perhaps you've heard about them.) When digging my tunnels I use my front paws together as if I was doing the breaststroke. Then I push the dirt down one side while I grip the walls with the strong claws of my back feet. When my tunnel is finished I can tear along it, if I have to, at a speed of about 5 kilometres an hour. I use my sensitive snout and tail for guidance then, because it is quite dark underground, which is why of course I don't like strong daylight very much.

My wife builds a nest in one of the high molehills that I have constructed above water level – I call it the fortress because it is much larger than the others, but it is possible to escape from it in an emergency. Our babies are pink and naked when they are born and we feed them for about 5 or 6 weeks, then they are on their own. They go off exploring of course, and I'm afraid that is when a lot of them get caught by foxes and owls – usually we are quite safe underground.

8 **Moles are generally found**
- A in small groups.
- B singly or in pairs.
- C in large colonies.
- D travelling in daylight.

9 **Soldiers generally march about one kilometre every 12 minutes. Is a mole**
- A faster?
- B slower?
- C about the same?
- D much slower?

10 **The breeding nest is dry during heavy rain because**
- A it is below the ground.
- B it is built like a fortress.
- C it has thick walls.
- D it has good drainage.

11 **All moles have**
- A exceptionally strong eyesight for underground vision.
- B weak vision and sensitive eyes.
- C a method of communicating using vibrations when in danger.
- D a fondness for soft grass and decomposing leaves.

12 **The 'molehills' that we have all heard of are made**
- A as a defence mechanism.
- B to get rid of excavated material.
- C to attract ground insects.
- D to let in oxygen

13 **The words 'partial to' in the passage mean**
- A a portion or piece of.
- B repelled by.
- C used to.
- D fond of.

The mole is seldom seen above ground.

GLACIER

EXERCISE 3

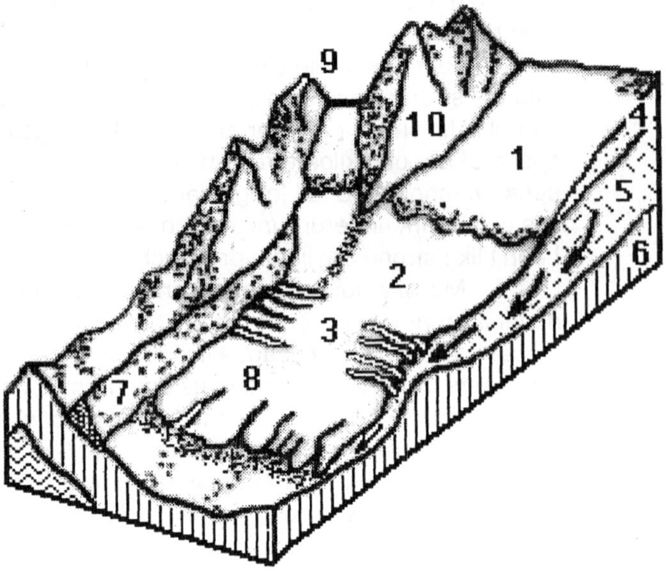

Key to Diagram

1 Snow Field accumulation zone where new snow is converted into ice.
2 Ablation zone where meltwater runs beneath the ice mass.
3 Crevasse area.
4 New ice.
5 Direction of ice flow.
6 Underlying bedrock.
7 Lateral moraine made of rock carried along by the glacier.
8 The toe or snout of the glacier.
9 Sharp pyramidal peak.
10 Truncated spur cut by glacier.

Use the diagram given to complete the following sentences:

14 The crevasses occur
- **A** where the new ice changes to old ice.
- **B** where the underlying bedrock causes a change in slope.
- **C** where the toe of the glacier retreats.
- **D** because of the lateral moraine.

15 The moving ice has the power to
- **A** move rock.
- **B** form sharp peaks.
- **C** cut through mountain ridges.
- **D** All of the above.

16 Because of the position of the lateral moraine and the toe of the glacier, it would seem that the glacier has been
- **A** advancing.
- **B** retreating.
- **C** stationary.
- **D** progressing.

17 From the diagram, meltwater streams would occur
- **A** on the ice field.
- **B** below the old ice above the bedrock.
- **C** in the crevasses.
- **D** along the moraine.

18 The word 'truncated' means
- **A** broken.
- **B** shortened.
- **C** elongated.
- **D** softened.

19 A moraine is
- **A** rock debris.
- **B** meltwater.
- **C** a dammed lake.
- **D** softer snow.

20 For glaciers to form there must be
- **A** many crevasses.
- **B** hard rock moraines.
- **C** ice lakes.
- **D** snow fields.

21 Glacial ice
- **A** moves laterally.
- **B** remains stationary.
- **C** moves downslope.
- **D** moves upslope.

GRIZZLY

EXERCISE 4

The grizzly bear is the dominant animal in the Rockies. However, popular conception of the habits and disposition of this impressive animal is generally inaccurate. Not a marauding, great hunter, the grizzly's diet is 90% vegetarian. Much of the meat it does eat is carrion, or kills 'strong-armed' from other animals. Although the grizzly has no natural enemies, it shuns others of its kind and is largely reclusive. It is easily distinguishable from the other bear of the Canadian Rockies, the black bear, by its distinctive shape.

The grizzly spends almost every waking moment in quest for food to tide it over the winter months. Berries, roots, herbs and the occasional rodent comprise the bulk of its diet.

The grizzly passes most of the winter in a state of dormancy. It digs a den in a steep hillside on a north-east-facing slope in the alpine ecoregion, where deep snow provides insulation. No food is cached in the den. Instead the grizzly lives off the fat gained in the previous summer and autumn. During denning, the grizzly's body temperature drops a few degrees and respiration subsides to 2-4 breaths a minute.

Because their behaviour is unpredictable, all bears are dangerous. Typically a bear will be more concerned with avoiding you than you are with avoiding it. However when a bear has learned to associate humans with easily obtained food, perceives a threat to its young or to a nearby food source, or is suddenly surprised on a trail, it may stand its ground and in some cases become aggressive. **{From Canadian Rockies SuperGuide by Graeme Pole)**

22 Despite what many people think, the grizzly
- **A** is an extremely aggressive animal.
- **B** has a great liking for fresh meat.
- **C** is a great, marauding hunter.
- **D** does not kill much of its own food.

23 The word in the passage that means that the grizzly is a solitary animal is
- **A** disposition .
- **B** unpredictable.
- **C** aggressive.
- **D** reclusive.

24 During the winter the grizzly
- **A** hibernates.
- **B** consumes large quantities of fat.
- **C** becomes aggressive.
- **D** looks for food around humans.

25 When a grizzly is confronted by a human
- **A** one cannot be sure what it will do.
- **B** its natural inclination is to attack.
- **C** it will associate the human with food and approach.
- **D** it will normally try to escape.

26 The grizzly's most constant activity is
- **A** denning.
- **B** searching for food.
- **C** dormancy.
- **D** marauding.

27 The grizzly cannot be confused with the black bear because of
- **A** its smaller body and pointed nose.
- **B** its larger body and humped back.
- **C** its pointed nose and longer tail.
- **D** its more aggressive behaviour.

28 In the passage the word 'strong-armed' means
- **A** stolen.
- **B** naturally.
- **C** found.
- **D** stored.

BIG ISN'T NECESSARILY BETTER

EXERCISE 5

Size is possibly the single most significant aspect of an animal's makeup. While humans instinctively associate large size with strength and resilience, the simple truth is that large size is a very risky card to play in the game of life. In the long run, few strategies are less likely to succeed. A truth well evidenced by the scarcity of big species alive in the world today. In modern Australia, for example, not a single land-living native species is larger than our own human species. In short, the aura of invincibility that surrounds giants is a sham. Low population sizes and reproductive potentials that typify large species leave them particularly vulnerable to the vagaries of an ever-changing planet.

However it is clear that there have been times when being big was not as peculiar as it is today. The age of dinosaurs is an obvious example. We don't have to go back 65 million years to find an abundance of giants in the fossil record. For most of the past 2 million years (the Ice Ages), the world has been dominated by conspicuous giants, most of them mammals. These have included high-profile behemoths – such as the woolly mammoth and sabre-toothed tiger on other continents – and the marsupial lion and rhino-sized Diprotodon here in Australia.

Collectively these are called megafauna and they must have been a wondrous sight to behold. Unfortunately over the last 100 000 years the world has been rocked by waves of selective extinction that have ruthlessly squeezed dozens of species weighing more than 45 kg into oblivion. This process devastated the megafauna of some land-masses more than others. Australia was hit hard.

Two major aspects of this mega-whodunnit are climate and humans. Cycles of aridity beginning at least 70 000 years ago culminated in the Last Glacial Maximum (Ice Age) about 20 000 years ago. In Australia this period was hellishly arid, with as much as 80 percent of Australia laid waste by vast, irrepressible sand dunes.

As for humans, the other possible culprit, many advocate a hypothesis widely known as "blitzkrieg", the notion being that when Ice Age humans invaded pristine environments they violently and almost instantaneously eliminated all species exceeding 44 kg.

(**From an article by Stephen Wroe and Judith Field.**)

The Diprotodon

29 The most important part of an animal's makeup is

A its skin. B its size.
C its defence. D its resilience.

30 In Australia during the last Ice Age, Australia became progressively

A wetter and colder. B drier and colder.
C wetter and warmer. D drier and warmer.

31 The last Ice Age occurred about

A 20 000 years ago. B 200 000 years ago.
C 2 million years ago. D 65 million years ago.

32 The two most popular reasons advanced for the extinction of large species are

A size and human interference. B human interference and low population.
C low population and reproductive rates. D climate change and human interference.

33 The 'blitzkrieg' concept says that
- **A** warfare caused the extinction of species.
- **B** mankind quickly wiped out many species.
- **C** climate changed too quickly for many animals to adapt.
- **D** many of the species were carnivorous and killed each other out.

34 The authors believe that these days being a large animal is
- **A** a recipe for disaster.
- **B** the most efficient way to survive.
- **C** an easy alternative.
- **D** better than being small.

35 Whales, elephants and rhinosceros are modern day examples of
- **A** multifauna
- **B** megafauna.
- **C** megaflora.
- **D** multiflora.

Choose the meaning which most closely matches with each of the following words from the text:

36 pristine. **A** clean **B** clear **C** ancient and unchanged **D** conserved

37 oblivion. **A** anxious **B** compression **C** most suitable **D** extinction

38 vagaries **A** unpredictable changes **B** strange motions **C** susceptible to injury **D** strength

39 behemoth **A** something unstoppable **B** a huge creature **C** easily seen **D** easily recognised

READING TEST 1 — THE WIND IN A FROLIC

EXERCISE 6

The wind one morning sprang up from sleep.
Saying. "Now, for a frolic! Now for a leap!
Now for a madcap, galloping chase!
I'll make a commotion in every place!"
So it swept with a bustle right through a great town,
Cracking the signs and scattering down
Shutters and whisking with merciless squalls
Old women's bonnets and gingerbread stalls.
Through forest it roared, and cried gaily , "Now
You sturdy old oaks I'll make you bow!"
And it made them bow without more ado,
For it cracked their great branches through and through.
Then it rushed like a monster on cottage and farm,
Striking their dwellers with sudden alarm,
And they ran out like bees in midsummer swarm;
There were dames with their kerchiefs tied over their caps
To see if the poultry were free from mishaps.

William Howitt

40 What time of day was it when the wind began to blow?
- **A** Early morning.
- **B** Mid morning.
- **C** Noon.
- **D** Evening.

41 To what does the poet liken the wind?
- **A** A squall.
- **B** A swarm of bees.
- **C** A monster.
- **D** A young man.

42 The oaks were sturdy. This meant they were
- **A** vigorous.
- **B** lively.
- **C** dense.
- **D** robust.

43 In the poem 'merciless squalls' means
- **A** frightening wind.
- **B** cruel gusts of wind.
- **C** dreadful mishaps.
- **D** moaning wind.

44 How did the women keep their caps on?
- **A** They held onto them.
- **B** They tied them down with string.
- **C** They secured them with their handkerchiefs.
- **D** They rushed inside.

PLAN AHEAD

EXERCISE 7

By PATRICIA JONES .

Citizens or permanent residents of the United States and Canada usually can cross the U.S./Canada borders without serious customs delays, but it's worth keeping a few things in mind.

In general, a driver's license is sufficient identification for adults who are U.S. or Canadian citizens. Canadian Customs officials however do suggest travellers also carry proof of citizenship, which could be either a birth certificate, a passport or naturalization papers. Passports and visas are not required by travellers, however non-citizens should have their Alien Registration Receipt Card or Landed Immigrant Visa. Naturalized citizens should carry a naturalization card or some other evidence of citizenship.

Adults travelling with children should bring the youngsters' birth certificates. In the case of a single parent or grandparents travelling with children, a notarised permission slip from absent parents may be necessary. This policy reflects heightened attention given to missing children, according to U.S. Immigration Inspectors.

Travellers with a criminal history, including drunken driving offences, are advised to call Canadian Customs (867) 862-7230, in advance of attempting to cross the border. Even offences that occurred 20 years ago may create problems at Canadian border crossings. Special permission must be obtained for travellers previously convicted and the lengthy process costs $200. Canadian Customs officials also check the amount of cash carried by travellers, to make sure enough funds are available to cover an urgent situation in that country. About $800 per person is required, or to be able to access that much money via credit card or bank debit card.

Pets travelling across the border should be accompanied with a rabies vaccination certificate signed by a licensed veterinarian. Firearms must be declared at U.S. border offices and certain types are restricted in Canada, including handguns, automatic weapons and some semi-automatic weapons. The spray, Mace, is also considered a weapon and is prohibited, unless the canister specifically identifies the chemical as a wild animal defence mechanism.

Both U.S. and Canadian customs stations on the Alaska Canada Highway are open 24 hours a day.

45 Overseas travellers going from the United States to Canada

- **A** do not require a passport or visa.
- **B** require a passport and visa.
- **C** must carry proof of citizenship.
- **D** require an Alien Registration Card or immigrant visa.

46 Single parents travelling with children should have a notarised permission slip from the other parent,

- **A** because they are too young to have a passport.
- **B** most parents forget these things.
- **C** because plane travel can be dangerous.
- **D** the children may be being abducted.

47 Pets

- **A** can be taken into Canada or the United States.
- **B** can only be taken to Canada.
- **C** have conditions attached to their entry.
- **D** can only be taken in by a licensed veterinarian.

48 When entering the United States, firearms and other weapons

- **A** must be declared.
- **B** are usually prohibited.
- **C** must be placed in a special canister.
- **D** must be left at the border and retrieved later.

49 Travellers to Canada must carry cash or credit cards

- **A** as evidence of good faith.
- **B** to spend in duty free shops.
- **C** in case of emergencies.
- **D** in order to gain a work permit.

50 It is likely that the article was written by

- **A** a customs or immigration officer.
- **B** a newspaper reporter.
- **C** someone who has had trouble crossing.
- **D** an airline official.

PANDORA'S BOX

EXERCISE 1

Hephaestus the god of fire, was also a blacksmith and one day he decided to make a metal statue of a woman in his forge. The statue was so beautiful that Zeus, the father of the gods, decided to give her life. All the other gods had to follow Zeus' example and showered gifts upon her. To her beauty was added grace, intelligence, skill, wit and persuasiveness. This was Pandora. But Hermes and Hera were more than a little jealous that a mere statue should be given life and made to be so like the gods, so Hermes also gave Pandora the gifts of cunning and falsehood while Hera gave her curiosity; curiosity that would never let her rest. After a while Pandora married Epimethus, and Zeus gave the happy couple a lovely box decorated with precious stones and gold. The box was locked but Zeus gave Pandora the key – he added the warning that if Pandora wished to remain happy with her husband, she must never open the box.

For a while Pandora lived quietly and happily with Epimetheus, but finally the curiosity that Hera had made part of her character became too strong. With great excitement she opened the box, but to her despair out flew all the miseries and misfortunes that have afflicted mankind ever since: dishonesty, unkindness, pain, disease and a thousand other evils. Hurriedly Pandora tried to close the box but she was too late. Fortunately one last apparition escaped just as she closed the lid. This was Hope, and Hope has enabled people ever since to bear the ills that befall the human race.

This of course is a story, but even today you will hear people say things like "If you do such and such, you will open a Pandora's box of trouble." By this they mean that curiosity is not always a good thing because we sometimes uncover things that are unpleasant when we investigate too much.

Pandora had to pay dearly for the gifts given to her by the gods. Here she is shown being moulded in the forge by the servants of Hephaestus.

1 Why did the other gods give Pandora so many gifts?
- **A** They had to follow the lead of Hephaestus.
- **B** They thought that Zeus would expect them to.
- **C** Pandora would not be complete without them.
- **D** They thought she was beautiful too.

2 Why were Hermes and Hera upset about Pandora?
- **A** The other gods gave better gifts.
- **B** They wanted a statue for themselves.
- **C** They were just naturally jealous gods.
- **D** They thought she should not have god-like powers.

3 What happened when the box was opened?
- **A** All the ills that have plagued mankind flew out.
- **B** Pandora was dismayed.
- **C** She tried to close the box but it was too late.
- **D** All of the preceding.

4 Zeus knew that Pandora would open the box, so how did he compensate mankind for the evils?
- **A** He gave Pandora the opportunity to become a statue again.
- **B** Most of the ills were easily caught.
- **C** He gave mankind Hope to overcome disaster.
- **D** He punished the other gods.

5 What has 'opening a Pandora's box' come to mean?
- **A** Curiosity can sometimes be a good thing.
- **B** There is always hope for the future.
- **C** Never put things off into the future.
- **D** Sometimes we can uncover more than we really bargain for.

BUYING A HOUSE

EXERCISE 2

What a person earns annually is of prime importance when applying for a housing loan. At the bank, building society, or other lending body, an officer will assess whether you will be able to make the necessary repayments.

A new home may be purchased at any stage of its construction, usually through an estate agent. An older house is worth considering because, with the help of qualified tradesmen, these can be restored to your own requirements and budget.

It is usually your solicitor who negotiates with the vendor for the settlement of the purchase of a property to take place. The waiting period while these matters are being attended to, however, tries the patience of most homebuyers.

It is unwise to saddle yourself with a huge loan. It does not make good economic sense to be paying out large amounts of interest over long periods. Legal fees and stamp duty have to be taken into consideration. Most lending bodies have a system that allows for mortgage repayments to be taken directly from your bank account. In general it is best to choose a lending body that has a low rate of interest repayments. You will need a Justice of the Peace to witness any financial arrangements that you may make and most banks, building societies and estate agents offer this service.

6 **The fitness of a person applying for a housing loan is usually determined by**
- **A** his or her marital state.
- **B** the size of the deposit.
- **C** his or her annual income.
- **D** the rate of interest.

7 **A home can usually be purchased**
- **A** only when it has reached 'lock up' stage.
- **B** even though it is not fully completed.
- **C** when the Estate Agent receives his commission.
- **D** without using a solicitor.

8 **Purchasing an older home has a number of advantages.**
- **A** It is usually cheaper and it can be restored to your own specifications.
- **B** There are more of them on the market and they are in better areas.
- **C** Most are close to public transport and it is fun to restore.
- **D** There are no government charges and councils are keen to help.

9 **An official loan to buy a house is called a**
- **A** bank loan.
- **B** mortgage.
- **C** repayment schedule.
- **D** saddle.

10 **The government charge that has to be paid when buying a house is**
- **A** a mortgage.
- **B** solicitor's fees.
- **C** stamp duty.
- **D** witness fees.

11 **Where can you go to get your signature witnessed by a Justice of the Peace?**
- **A** A bank.
- **B** A building society.
- **C** An estate agent.
- **D** Any of the preceding.

EXERCISE 3 OLD SHELLOVER READING TEST 2

Old Shellover

'Come!' said Old Shellover.
'What?' says Creep.
'The horny old Gardener's fast asleep;
The fat cock Thrush
To his nest has gone;
And the dew shines bright
In the rising moon;
Old Sallie Worm from her hole doth peep:
Come!' said Old Shellover.
'Ay!' said Creep.

Walter de la Mare

12 **What does the poem describe?**
- **A** A conversation between a worm and a snail.
- **B** A conversation between a gardener and his friend.
- **C** A conversation between two worms.
- **D** A conversation between two snails.

13 **Why did Old Shellover think it time to go out?**
- **A** The gardener was asleep.
- **B** The thrush had retired for the night.
- **C** The dew was on the grass.
- **D** All of the preceding.

14 **How did Shellover know there was dew?**
- **A** It shone in the moonlight.
- **B** It was wet.
- **C** It was the right time.
- **D** Creep agreed to go with him.

READING TEST 2

THE CLIMATE OF MT ISA

EXERCISE 4

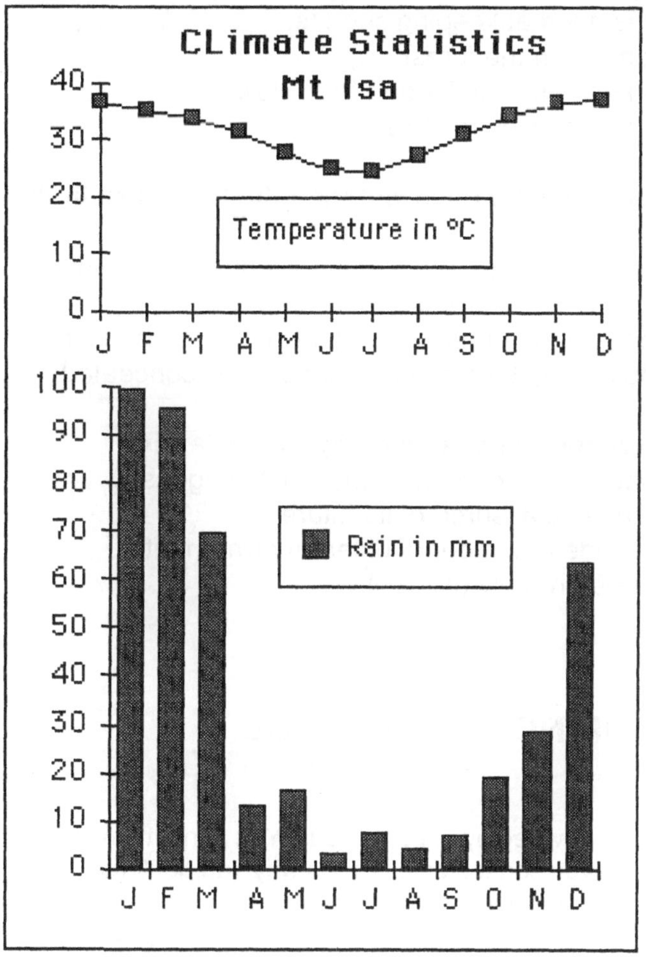

Use the statistics given to answer these questions about the climate of Mt Isa.

15 What is the coldest month of the year at Mt Isa?
A May. **B** September. **C** July. **D** June.

16 From the graph we can tell
A Mt Isa has a marked dry period.
B Mt Isa has a marked wet period.
C Mt Isa has both a wet and a dry period.
D Mt Isa has a uniform rainfall regime.

17 What is the approximate range of temperature in Mt Isa?
A 12°C **B** 15°C **C** 20°C **D** 23°C

18 The winter season in Mt Isa is
A cold, windy and wet conditions.
B mild with many sunny days.
C warm with many cloudy or rainy days.
D dry and cold.

19 In what hemisphere is Mt Isa located? How can we tell?
A In the southern hemisphere because autumn is in September.
B In the northern hemisphere because July is a cold month.
C In the southern hemisphere because December is hot.
D In the northern hemisphere because January is hot.

READING TEST 2 — TRACTOR

EXERCISE 5

Dragging an iron rake the tractor wallows
across the ocean of the paddock
with a fine excitement of gulls in its wake.
It has two large paddle wheels,
a funnel, with smoke;
and the captain is on the bridge.
Having cast off a couple of moments ago,
he sets a course for the opposite hedge.

William Hart-Smith

20 In the poem, the tractor is compared to
A a rake. **B** a ship.
C a paddle. **D** a wallow.

21 The captain on the bridge was really
A an engineer. **B** a navigator.
C a bird-trapper. **D** a farmer.

22 The birds were excited because
A they were sea birds and could see the ocean.
B the captain had cast off.
C they could find insects that had been disturbed in the 'wake'.
D the paddock was like an ocean.

THE RIFLE BIRD

EXERCISE 6

'Secretive' is perhaps the word
Best fitted to the Rifle Bird.
Its armaments to casual eyes
Seem lighter than the name implies
Savants to whom we have appealed
Assure us they are well concealed;
But records do not indicate a
Very happy wealth of data;
And scientists who've lain in wait
To watch it in its native state
Have not so much as caught an
eyeful
Of the furtive creature's rifle.

Leon Gellert.

23 The author thinks that 'secretive' is a good word to apply to the Rifle Bird because

A it is good at keeping secrets.
B it hides in the forest.
C it keeps its rifle hidden from view.
D it is a native creature.

24 Scientists who have watched the Rifle Bird in the forest

A have not seen much data to support their views.
B are unable to report any secret activity.
C have been unable to catch sight of the bird's rifle.
D assure us that they have been well concealed.

25 The weapons possessed by the Rifle Bird

A seem less than the name would suggest.
B make us assured of its future.
C include a number of different armaments.
D are extremely destructive.

READING TEST 2
EXERCISE 7

BELIEVE IT OR NOT - THE NOSE

You probably already know that the nose is an important organ of the body, but do you realise just how important? Here are some interesting facts about smell and taste.

Did you know that your sense of taste and smell are complementary? Its true, when your sense of smell is not working properly then you cannot taste as well. In fact a lot of what you taste when eating is really what you smell. When you have a heavy cold, the cell receptors for smell located on the surface of the inner nasal cavity are covered by extra mucous. You cannot smell and so you cannot taste. This is why you don't feel hungry when you have a cold.

Your nose is always adjusting to changes in the environment. Dust, germs, temperature, pollen, chemical smells, even spicy food can upset your nose. The nose tries to protect itself in these situations by shrinking or by manufacturing more mucous. Then we start to sniff and say we have an allergy.

26 The senses of taste and smell are said to be complementary because

A they are located adjacent to each other.
B they are connected to the brain along a common nerve channel.
C the operation of one affects the other.
D the nose reacts to a bad smell.

27 When your nose runs after eating a kind of food, we say that this is

A unfortunate. **B** unsatisfactory. **C** unlikely. **D** an allergic reaction.

28 The production of mucous during a cold

A acts to reduce your appetite.
B is a reaction to germs or viruses.
C stops the nasal receptors of smell from working properly.
D All of the preceding.

READING TEST 2

MURDER MOST FOUL

EXERCISE 8

Inspector Ferret looked around. On the table were two glasses, one with ice still in it. The window pane was broken and it was snowing lightly outside, but the room still felt warm. The body of Colonel Entwhistle was slumped forward over the desk clutching a pistol in his left hand. Next to his right hand was a cheque book in which there was an uncompleted cheque. There were two cigarette butts in the ashtray and ink stains on the Colonel's right index finger.

Ferret looked closely at the white shirt of the Colonel and observed black powder burns on it next to a red bloodstain on the left side over the heart. Next he sniffed and Ferret fancied that he could detect a faint aroma of perfume. Crossing to the window he looked out and saw broken glass lying on the lawn as if indicating the direction that the burglar had taken. On the far side of the lawn a gravel path led to the street. The safe door swung on its hinges and the safe was empty, but the safe door itself had not been forced. There was no key in evidence.

"Who found the body?" he asked.

"I did," replied the housekeeper, a young woman in her early twenties. " I heard a shot and came running in from the kitchen. The Colonel was slumped over the desk. I couldn't see anyone, but I was in time to hear someone running down the path on the other side of the lawn."

" Do you smoke by the way?" questioned Ferret.

"Of course not, sir," said the housekeeper angrily.

" Ah," said the Inspector with a grim smile, " Then I am afraid I must place you under arrest for the murder of Colonel Entwhistle. Now to find your accomplice," he added.

29 The inspector knew the murder had just been committed because

- **A** there were cigarette butts in the ashtray.
- **B** the safe door was open.
- **C** he could smell the faint scent of perfume.
- **D** the ice had not quite melted.

30 He knew that the Colonel had been shot at close range because

- **A** the glasses were still on the table.
- **B** the body was slumped over the desk.
- **C** only the blood was on the desk.
- **D** there were powder burns on the shirt.

31 The inspector knew that no-one had come in from outside because

- **A** the broken glass was on the lawn.
- **B** the room was still warm.
- **C** there was no gravel on the carpet.
- **D** the path was made of gravel.

32 The inspector knew it wasn't a case of suicide because

- **A** there were two glasses on the desk.
- **B** the gun had been fired.
- **C** the gun was in the Colonel's left hand.
- **D** there were butts in the ashtray.

33 Inspector Ferret knew that someone inside the house was guilty because

- **A** the maid said she heard the burglar running away.
- **B** the Colonel had just begun to write out a cheque.
- **C** the broken glass was only on the lawn.
- **D** Both 'A' and 'C'.

34 The inspector's smile was grim because

- **A** he knew that he would soon find the key to the safe.
- **B** he knew he was right but he was after all in the presence of a murderer.
- **C** it had only taken a short time to solve the case.
- **D** not all murder mysteries were as simple.

35 Inspector Ferret thought that

- **A** the housekeeper had acted alone.
- **B** it was likely that the maid had had someone to help her murder her employer.
- **C** it would be impossible to find the person who had helped the housekeeper.
- **D** he already knew who had helped the housekeeper.

LAND GRANT 1

EXERCISE 9

James Ruse

James Ruse was born in Cornwall in 1760. Although not a landowner himself, he was born of farming stock. When he was 22 years of age he was sentenced to 7 years transportation for stealing. Luckily for him, he escaped being sent to Africa where the life expectation for transported convicts was low. Instead, because the regular prisons were overflowing, he spent the first 5 years of his sentence on a prison hulk moored in the River Thames, before being sent to Australia with the First Fleet.

When the first group struggled ashore at Sydney Cove on 26th January 1788, Colonel Johnston of the New South Wales Corps claimed the distinction of being the first person to set foot in the new colony, but actually he was carried ashore on the back of convict James Ruse who really deserved the title of 'First in the Colony.'

James Ruse was destined for further fame. The early colony was desperately short of food and Governor Phillip, as an experiment, offered title to land to any person who could grow enough food to become independent of the Government Stores. James Ruse, who by this time had only one year left of his sentence to serve, asked the Governor for permission to try. On learning of Ruse's farming background Phillip was keen to allow him a chance, but there was one small problem. Phillip could not give a land grant to a convict and he had no way of knowing when Ruse's time would finish because there were no records sent with the convicts of the First Fleet. In the end Phillip promised Ruse that he would get his grant if, when his sentence had been served, he could prove that he was self-sufficient in food production.

Ruse was given land on the banks of a small creek, Clay Cliff Creek, which flowed into the Parramatta River. He was also given assistance in clearing the land, some seed and some basic tools for his task. Unlike the other convicts on the government farm that was nearer to the Parramatta River, Ruse, because he was working for himself, used his farming knowledge and cultivated the land well. Rather than just scratching the surface like the lazy workers at the nearby Government Farm, he turned the land over properly and added whatever fertilisers he could find. He was so successful that at one stage Ruse had cause to complain because the other convicts were stealing the food that he grew. He built a slab hut and within eighteen months he was able to announce to Governor Phillip that he was able to feed himself. Phillip was true to his word and gave Ruse 30 acres, Land Grant 1, the first in the colony.

It may seem strange that Ruse secured the first grant of land ahead of any of the 'free' men serving in the New South Wales Corps, but that is what happened. But the story of Ruse is not quite finished. Ruse married a young girl who had also just finished her sentence and so he became the first person in the colony to marry an emancipist. Together they worked day and night to improve the farm that became known as Experiment Farm. Ruse realised however that the land that he had been given was not nearly as good as other newly-found land to the west along the Hawkesbury River. In 1793 he sold Experiment Farm to Surgeon John Harris and moved to the Hawkesbury.

Ruse died in 1837 and was buried at Campbelltown. A character to the end, Ruse carved his own tombstone, leaving it to others to fill in the last important date upon it!

36 An emancipist was

A a convict who had escaped. B a supervisor of convicts.
C a convict who had served his/her sentence. D a convict farmer.

37 Ruse was given a land grant because

A he had previous experience. B he was a hard worker.
C he knew how to grow wheat. D he proved he could become self-sufficient.

38 What was Ruse's 'last important date'?

A 1760 B 1837 C 1788 D 1793

39 Phillip wanted to give out land grants

A to keep the convicts happy. B to make the job for the warders easier.
C to establish a storehouse. D because food was in short supply.

40 Phillip initially gave Ruse

A 11 acres. B 30 acres. C 300 acres. D 15 acres.

41 The farm became known as Experiment Farm because

A Ruse and his wife experimented with many different crops.
B it was a trial to see if anyone could become independent of the Government Store.
C Ruse used a lot of new methods when he was cultivating.
D Ruse added many new ingredients to the land.

42 Yields were low on the nearby Government Farm because

A the soils were poorer. B they were not near a reliable water supply.
C the convicts, not working for themselves, were lazy.
D they did not get the help that Ruse did.

44 We can assume that a prison hulk was

A an old ship that had been fitted out as a prison.
B the remains of an old stone prison .
C one of the ships of the First Fleet.
D the first prison to which all convicts were sent.

BELIEVE IT OR NOT – THE TONGUE

EXERCISE 10 **READING TEST 2**

How is it that a cold chilli can taste hot when you bite it? What happens when you taste a lemon? I'm glad you asked these important questions. The answers go like this. On the surface of the tongue, mostly towards the back, are a number of taste receptors, called taste buds. Their job is to sense information about what you are eating or drinking. Some detect heat, some detect cold, while others are responsible for sensing sweet and sour. Hot peppers and chillies have a chemical called capsaisin which is a weak acid that burns your skin. Presto, the receptors for heat and pain are turned on.

If you eat lemons, the sense of sourness causes the side of the mouth to contract, thus affecting the salivary glands located on each side of the mouth. More saliva is squeezed out which then dilutes the lemon juice. The juice tastes less sour.

45 The fact that a cold chilli can taste hot, on the face of it, seems

A an absurd statement. B an important question. C a sensitive statement. D a qualification.

46 The sourness of lemon juice

A is lessened by the production of extra saliva.
B causes an automatic response in the mouth.
C makes the salivary glands contract.
D All of the above.

EXERCISE 11 TEMPERATURE

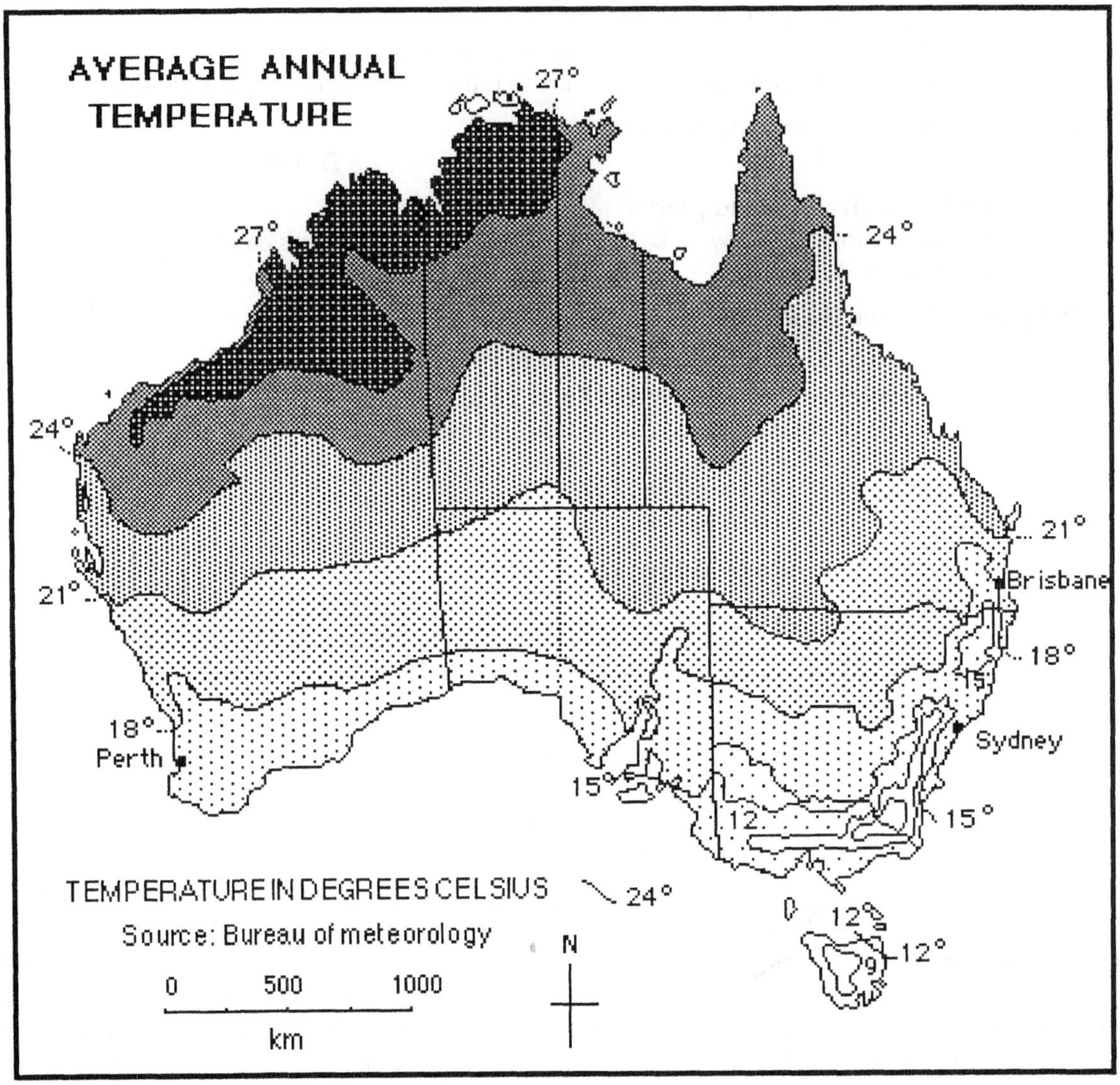

47 The hottest average temperatures are found in

A northern Australia. **B** north-western Australia. **C** central Australia. **D** eastern Australia.

48 The average temperature generally

A decreases from south to north. **B** increases from north to south
C decreases from north to south. **D** decreases from east to west.

49 The average annual temperature at Perth is between

A 6°-9° C. **B** 9°-12° C. **C** 12°-15° C. **D** 15°-18° C.

50 The temperature which Brisbane experiences is

A similar to that of Perth. **B** warmer than that of Sydney but not that of Perth.
C colder than Perth. **D** warmer than both Sydney and Perth.

READING TEST 3

NORFOLK ISLAND

EXERCISE 1

In 1814, the evacuation of the convict settlement at Norfolk Island, (begun just a few short weeks after the settlement at Sydney Cove), was complete. The forests on the island had been substantially cleared, and more than 200 farms for emancipated convicts whose time had elapsed, and free settlers had been established. All -- houses, farms and most livestock -- all were abandoned because large acres of arable land had been found on the mainland within easy reach of Sydney. The principal reasons for the establishment of the colony, the procurement of naval spars from the large pine trees growing in abundance and to make sail cloth from the native flax plant had not proved successful – the spars were brittle and easily snapped while no one knew how to process the strong flax fibres.

Before the unwilling inhabitants left for their new homes in Van Diemen's Land (Tasmania) the buildings of the island were knocked down to prevent their possible use by the French who were aware of the island's existence. For eleven years Norfolk Island was deserted except for occasional visits by whaling vessels taking on wood and water.

But then there was a reversal. A decision was made to re-settle the island as a prison for the most dangerous and desperate characters in New South Wales; "Capital Respite" convicts who had committed new offences while convicts, and been sentenced to death only to have their sentences commuted to life imprisonment. Earl Bathurst in England wrote to Governor Brisbane about the unlucky convicts saying "I wish it to be understood that no hope of any mitigation of their sentences should be held out to them, but if any convict should be withdrawn from Norfolk Island, it should only be after detention of ten years."

The Commandant was a cruel disciplinarian and so a tragic and horrible chapter in the history of penal settlement in Australia began. Located over 1500 kilometres from Sydney in the middle of the Pacific Ocean, surrounded by steep cliffs and with no safe anchorages, it was surely a case of 'Abandon hope all ye who enter here'.

1 In 1814, the convict settlement on Norfolk Island, was
- **A** dismantled.
- **B** renewed.
- **C** strengthened.
- **D** fortified.

2 'Capital Respites' were
- **A** convicts who had been pardoned.
- **B** convicts who had had their sentences reduced.
- **C** repeat offenders while still under sentence.
- **D** lazy convicts.

3 The second settlement at Norfolk was made to
- **A** accommodate the very worst offenders.
- **B** encourage free settlers once more to return .
- **C** frighten the other convicts.
- **D** repair the buildings that had previously been destroyed.

4 The houses and farms were destroyed
- **A** to prevent the convicts who had escaped from using them.
- **B** to render them useless to the French.
- **C** so that no one would be tempted to return to the island.
- **D** as there were no more trees left for building purposes.

5 In the passage, the word 'substantially' means
- **A** solidly.
- **B** hopelessly.
- **C** mostly.
- **D** most favoured.

6 The word 'mitigation' means
- **A** lessening.
- **B** anger.
- **C** reversal.
- **D** continuance.

7 Why was it a case of 'Abandon hope all ye who enter here' for convicts of the second settlement ?
- **A** The Commandant was particularly strict.
- **B** Norfolk was an isolated island with steep cliffs.
- **C** The minimum sentence was for 10 years .
- **D** All the above.

The precipitous West Coast with one of the famous Norfolk Island pine trees.

WILLIAM JAMES FARRER

EXERCISE 2

William James Farrer

William James Farrer is one of the most important persons in the history of Australia. Yet few people know about this quiet, unassuming man. Single-handedly, with great skill and foresight, painstaking research and long work hours, he was able to rescue the Australian wheat industry from collapse, and establish Australia as one of the great wheat-growing nations of the world.

Farrer was born on a farm near the town of Kendall in England in 1845. He was a sickly boy and wanted to be a doctor but because of a lung disease, it was recommended that he go to Australia where the climate was drier. He took a job at Duntroon (a famous country property occupied by the Australian Defence Academy today in Canberra) and saved up to buy a farm near Dubbo, New South Wales.

The wheat seeds that had been brought out from England by the early farmers were just not suitable for Australian conditions. They were unreliable. When rainfall was good the wheat plants were susceptible to a tiny insect called the rust parasite; in years of low rainfall, the crops were burnt off by drought. The wheat industry was facing complete disaster when Farrer decided to do something about the situation. Little did he guess that breeding of strains of wheat to combat both rust and drought was to be his life's work.

Farrer began by procuring wheat seeds from all over the world. He wrote to India, Egypt, Canada and the United States asking for seeds. He treasured the seeds and planted them. Year after year, he patiently crossed hundreds of varieties of wheat, each time keeping the seeds of the best plants to grow again the following year. His notebooks were his computer and in them he recorded the life cycle of every seed planted; where it came from, where it had been planted, what it had been crossed with, what the weather was like that season and how well it had grown.

The farmers from nearby properties, when they saw Farrer down on his hands and knees, carefully transferring pollen from one plant to another, thought he was mad. He had thick glasses, wore a long grey coat and had sewed leather patches on the knees of his trousers so they wouldn't wear out. But he was far from mad. As the years passed and Farrer's wheats grew better than any others, the flow of seeds was reversed as farmers from overseas began asking Farrer for some of his seed to start their own experiments.

Altogether Farrer released over thirty wheat varieties, all especially bred for Australian conditions. The most successful, called Federation, was released in 1902. William Farrer was a truly great Australian. Single-handed, without government assistance, (although he later became director of the Wheat Research Institute at Dubbo), he showed that wheat varieties could be bred to withstand drought and disease, and he saved the Australian wheat industry. He died in 1906 but his wheat lives on, and so must his work because the rust parasite is eventually able to overcome even resistant strains of wheat. New varieties must be constantly developed. A scientist named Walter Waterhouse took up Farrer's work and today the scientific breeding of wheat strains to combat changing patterns of disease is carried out by the Commonwealth Scientific and Industrial Research Organisation (CSIRO).

8 It was recommended that Farrer go to Australia

A for his health. B to study wheat diseases. C as a migrant. D to be nearer to India.

9 His research records were

A extremely painful. B computerised. C meticulous. D final.

10 Farrer's neighbours thought that he was
A law abiding. B conscientious. C religious. D insane.

11 The rust disease in wheat is brought on by
A a germ. B a bacteria. C a parasitic insect. D neglect.

12 The artificial fertilisation of wheat plants involves
A painstaking research. B the transfer of pollen by hand.
C foresight. D access to foreign seeds.

13 Wheat research must continue
A as old varieties become susceptible to rust. B to cross new varieties.
C to keep Farrer's name alive. D to be consistent.

14 The flow of wheat seeds was reversed
A so that Farrer could keep his research going. B to keep Farrer's promises.
C when the drought became bad. D as researchers overseas became aware of Farrer's work.

15 Farrer continued his work
A regardless of people's opinions. B all his life.
C without much help. D A, B, and C.

THE BANDICOOT

READING TEST 3

EXERCISE 3

The Bandicoot

All people should refrain from shooting
The bandicoot when bandicooting;
For though he may up-end the land he
Will never bite nor is he bandy.
Just watch him prod and plough and riot
Among the grubs that are his diet,
As, with his strong bull-dozing snout,
He turns the landscape inside out.

Leon Gellert.

16 Which of the following statements does the poem suggest are true?
A All bandicoots should be hunted and shot.
B Bandicoots are harmless and should not be shot.
C We should provide grubs for the bandicoot to eat.
D Most people dislike bandicoots.
E The bandicoot is a ground feeder.
F A bandicoot would be very destructive in a suburban garden.
G Bandicoots can be quite ferocious if cornered.

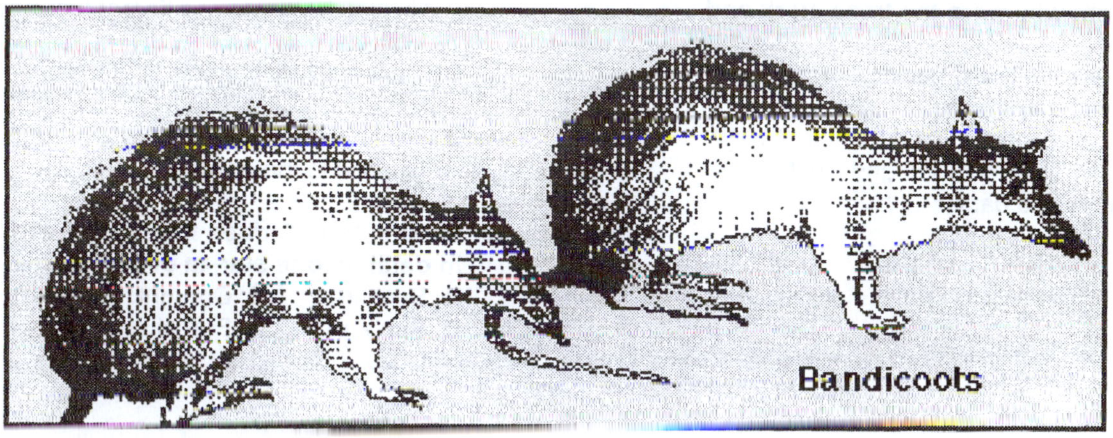

MY COUNTRY

EXERCISE 4

The love of field and coppice,
Of green and shaded lanes,
Of ordered woods and gardens,
Is running in your veins.
Strong love of grey-blue distance,
Brown streams and soft, dim skies—
I know, but cannot share it.
My love is otherwise.

I love a sunburnt country,
A land of sweeping plains,
Of ragged mountain ranges,
Of droughts and flooding rains.
I love her far horizons,
I love her jewel sea,
Her beauty and her terror—
The wide brown land for me!

The stark, white ring-barked forests ,
All tragic to the moon,
The sapphire-misted mountains,
The hot gold hush of noon.
Green tangle of the brushes,
Where lithe lianas coil,
Where orchids deck the tree-tops,
And ferns the warm dark soil.

Core of my heart my country!
Her pitiless blue sky,
When, sick at heart, around us
We see the cattle die—
But then the grey clouds gather,
And we can bless again
The drumming of an army,
The steady soaking rain.

An opal-hearted country,
A wilful, lavish land—
All you that have not loved her,
You will not understand—
Though Earth holds many splendours,
Wherever I may die,
I know to what brown Country
My homing thoughts will fly.

Dorothea Mackellar

17 In the first stanza the poet was telling of the love some people have for
- **A** England. **B** Australia.
- **C** Indonesia. **D** Alaska.

18 In the second stanza the poet was telling of her love for
- **A** England. **B** Australia.
- **C** Indonesia. **D** Alaska.

19 In the poem why were the trees stark and white?
- **A** They were ghost gums.
- **B** It was a full moon.
- **C** The artist had painted them that way.
- **D** They had been killed and lost their leaves and bark.

20 Why were the people sick at heart?
- **A** The cattle were dying.
- **B** The sky was cloudless.
- **C** The farmers had no pity.
- **D** There was a drought.

21 Why do you think the poet describes Australia as 'opal-hearted'?
- **A.** Australians are kind and considerate.
- **B** Like the opal, the Australian land and its peoples have many different features and aspects.
- **C** There are many precious stones in Australia.
- **D** You have to be physically strong to survive in the Australian outback.

22 Which "terror" does the poet describe in detail in one stanza of the poem?
- **A** Bushfire. **B** Drought.
- **C** Sunburn. **D** Forest clearance.

In the 1930s a well-known photographer, Cazneaux, took a picture of a tree in the Flinders Ranges, South Australia. The photograph, which he entitled 'The Spirit of Australia', became famous around the world. A number of times since the time of the original photograph, the tree has had to battle with drought, wind and flood, but it has always managed to struggle on. The tree is still alive today and Dorothea Mackellar has passed on. If she were alive however, she would no doubt be thrilled to be given a copy of this photograph.

The Cazneaux Tree in 2000

23 Dorothea Mackellar would be thrilled if she were given a copy of the Cazneaux' photo today. Why?

A It is a very good photograph.
B The tree has been able to win its battles.
C Most people would agree with Cazneaux.
D The photo captures her ideas in photo form.

READING TEST 3 STORMS OF FURY

EXERCISE 5

The largest and strongest of all storms are tropical cyclones, also known as hurricanes or typhoons. They form over warm seas in summer and early autumn. They begin near the equator and move south or north depending on the hemisphere they are in – they never cross the equator.

Tropical cyclones contain vast amounts of energy which they get from the Sun and through evaporation of water from the warm ocean. Most of these huge storms are over 200 kilometres wide. In the centre of the storm is a small, calm area called the 'eye'. The eye is surrounded by a wall of gale-force winds with heavy cloud and torrential rain. Near the eye, wind speed may exceed 300 kilometres per hour.

The whole system of swirling cloud, wind and rain moves erratically and so it is difficult to predict exactly where a tropical cyclone will go and how fast it will travel. When it moves into an area of cool sea it decays or weakens as it loses its source of energy. If it crosses land it also weakens, but not before it causes great damage with fierce winds, hail and torrential rain. Often a tropical cyclone whips up giant storm waves into what is called a 'storm surge'. When this happens, ships are driven aground and much damage is done to coastal areas. **Nature the Annihilator. G. Wilson**

24 The tropical cyclone

A has a number of names.
B usually forms in autumn and winter.
C begins in the Southern Ocean.
D None of the above.

25 The necessary conditions for tropical cyclones to develop are

A rain and strong winds.
B warm seas and sunlight.
C wind and vast amounts of energy.
D strong winds and large waves.

26 It is difficult to predict the path of the tropical cyclones because they

A often cross the equator.
B wander erratically.
C are surrounded by cloud.
D move so quickly.

27 Tropical cyclones begin to dissipate when

A they have used all their water content.
B the eye has passed.
C they cross land or move away from the equator.
D ships send up carbon dioxide rockets.

PINCHGUT

EXERCISE 6

Pinchgut or Fort Denison

Using the language of a sailor, a 'pinchgut' is a constriction in a harbour, but if you were a convict chained in a damp, dark cell without much food, the term would have a different meaning altogether. Whatever the reason for its name, 'Pinchgut' the small rocky island in Sydney Harbour located just before it narrows under the Harbour Bridge, has gained a new lease of life. It has become one of the city's most unique and exclusive restaurants. Patrons searching for that something a little different will certainly be lured there. Just think of it - a summer night and as you lift the oyster to your mouth, or you sniff the aroma of your seafood bisque, your eyes stray to the nearby Bridge, or to the myriad lights of Sydney's skyscrapers – the ambience is magic! Or perhaps yours is a day visit – if it's your birthday you may be lucky enough to fire the gun signifying one o'clock, because they usually select volunteers that way. The gun, which makes quite a bang, was fired in olden days to allow ships to set their chronometers. The calculation of both latitude and longitude depended upon the accurate telling of the time.

Pinchgut was originally called Mattewai meaning 'small, rocky island' by the aborigines. It was noted by Governor Phillip, and a convict was confined to it for a week for stealing biscuits from a fellow prisoner. The island was irregularly used in this fashion over the next eight years. Perhaps around about this time it earned the name of Pinchgut. In 1796 a convict was hanged on the island, but as time passed the island outgrew its usefulness as a prison. In 1842 it was converted into a fort with cannons as protection for the city. Shortly after, in the 1850s with the outbreak of war between Russia and England, a gun tower, called a Martello, was added. In 1857 it was renamed Fort Denison and manned by a small contingent of the British Royal Artillery until 1869. No shots were ever fired in anger however from the fort and, due to the introduction of improved weapons and the development of iron-clad warships, the island was abandoned as a defensive installation in the 1870s.

As a matter of interest, the rise and fall of the tides in N.S.W. are measured from Fort Denison. Places that are east of Fort Denison are given a figure of 'minus so many minutes.' Those coastal areas that are west of it have a plus measurement, signifying a later tide. During World War II the Martello tower was hit by a shell from an American warship fired at a Japanese midget submarine. Luckily the circular sandstone walls were strong enough to withstand the blast.

Original Cannon

28 In nautical terms 'pinchgut' means

- **A** a narrow stretch of water.
- **B** a time when rations are reduced.
- **C** a treacherous current.
- **D** a small cell.

29 From the passage you can tell that the word 'ambience' most likely means

- **A** the smells of cooking.
- **B** the city lights at night.
- **C** the general atmosphere or feeling of a place.
- **D** a vivid imagination.

30 A Martello Tower is

- **A** circular in shape.
- **B** rectangular in shape.
- **C** a level firing platform.
- **D** a sandstone platform.

31 As a prison, Fort Denison was
- **A** never used.
- **B** seldom used.
- **C** only used briefly.
- **D** often used.

32 The gun was fired each day
- **A** to allow ships to calculate their position.
- **B** as a warning to shipping of the constriction in the harbour.
- **C** to allow captains to check the ship's clock.
- **D** to test the gun's readiness.

33 As a fort, Fort Denison was
- **A** made obsolete by advances in naval weaponry.
- **B** re-armed with armour piercing shells during World War II.
- **C** made less efficient with the addition of the Martello tower.
- **D** dismantled and its guns taken away in the 1870s.

34 Places along the NSW coast that have a more easterly longitude
- **A** experience later tides than Fort Denison.
- **B** experience earlier tides than Fort Denison.
- **C** can no longer receive accurate tidal information.
- **D** depend on the daily cannon firing for accurate tidal information.

READING TEST 3

COAT OF ARMS

EXERCISE 7

Australia

A coat of arms is like a badge or emblem. Originally placed on a herald's tabard or the shield of a knight as a means of identification, it is used in a similar way today on flags, official documents, buildings and the like, to show ownership. The Coat of Arms of the Australian Government has on it a kangaroo and an emu, with branches of wattle. The wattle was chosen because it is a native flower found in all States. The two indigenous animals however were chosen because neither can walk backward, and Australia's motto is 'Advance Australia Fair.'

35 Over the years the purpose in having a coat of arms
- **A** has changed little.
- **B** has changed markedly.
- **C** can never be changed.
- **D** is now accepted.

36 The emu and kangaroo were chosen because
- **A** they are both native animals.
- **B** these native animals cannot walk backward.
- **C** they are so well known.
- **D** one is a bird and the other a land animal.

37 The wattle was chosen because
- **A** it is a common, indigenous species.
- **B** its colours blended in well.
- **C** Australia's colours are green and gold.
- **D** it is easily recognized.

THE GULF STREAM

EXERCISE 8

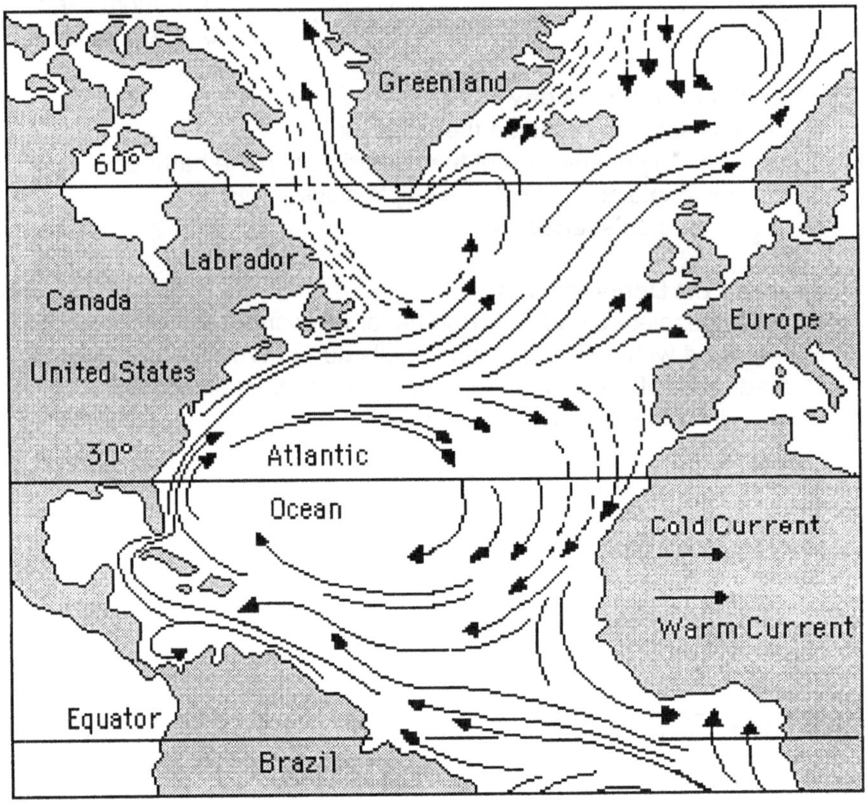

The Gulf Stream (or North Atlantic Drift) is the name given to the warm ocean current which flows in a north-easterly direction across the Atlantic Ocean from North America towards Europe. The name would suggest that this current is formed in the Gulf of Mexico, but it is really an extension of the Equatorial Current. The Equatorial Current is formed by strong Trade Winds which blow onto the north-east coast of South America.

The current of the Gulf Stream has a temperature of about 28° C and a speed of about 8 kilometres an hour. It is about 80 kilometres wide at the Equator and 470 metres deep as it passes the tip of Florida. Just north of Florida it is joined by another warm current, the North Equatorial Current. Both flow along the coast of North America until they are diverted to the east by the shape of the land and the westerly winds that blow at latitudes around 40°. When the combined current reaches the British Isles it divides again, part going north-east through the British Channel and part, the larger part, going on to Norway. The warm waters of the Gulf Stream finally peter out in the cold seas of the North Atlantic.

Not only are the coastal bays and inlets of Britain, France, Denmark and Norway kept free of ice in winter, but the westerly winds that blow over the current are warmed by the Gulf Stream too. They pick up and carry much more moisture than they would otherwise and so the high rainfalls of Western Europe depend in large part upon the presence of the Gulf Stream.

38 What is the alternate name for the Gulf Stream?

- **A** The Equatorial Current.
- **B** The North American Current.
- **C** The North Atlantic Drift.
- **D** The North Equatorial Current.

39 What causes the Gulf Stream to change direction towards Europe?

- **A** The shape of the land.
- **B** The westerly winds.
- **C** Pressure from the Labrador (cold) current.
- **D** The land direction and the westerly winds.

40 What effect does the Gulf Stream have upon the ports of Western Europe?

- **A** There is very little effect.
- **B** It helps to keep them free of ice.
- **C** It causes high rainfall totals.
- **D** It helps the fishing industry.

41 What happens to the westerly winds as they blow over the Gulf Stream?

- **A** They become colder.
- **B** They become warmer and drier.
- **C** They lose moisture.
- **D** They become warmer and pick up moisture.

42 What is the most important effect of the Gulf Stream?

- **A** To change the climate of Western Europe.
- **B** To increase rainfall in Western Europe.
- **C** To increase temperature in Western Europe.
- **D** To cause North America to be colder.

43 What does 'peter out' mean?

- **A** Augment.
- **B** Dissipate.
- **C** Divert.
- **D** Avoid.

THE GOPHER OR GROUND SQUIRREL

EXERCISE 9

Gophers, or ground squirrels, are herbivorous inhabitants of the prairies of western Canada and the United States. They form loose colonies in the short grass plains and there are usually two or three of these quaint little animals on the watch for danger at any given time during the day. From a distance their erect posture makes them look like small, upright stakes stuck into the plain, giving rise to one popular name, 'pocket pin squirrel'.

To early settlers of the prairies, any native creature that ate grass and dug holes was considered vermin and in Canada as a specie they were nearly extirpated. Their preference for living close to the edges of grain fields, golf courses and lawns, where they eat so much and thrive so well, causes them to be considered still as agricultural pests. Over the years these little rodents have been subject to a wide range of persecutions – from bounty hunters, poisoning campaigns and target shooters, but still they thrive. As well as their cautious nature, their success in part is due to their capacity for reproduction. A female may give birth to as many as eleven offspring each year.

In late summer and autumn the young gophers disperse to found their own colonies and become extremely vulnerable at this time to predation by hawks, falcons, weasels, coyotes and any other animal that fancies a nice plump ground squirrel, fattened by summer grasses, for dinner. Cruel though it may sound, it is just as well that these small animals are available as food, because many of the predators rely on them to build up their reserves of body fat for the long, hard winter that is soon to come. Gophers do not have to worry about the winter as they are true hibernators. With the onset of cold weather they vanish underground not to be seen from October to March each year. However, early risers after their winter sleep become exposed on late winter snow drifts, and fall prey to migrating bald and golden eagles at this time.

Choose the best answer to complete the following sentences.

44 Gophers live in
- **A** colonies.
- **B** small family groups.
- **C** pairs.
- **D** single units.

45 Like rats and rabbits, they
- **A** are quick runners.
- **B** are rodents.
- **C** make good pets.
- **D** have long ears.

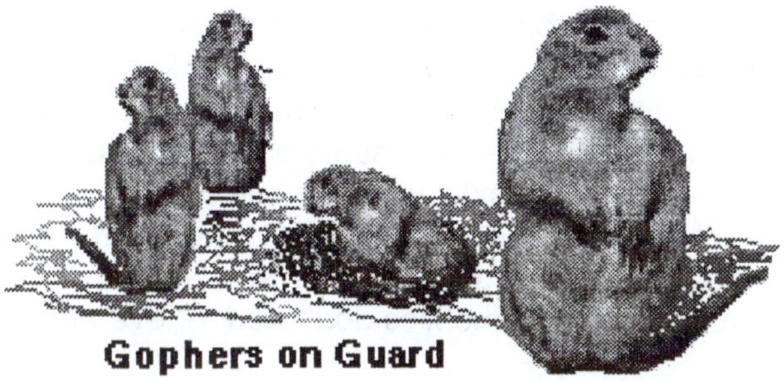

Gophers on Guard

46 The early Canadian settlers regarded them as
- **A** poisonous and dangerous.
- **B** animals good for hunting.
- **C** vermin to be exterminated.
- **D** small, endearing and 'quirky' animals.

47 In the autumn, the young ground squirrels are
- **A** getting out to found new colonies.
- **B** vulnerable to attack from predators.
- **C** fat from the grasses of summer.
- **D** All of the above.

48 Because of their life routine, ground squirrels are classed as
- **A** true hibernators.
- **B** native dogs.
- **C** native rodents.
- **D** simple herbivores.

49 The large supply of ground squirrels each year is important to the maintenance of
- **A** recreational hunting programmes.
- **B** a meat supply for American Indians.
- **C** quality fairways on many American golf courses.
- **D** biodiversity in the prairies.

50 From the passage, the word "extirpated" means
- **A** eliminated.
- **B** hunted.
- **C** appreciated.
- **D** persecuted.

CHICKEN, ALASKA.

EXERCISE 1

Why do they call it "Chicken?" Good question. In the late 1800's, early miners travelled far into the cold wastes of Canada and Alaska in search of gold. Food was sometimes scarce, but a particular area near the South Fork of the 40-Mile River was abundant in ptarmigan, now recognised as the State bird. Ptarmigan, which bear a resemblance to chicken, helped to keep the miners alive (if you consider being eaten as helping).

In 1902, Chicken became incorporated as a town, only the second town in Alaska to do so. The name "Ptarmigan" was suggested for the new town. Many people liked the name, but felt the quotation marks were too presumptuous, so the name was shortened to Ptarmigan. The only problem was that nobody could agree on the correct spelling. They didn't want their town name to be the source of ridicule and laughter, so they decided on Chicken.

The main (only) shops in Chicken.

At Chicken, the climate in winter is bitterly cold with temperatures many degrees below freezing point, but, as you can see, (note the modern jet aircraft approaching the aerodrome), Chicken is an up-to-date, thriving, metropolis, replete with every modern convenience. Nearby towns, equally as progressive, are named Eagle and Tok. The township of Chicken was immortalised in the book “Tisha” which was the story of the first school teacher to come to town. The frozen town is also famous for the saloon that has its walls lined with paper money contributed by visitors passing through from every place on earth.

Jokes aside, when you arrive in Chicken after many hours of driving along the deserted Alaskan Highway, the township is a welcome respite. And I can definitely recommend the homemade blueberry, loganberry and currant pies on sale at the café – but be quick, they don’t keep a lot of stock. And don’t count on calling home as mobiles don’t work - even the businesses don’t have a phone.

1 The story of the naming of Chicken is

A humorous. **B** tragic. **C** satisfying. **D** superstitious.

2 The area was vital to the early miners because

A it was adjacent to the goldfields. **B** the ptarmigans were a food source.
C it was on the Alaskan Highway. **D** it wasn’t as cold as other parts of Alaska.

3 When Chicken was incorporated it became

A a sample for other towns to follow. **B** officially a town.
C surrounded by a fence. **D** a place for aeroplanes to land at.

4 The township is a welcome respite to highway travellers because

A the township sells good pies. **B** they have been travelling for a long time .
C the saloon is unique. **D** All of the preceding.

5 The word “presumptuous” means

A unduly ugly. **B** unduly boastful and arrogant. **C** unduly uncertain. **D** unduly vague.

6 The shops only operate in the summer because

A the townsfolk go south for their holidays.
B there is no passing traffic.
C the town is snowed-in during winter.
D there are no berries.

7 The word "immortalised" means

A only found there.
B a reading manual.
C remembered for ever.
D known about.

READING TEST 4

QUICKSAND

EXERCISE 2

If you are a long-time fan of bad, B-grade movies, you will, no doubt, have seen a variety of people disappearing into a quicksand morass. The 'goodies' usually manage to survive by grabbing hold of a conveniently-placed branch or vine, while the 'baddies' are sucked to a timely and well-deserved death. Nothing remains of them except a few satisfying bubbles and a floating hat.

Not really. Quicksand is so much denser than water, fresh or salt, that is impossible for a human body, which is marginally less dense, to sink completely. This not to say that something really dense, like a train or a car, can't sink in quicksand. Nor is it to say that you won't die if you fall in. Quicksand clings, and if you can't get out within a reasonable time, the hydrostatic pressure on the body can eventually render mortal damage to internal organs and quite possibly prevent you from breathing.

Adventurers planning to travel alone through known quicksand territory should carry a strong pole, not so much to test the sand, but to assist you to get out if need be. The trick is to try to flop backwards on the stick, then, once your rate of sinking has stabilised, try to manoeuvre the pole so that it is under your hips. Then slowly try to free your legs fully. Once you achieve this you are as good as out. Carefully roll across the top of the quicksand to the nearest solid ground.

Few animals can rescue themselves from quicksand. A dog might if someone is there to encourage it to work towards a given point. A horse will manage too, but quickly becomes exhausted without guidance. Cattle almost always panic and drown in quicksand. The only way to get them out is by getting a rope around their neck and pulling. However, once on dry land, don't be too surprised if they attack you – they have no sense of gratitude. - **Based on an article by Dr Karl Kuzelnicki.**

8 The article explains that

A it is quite possible for people to disappear completely in quicksand.
B it is unlikely that a human will disappear beneath the surface of quicksand.
C 'baddies' are only found in B-grade movies.
D 'goodies' deserve to be rescued.

9 The article explains that

A it is impossible to escape from quicksand.
B the best way to get out is to work towards a point.
C hydrostatic pressure can cause death by suppressing body functions.
D to avoid danger you must control your breathing.

10 From the article one can infer that the key to survival is to

A call quickly for help.
B try to get on top of a pole by flopping backwards on it.
C wait until you float back to the surface.
D use a rope to pull yourself out.

11 In the passage the word 'mortal' means

A inoperable.
B sufficient .
C casual.
D deadly.

RAINFALL IN AUSTRALIA

EXERCISE 3

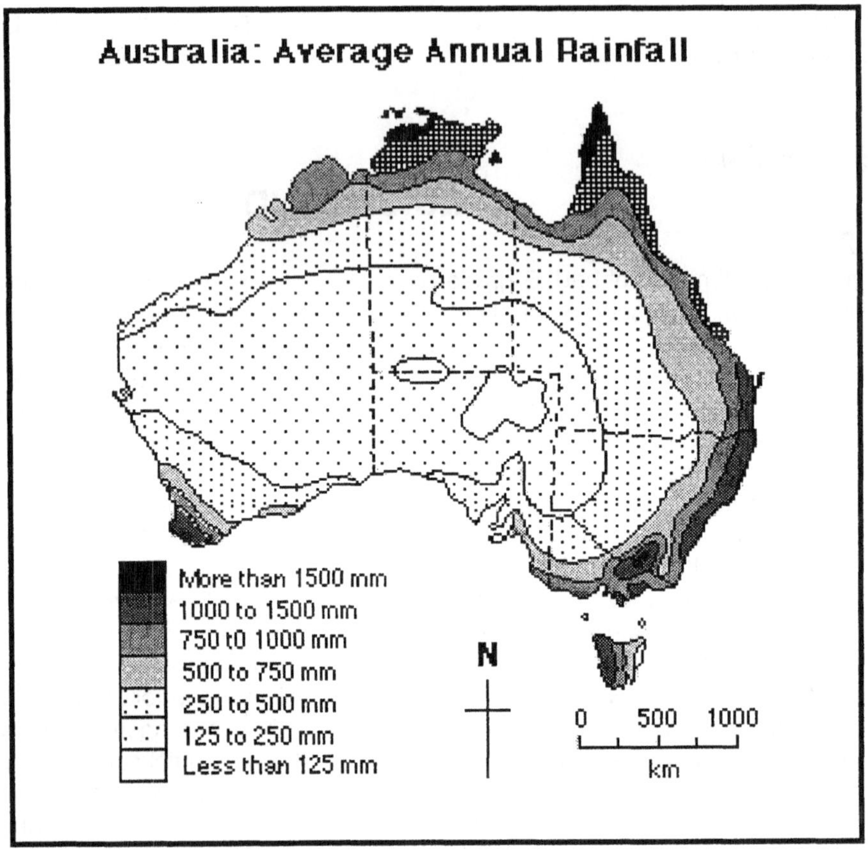

Use the map to answer the following questions:

12 The areas of Australia which receive the heaviest rainfall are located mainly in the
A north. **B** south. **C** east. **D** west.

13 In northern Australia, rainfall totals decrease as you travel from
A south to north. **B** west to east.
C north to south. **D** east to west.

14 Central Australia is best described as
A very wet. **B** wet.
C dry. **D** very dry.

15 The driest State appears to be
A Western Australia.
B South Australia.
C Tasmania.
D Victoria.

16 Areas of heaviest rainfall receive in excess of
A 1500 mm. **B** 1000 mm.
C 750 mm. **D** 500 mm.

17 These areas of heaviest rainfall are located
A inland.
B near the coast.
C in southern Western Australia.
D in northern Tasmania.

THE RIME OF THE ANCIENT MARINER.
(Lines 103 – 122, 145 – 148)

EXERCISE 4

The fair breeze blew, the white foam flew,
The furrow followed free;
We were the first that ever burst,
Into the silent sea.

Down dropt the breeze, the sails dropt down,
'Twas as sad as sad could be;
And we did speak only to break
The silence of the sea.

All in a hot and copper sky,
The bloody sun, at noon,
Right up above the mast did stand,
No bigger than the moon.

Day after day, day after day,
We stuck, nor breath nor motion;
As idle as a painted ship
Upon a painted ocean.

Water, water, everywhere,
And all the boards did shrink,
Water, water, everywhere,
Nor any drop to drink.

And every tongue, through utter drought,
Was withered at the root;
We could not speak, no more than if
We had been choked with soot.

Samuel Taylor Coleridge

18 Why was the ship idle?
- **A** The sailors were lazy.
- **B** The sails had been torn.
- **C** There was no wind.
- **D** There was too much foam.

19 Why did the ship look as if it was in a painting?
- **A** Nothing was moving, even the sea was still.
- **B** The ship had been painted recently.
- **C** The sun had made everything a reddish colour.
- **D** Everything had dried out.

20 What was the water that was 'everywhere' but couldn't be drunk?
- **A** The water in the clouds.
- **B** The sea water.
- **C** Rainwater.
- **D** The water that had been filled with soot.

21 Why couldn't the sailors talk?
- **A** They were frightened by the silence.
- **B** Their mouths were choked with soot.
- **C** They had drunk too much sea water.
- **D** They had nothing to drink.

22 How true to the text of the second verse is the illustration?
- **A** It is a good representation.
- **B** It contains many errors.
- **C** It is error free.
- **D** The sea is too calm.

WARATAH

EXERCISE 5

The Waratah

Telopea speciosissima is better known as the waratah. This magnificent shrub grows on the sandstone areas of the central coast and mountains to the north and south of Sydney. Its common name, waratah, was adopted by the early settlers at Port Jackson from the aboriginal word for this magnificent plant.

The waratah is a tall, erect shrub that may grow to 4 metres in height with a width of 1.5 metres. The crimson flower, which can be 10 cm in diameter, is surrounded by bracts, about 5 to 7 cm long. It flowers from September to November and is pollinated by nectar-seeking birds. The waratah has been able to resist destruction by bushfire by regenerating from rootstock when the bushfire period is past. A mature plant before a fire can return to flowering size two years after being burnt to the ground.

The botanical name 'telopea' means 'seen from afar' and the striking red flower heads of the waratah certainly fill that description. The waratah is one of the world's most beautiful flowers. In 1962 the waratah was made the official emblem of the State of New South Wales but its spectacular rounded flower has been used for designs in arts and crafts, such as stained glass and wall paper patterns, for many years. A Sydney railway station has been named after this striking flower and a department store has adopted it for its logo; there is even a waratah postage stamp.

The waratah can be a spectacular as a garden shrub but only in suitable soil and climate. When established however, it is long-lived and flowers prolifically. Seeds should be sown in a coarse, sandy soil and soon after germination the seedlings should be transplanted into individual pots of similar soil. Propagation by cuttings is also possible. New, hardy varieties of waratah are now being bred for overseas markets.

23 A good word to use to describe the waratah flower would be
A pretty. **B** distinctive. **C** useful. **D** erect.

24 A good word to use to describe the waratah plant would be
A erect. **B** mature. **C** delicate. **D** pretty.

25 After fire the waratah is able to
A flower prolifically. **B** be transplanted. **C** set seeds. **D** regenerate.

26 In the average garden the waratah would be
A easy to grow. **B** difficult to grow. **C** not worth growing. **D** far too large.

27 The waratah can be grown from
A seeds only. **B** cuttings only. **C** rootstock. **D** seeds and cuttings.

28 The waratah flower head has been often used
A for art designs. **B** for stained glass patterns.
C in many decorative situations. **D** for logos.

29 Around the world, waratahs are now
A no longer popular. **B** becoming popular.
C used for medicines. **D** unknown.

30 The word 'prolifically' means
A abundantly. **B** sporadically. **C** infrequently. **D** satisfactorily.

WIND MINING

EXERCISE 6

There's gold in the air above Mount Foster – cold, clear wind blowing at the highest measured speed in the State (N.S.W.), making a hill on the Wass family property a sky miner's dream. The Sustainable Energy Development Authority (SEDA), assisted by the CSIRO, has installed in areas as far a-field as Lord Howe Island and Bourke, twenty-five 40-metre towers with wind measuring instruments at their summit. The aim is to prepare a State Wind Atlas as a resource for energy companies.

Just a year into the study, scientists have already uncovered a few breezes from 'left field'. The scientists have revealed the extent of last month's gales; the State's windiest area, Mount Foster, has an average wind speed of 6.82 metres a second (24.6 km/ph), and the stillest, Orange, which has an average wind speed of 3.7 metres a second (13.3 km/ph)

The gustiest site in the study was Lake Bathurst near Goulburn, where a burst of wind sent the scientists' monitors into a spin of 165 kilometres an hour at 11 a.m. 12 days ago. According to the Bureau of Meteorology, the single strongest gust of wind recorded in NSW was 171 kilometres an hour at Newcastle in 1974. The NSW Energy Minister, Mr Yeadon, said energy utilities could invest hundreds of millions of dollars to set up wind farms in high wind areas.

The director of the CSIRO's wind energy unit, Dr Peter Coppin, said that he expected a cleared location in the southern or northern tablelands at an elevation of above 1 000 metres would have had the highest average wind in the study. " Mount Foster's obviously a fantastic hill; it's like an aircraft wing: it's got the right shape to speed the wind up." Dr Coppin's research has also discovered that while coastal sites in NSW often feel tremendously windy, the seaside is in fact less consistently blowy than many inland areas.

SEDA's manager of wind power, Mr Andrew Williamson said "We are prospecting for good wind potential. The knowledge of where you would go to mine the wind is incredibly valuable to both the community and the environment. It's a race to tap the resource."

James Woodford.
Sydney Morning Herald, Sept 1, 2001

31 Why have the towers been constructed?
- **A** To transport electricity.
- **B** To monitor wind speeds around the State.
- **C** To provide jobs in depressed areas.
- **D** To provide a data resource for energy companies.

32 Which site experienced the most sudden bursts of wind?
- **A** Newcastle.
- **B** Lake Bathurst.
- **C** Mount Foster.
- **D** Orange.

33 What did research show about the relative 'windyness' of coastal areas?
- **A** Coastal areas are not windy.
- **B** Coastal areas are extremely windy
- **C** Coastal areas are not as windy, comparatively, as one might expect.
- **D** Wind measurements from coastal areas are not reliable.

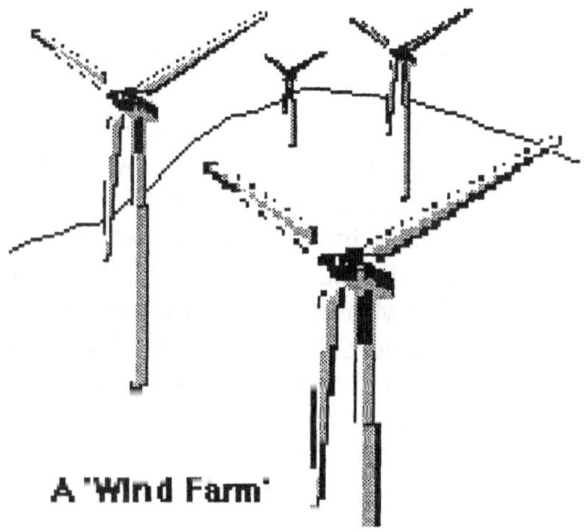

A 'Wind Farm'

34 From the passage we can infer that
- **A** wind speed decreases over flat, cleared land.
- **B** the shape of a hill does not influence wind speed over it.
- **C** coastal areas are consistently the most windy of all sites.
- **D** None of the above.

THE SINKING OF THE QUETTA

EXERCISE 7

The loss of R.M.S. Quetta as portrayed in newspapers of the time.

The Royal Mail Steamer Quetta pushed towards Adolphus Channel making a fast 13 knots on her run up to Thursday Island in Torres Strait.

Almost a hundred years earlier, because of its hidden reefs, submerged rocks and shallows, Matthew Flinders had said that he knew of 'perhaps no space of three and a half degrees in length that represents more danger than Torres Strait'. Yet Captain Sanders was not unduly worried, even though night passages of Adolphus Channel were not recommended. After all it was bright moonlight, the sea was flat and the ship was only seven years old. Besides he had on board an experienced pilot who had made the run through the channel 23 times before. The position of the only navigational hazard, a submerged rock midway in the channel, was well known to both the Captain and the pilot.

The passengers promenading on the decks certainly had no inkling of impending disaster. Dinner was over and it had been a hot day, so they were on deck to catch the breeze of the ship's way, and to admire the line made by the bright three-quarter moon on the placid sea. Families strolled while the children laughed and played hidings in and out of the deck equipment.

Circumstances were soon to change however as the ship entered Adolphus Channel. At 9.14 p.m. February 28th 1890, R.M.S. Quetta struck a previously-unknown submerged, granite pinnacle. The speed of the ship carried it forward causing the rock to slice neatly open the bottom of the ship. There was little impact, only a slight jar was felt above deck. The heavily laden ship continued onwards. Within three minutes, less time than it takes to boil an egg, it had heeled over to port and sunk, taking all its cargo, mails, and half of the passengers and crew with it.

The fact that there had been little impact probably contributed to the death toll aboard the Quetta. Passengers simply couldn't believe that the ship was sinking. As the ship began to dip at the bow they moved in an orderly fashion to the back of the ship to await further orders. Then the sinking bow struck the bottom of the channel some twenty metres below. The ship at this stage was still moving forward, being borne along by the strong tide in the channel. The rip swung the ship on its side emptying the grouped passengers into the sea then collapsing on them.

Altogether that night 134 people drowned out of a total of 292 on board. It was, and still is, Australia's worst peace-time maritime disaster. At the enquiry held after the disaster there were no allegations of fault made against the captain, pilot or officers of the ship. Divers found that four of the Quetta's watertight compartments had been opened up in the accident and that more than one would have been enough to sink the ship. A later survey found that the offending rock, now known as Quetta Rock, was only 10 metres wide at the top and 3 metres below the surface at low tide.

Following a thorough re-survey of Torres Strait charts of the area have been adjusted, but vessels still use Adolphus Channel.

35 Captain Sanders was not worried about Adolphus Channel because

A he had an experienced pilot on board.
B it was bright moonlight.
C the sea was calm.
D All of the preceding.

36 The position of 'Quetta Rock' was

A well known to the captain.
B was well known to the captain and the pilot.
C was not known to the captain.
D was not known by the captain or the pilot.

37 When the bow section hit the bottom

A the passengers ran to the front of the ship.
B the aft (rear) section was swung around.
C the captain sounded the alarm.
D the lifeboats were immediately launched.

38 From your reading of the passage would you say that the Quetta was

A sailed negligently.
B sailed cautiously.
C unlucky to hit the rock.
D sailed recklessly.

39 Many of the passengers were on deck before the disaster because

A it was a moonlight night.
B it had been a hot day.
C the ship was going so fast.
D Both 'A' and 'B'.

40 The ship sank very quickly because

A the ship was old.
B it was made of iron.
C the bow section was holed.
D the bottom was ripped out.

41 Due to the wreck of the Quetta

A large ships no longer use the Adolphus Channel.
B Torres Strait is no longer used by large ships.
C the whole area was re-surveyed and re-charted.
D the captain lost his command.

The Quetta Memorial Church, Thursday Island.

42 From a reading of the story it is apparent that

A the findings of the maritime enquiry were correct.
B the Captain was lucky to be exonerated
C some penalties should have been attached to the entire crew.
D the passengers behaved badly.

43 Find words in the passage that mean

A a sharp peak
B charges
C about to occur
D without panic

THE GOLDEN APPLES OF THE HESPERIDES

EXERCISE 8

The illustration shows Atlas offering the golden apples to Heracles who is holding the sky on his shoulders while Athena helps.

Far away in the foothills of the Atlas Mountains, was the Garden of the Hesperides with its golden apples. The daughters of Atlas were forever trespassing in the garden and stealing the apples, so Hera, the wife of Zeus, gave the task of guarding them to an immortal dragon which had a hundred heads and which was assisted by three Nymphs. These were the Hesperides.

Now the brave hero, Heracles, who was already a demi-god, had been given a series of labours to carry out by Eurytheus. Heracles' labours were designed to prove whether he was fit to become a fully immortal god because he had already performed one bad deed. One of the labours imposed upon him was to fetch three of the golden apples from the Garden of the Hesperides. His first task of course was to find the location of the Garden, which he eventually did, but getting there involved Heracles in many adventures along the way. One adventure involved the freeing of the god Prometheus, who had been chained to a mountain by Zeus.

Out of gratitude for his release, Prometheus advised Heracles not to pick the apples himself, but to ask the giant, Atlas, to do it for him as a favour. Atlas was responsible for holding the sky upon his shoulders, so Heracles offered to relieve him of his burden, while he went to get the apples. Atlas fetched the apples, but was then unwilling to resume his burden, offering instead to take the precious fruit to Eurytheus. The demi-god was forced to use cunning: he asked the Giant to hold up the dome of the heavens for a moment while he, unused to such a huge weight, put a cushion on his shoulders. Atlas, unsuspecting, resumed the burden - only to discover that Heracles had snatched up the apples which Atlas had laid down, and taken to his heels.

Well, after all that, Eurytheus got his apples, but then didn't know what to do with them. So he gave them to Athena,who took them back to the Garden. Such fruit, she knew, should not be kept anywhere but in a divine place.

44 It was the responsibility of the giant Atlas to

- **A** pick the golden apples for Heracles.
- **B** shoulder the weight of the heavens.
- **C** report upon the misdeeds of Heracles.
- **D** return the apples to Eurytheus.

45 Heracles' labours involved him in

- **A** close contact with Hesperides.
- **B** a fight with the immortal dragon of the Garden.
- **C** many strange adventures.
- **D** being sympathetic to the Hesperides.

46 Prometheus helped Heracles because

- **A** he was grateful for his release.
- **B** Zeus had imprisoned him.
- **C** he was a semi-mortal himself.
- **D** no-one else would help him.

47 In the passage, 'took to his heels' means

- **A** at his feet.
- **B** nearby.
- **C** ran away.
- **D** unsuspecting.

48 When Atlas resumed his burden, he
- **A** put the apples in his robe.
- **B** accepted the dome of the sky again.
- **C** went to Eurytheus.
- **D** put a cushion on Heracles' shoulder.

49 Heracles' many labours were imposed
- **A** as a punishment and a test of his fitness to become fully immortal.
- **B** because he was stronger than the giant Atlas.
- **C** because he was a hero of the people.
- **D** to satisfy Hera.

50 In the passage the word 'divine' means
- **A** beautiful.
- **B** special.
- **C** magic.
- **D** belonging to the gods.

READING TEST 5

READY, AIM, FIRE!

EXERCISE 1

In the steamy Indonesian darkness a Sumatran rhinoceros slops through a swamp. Click! High on an icy ledge in the Himalayas a snow leopard sniffs a scent mark on a rock. Click! In the hills near San Diego, California, a mountain lion lopes along a trail. Click!

From the depths of South Asian rainforests to the shrinking patches of wilderness tucked in California's megalopolises, automated cameras have become a preferred tool, of conservation biologists trying to study rare and reclusive animal species.

Starting in the early 1900s, biologists began experimenting with cameras triggered by trip wires and, later, photo-electric cells to photograph tigers, bats, birds and other wildlife. But early efforts were severely constrained by clunky equipment that would waste film shooting falling twigs. Over the past 15 years however the equipment has become far more sophisticated, rugged, and easy to use, thus allowing biologists to record the passage of particular species at particular times of day, and to train local residents to take over the day-to-day work of reloading cameras.

Usually scientists have to spend months or years studying wildlife in dense greenery, and hardly ever see their quarry. The weatherproof, infrared cameras are going to revolutionise the study of rainforest biology because so many more animals will be seen. The next step, researchers hope, will be figuring out how to use cameras that can store and transmit data digitally.

1 The rare and reclusive animals are 'shot' using a
- **A** long range rifle.
- **B** waterproof camera.
- **C** bow and arrow.
- **D** sling.

2 What was wrong with the early automated cameras?
- **A** They were bulky.
- **B** They wasted film.
- **C** They were hard to use.
- **D** All of the preceding.

3 The cameras are of the greatest help in
- **A** deserts.
- **B** urban areas.
- **C** rainforests.
- **D** tree tops.

4 In the passage, the word 'sophisticated' means
- **A** delicate.
- **B** simple.
- **C** proficient.
- **D** generalised.

5 The use of digital transmitter cameras will be a big step forward because they will
- **A** allow the researchers to work at a distance from the site.
- **B** allow local residents to load and unload the cameras.
- **C** notify the researchers when there is an emergency.
- **D** protect the animals from native poachers.

JAMES BOND, 007

EXERCISE 2

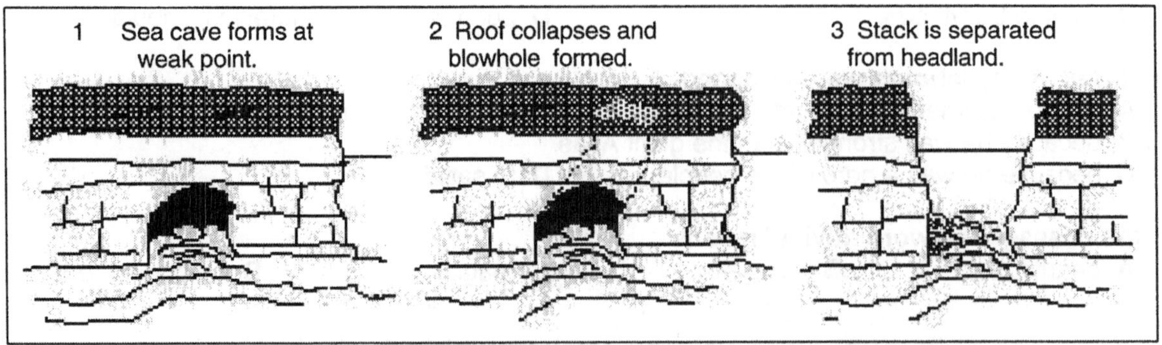

How Sea Caves, Blowholes and Sea Stacks are formed.

A headland is a finger of land that juts out into the sea. When a weakness exists in the rock strata at the side of a headland, waves can eat their way into the side of it and make a cave. Sometimes part of the cave's roof falls in and a hole is made through to the surface of the headland to form a 'blowhole'. If the weakness in the rock strata goes right through, and the headland is attacked by the waves from both sides, a natural bridge can be formed. When the bridge eventually collapses from undercutting, a large piece of headland with steep sides is left standing in the sea. This is called a 'stack'. Sea stacks are fairly common especially in areas where there are beds of horizontal limestone or sandstone.

Now what may you ask has 007 to do with all this? Well perhaps the most famous sea stack in the world is found, with a number of others, in a limestone area in the Andaman Sea on the west coast of Thailand. James Bond Island, as it is now called, is a sea stack and it was used in the filming of the James Bond film, Goldfinger. A number of large sea caves in this region are a source of the nests used to make birds' nest soup.

Australia has its own famous series of limestone sea stacks along the southern coast of Victoria near Port Campbell, called the 'Twelve Apostles'. In the days of sail and early steam this region of very rough seas was the scene of a number of tragic shipwrecks. One shipwreck, the Loch Ard, claimed the lives of all aboard except for the cabin boy and one young female passenger. These two had great difficulty climbing the steep cliffs to reach safety. Bodies from this wreck were washed into a long blowhole called Devil's Hole. One famous formation in the same area, a bridge called London Bridge, has now collapsed and some of the original Twelve Apostles have also been worn away by the rough seas.

In New South Wales the well-known Kiama blowhole has been formed in an area of basalt lava flows. It functions when strong southerly seas are running. In one recent accident, a family of newly arrived migrants to Australia was drowned there in 1992. They had foolishly climbed over the safety fence to see how it worked.

There are many sea caves and stacks along the coast of Devon in Britain and the coast of Normandy in France. Here the sea has cut into cliffs formed of soft chalk.

6 A headland is
- **A** a piece of land with sea caves.
- **B** a long neck of land almost surrounded by sea.
- **C** a narrow piece of land made up of high cliffs.
- **D** a neck of land undercut by the ocean.

7 A blowhole is formed
- **A** when the sea comes from a constant direction.
- **B** when erosion of the headland occurs.
- **C** only in sandstone areas.
- **D** when the roof of a sea cave collapses.

8 How did James Bond Island get its name?
- **A** It was discovered by James Bond.
- **B** It was used in a James Bond film.
- **C** James Bond was imprisoned there.
- **D** The sea stacks became 'bonded' to each other .

James Bond Island today.

9 The Twelve Apostles probably get their name from

A the twelve biblical disciples.
B a town called Apostles in Victoria.
C their steep sides.
D the fact that there were more of them.

10 Devil's Hole turned out to be an appropriate name because

A it was hard to get out of.
B some of the bodies were washed into it.
C some of the rescuers lost their lives there.
D it was connected to the sea by a long tunnel.

11 The Kiama blowhole has been the scene

A of a variety of water sports.
B of demonstrations against the Kiama council.
C of the collapse of many sea stacks.
D of a number of tragedies.

12 Sea stacks are found

A only in southern Australia.
B only in Victoria.
C only in the Andaman Sea.
D in a number of places around the world.

READING TEST 5

BELIEVE IT OR NOT - SALIVA

EXERCISE 3

Saliva, the common name is spit, is produced by glands inside the mouth. Saliva secreted by these glands is injected into the mouth when required by the chewing action. Saliva's main job is to lubricate food that has been masticated so that it will pass more easily down the oesophagus to the stomach. A secondary function is to help carry flavour to the taste buds located on the tongue.

Saliva also contains enzymes which are chemicals manufactured by the body to assist in the break down and digestion of food, so this is a third function of saliva. If you continued to chew a dry cracker biscuit it would eventually begin to taste sweet. This occurs because the starch in the biscuit is being broken down by the saliva into sugars.

Most animals have some form of saliva containing enzymes. The fly, for example, although it has no teeth or jaws to masticate food, secretes saliva directly onto food to liquefy it, then sucks up the resulting mixture.

13 The most important function of saliva is

A mastication.
B tasting.
C enzyme production.
D lubrication.

14 Enzymes are

A manufactured by the body.
B found in saliva.
C an aid to digestion.
D All of the preceding.

15 The tube connecting the mouth and the stomach is called

A the tongue.
B the canal.
C the oesophagus.
D the neck.

16 The word 'masticate' means

A lubricate.
B spit.
C produce enzymes.
D chew.

17 The enzymes in saliva have the ability to

A make food more slippery.
B convert starches into sugars.
C produce chemicals in saliva.
D transfer flavour to the taste buds.

ASH WEDNESDAY

EXERCISE 4

DEATH IN THE DANDENONGS.
At 2 p.m. 16 February, 1983, Cockatoo was a normal, sleepy Australian country town nestling in the Dandenong Ranges just east of Melbourne. By 3.30 p.m. it resembled a war zone . Destroying everything in its path, Victoria's worst ever bushfire descended on the township, claiming 29 lives ....

KANGAROOS PREFER DROWNING.
Terrified holiday makers sheltering on the beach at Aireys Inlet could only watch helplessly as kangaroos jumped from nearby cliff tops to escape yesterday's searing bushfire. Women wept openly as they watched from the beach.............

Of all the acts of Nature, nothing is more terrifying or destructive than a bushfire. A fire can race unchecked through huge areas of bush and forest land, burning everything in its path. In some parts of the world the native bush catches fire easily and burns with great intensity.

For obvious reasons, when people unwisely build their homes close to the bush, great loss of life and property can occur. When a bushfire breaks out in an area of old forest, many valuable trees are lost, and rare species of animals and plants wiped out.

The largest bushfire ever to occur was in Borneo in 1983 when over 30 000 square kilometres of rainforest were burnt out. The three worst bushfire areas in the world are the forested parts of Australia, California, and the French Riviera. Hardly a year passes without a major fire occurring in these places.

February 16,1983 was Ash Wednesday, the first day of Lent in the Christian calendar for that year. In Lent, Christians commemorate the time that Christ spent wandering in the desert. Ash Wednesday got its name from the practice of placing ashes on the heads of Christians who were asking for forgiveness at the beginning of Lent. There were plenty of ashes available for use on Ash Wednesday in 1983.

February 16,1983 was also the hottest February day ever recorded in Victoria and South Australia. The weather forecast was bad enough – strong, dry northerly winds, low humidity and a temperature of 37° C, but no one was prepared for the conditions that actually came. By midday the temperature across most of the two States had reached 43 °C and a wild north wind was blowing in from inland areas, with gusts in excess of 50 km per hour. Power lines snapped in the heat and wind and major fires started in nine locations. Moving with terrible speed the fires engulfed all in their path.

From 'Nature the Annihilator'
G.Wilson

18 Great loss of life and property can occur when

A people do not take care with matches.
B people locate their houses in bush settings.
C people do not check the weather forecasts.
D when the fire brigade is not notified.

19 In France, an area badly affected by bushfires is

A the forested area of southern California.
B the Riviera coastline.
C the forested area of the east.
D the Borneo rainforest.

20 In Victoria and South Australia hot weather is usually brought by winds from

A east . **B** south. **C** west. **D** north.

21 When we say the humidity is low, it means

A there is a lot of moisture in the air.
B the air is very dry.
C the air is very hot.
D the air is very cold.

22 It is a great pity when an area of old growth forest is burnt out because
A valuable trees are lost.
B rare fauna and flora may be wiped out.
C breeding sites for native animals are lost.
D All of the preceding.

23 The hottest February day ever recorded in Victoria was in
A 1983. B 1993. C 1984. D 1923.

24 The women on the beach at Aireys Inlet were affected because of
A the heat from the flames.
B the sight of the desperate kangaroos.
C the war zone that they could see.
D the strong winds.

25 The township of Cockatoo is
A in inland Victoria.
B on the coast.
C near Melbourne.
D a suburb of Melbourne.

26 The use of the title 'Ash Wednesday' to describe the fire disaster was
A simple. B apt. C a warning. D a sign.

READING TEST 5

THE GODS MUST BE ANGRY

EXERCISE 5

Thor was the god of war. He was also a blacksmith who worked in his smithy located on the edge of the dark North Sea. When he wielded his great hammer and slammed it onto the huge anvil in his forge to make Viking war swords, sparks flew and the noise of each blow rolled across the frozen hillsides. The thunder and lightning so created set off the great storms which often swept down the North Sea from the Arctic – or so the Scandinavians (the people from Norway, Sweden and Denmark) believed.

In the week beginning 30 January 1995, Thor must have been very busy and very angry because the weather was terrible. A series of storms pounded the Netherlands coast and mountainous waves, pushed along by gale force winds, were hurled against the Dutch dike system. The dikes were breached and the sea swept inland.

Jan Hendriks and his wife Olga hadn't had much sleep that week. They lived in Nijmegen, a town close to one of the river dikes, and it had been raining for days. On the night of 3 February, Jan woke at 3 a.m. Sensing that something was wrong he leaned over to switch on the light on his bedside table. It wasn't working. Straightaway Jan knew that he and Olga were in trouble – deep, wet, trouble as it happened.

From Nature the Annihilator. G.Wilson.

27 What did people believe set off the Arctic storms?
A The gale force winds that pounded the coast.
B The hammer blows in the forge.
C The thunder and lightning.
D The war between the gods.

28 Why did they think Thor was so angry at the end of January 1995?
A The Dutch people couldn't sleep.
B The weather was particularly bad.
C There had been a lot of lightning.
D There was a gale blowing.

29 What was the deep trouble that had happened in Nijmegen?
A Electricity failure.
B Lightning strike.
C The river dikes had broken.
D Jan and Olga had overslept.

THE TEAMS

EXERCISE 6

A cloud of dust on the long, white road,
And the teams go creeping on
Inch by inch with their weary load;
And by the power of the green-hide goad
The distant goal is won.

A teamster at work

With eyes half-shut to the blinding dust,
And necks to the yokes bent low,
The beasts are pulling as bullocks must
And the shining tyres might almost rust
While the spokes are turning slow.

With face half-hid by a broad-brimmed hat,
That shades from the heat's white waves,
And shouldered whip with its green-hide plait,
The driver plods with a gait like that
Of his weary, patient slaves.

He wipes his brow, for the day is hot,
And spits to the left with spite,
He shouts at Bally and flicks at Spot,
And raises dust from the back of Scot,
And spits to the dusty right.

He'll sometimes pause as a thing of form
In front of a settler's door,
And ask for a drink, and remark "It's warm,"
Or say "There's signs of a thunderstorm;"
But he seldom utters more.

The rains are heavy on roads like these
And, fronting his lonely home,
For days together the settler sees
The wagons bogged to the axletrees,
Or ploughing the sodden loam.

And then, when roads are at their worst,
The bushman's children hear
The cruel blows of the whips reversed
While bullocks pull as their hearts would burst,
And bellow with pain and fear.

And thus – with glimpses of home and rest -
Are the long, long journeys done;
And thus – ' tis a thankless life at the best! –
Is Distance fought in the mighty West,
And the lonely battle won.

Henry Lawson

30 What was the green-hide goad?
A A rope. **B** A sling. **C** A whip. **D** An axle.

31 Why were the bullocks' eyes half-shut?
A They were tired and bored. B It was dusty. **C** It was sunny. **D** Their eyes were sore.

32 Why might the iron tyres almost rust?
A There had been wet weather.
B The wheels turned so slowly.
C They were made of iron.
D They were difficult to clean.

33 In the early part of the poem, what kind of day was it?
A Hot and wet. **B** Hot and humid. **C** Dry and cool. **D** Hot and sunny

34 Why was the wagon 'ploughing the sodden loam'?
A The bullock driver was helping the farmer.
B The bullock driver was good at ploughing.
C The wagon's axles had broken.
D The wagon was bogged.

35 What kind of a life does a bullock driver have?
- **A** Lonely and simple .
- **B** Superstitious and strange.
- **C** Friendly and companionable.
- **D** Careful and hopeful.

36 Why were the whips reversed?
- **A** The bullocky had to force the bullocks to work.
- **B** The bullocky was cruel.
- **C** To pull the bullocks out of the mud.
- **D** It made it easier for the bullocks.

37 What is a 'gait'?
- **A** A kind of wrapping around the foot.
- **B** A kind of shoe.
- **C** A way of walking.
- **D** A kind of grunt.

38 What was the 'yoke'?
- **A** The shaft tying the bullocks to the wagon.
- **B** The shaft tying each pair of bullocks together.
- **C** The brake shaft that slows the wagon down.
- **D** The front of the wagon.

39 Why did the bullocks have their necks bent low?
- **A** They were tired and dispirited.
- **B** It was extremely hot.
- **C** They could see better that way.
- **D** They could pull better that way.

40 In those days what was the biggest problem in the opening up of the west?
- **A** The climate.
- **B** The long distances.
- **C** The thankless tasks.
- **D** The lack of food.

READING TEST 5

THE BOLL WEEVIL

EXERCISE 7

A Boll Weevil

One of the most destructive of all insect pests, the boll weevil lays its eggs inside the buds and ripening bolls (fruits) of the cotton plant. The adult insect has a long snout, is grayish in color, and is usually less than 6 mm long. The time from egg to egg-laying adult is about three weeks so four or five generations may breed in one season. The larva, a fat, white maggot, lives on the internal tissues of the buds and bolls. An infested bud usually drops, but most of the damaged bolls remain on the plant where they become stunted and dwarfed, thus hindering harvesting. Adult weevils that emerge in the autumn hibernate over winter in grass, old bolls or other vegetation, or in the seeds around the cotton gins. They reappear in spring. Native to Central America and the West Indies, in 1892 it spread across the Rio Grande into the cotton-growing districts of the United States.

41 The boll weevil was originally from
- **A** the United States.
- **B** Central America and The West Indies
- **C** Canada.
- **D** Brazil.

42 The boll weevil ruins
- **A** the harvest.
- **B** the young buds .
- **C** the cotton fibres in the boll.
- **D** All the preceding.

43 Perhaps its worst feature is
- **A** its tolerance to insecticides.
- **B** its offensive odour.
- **C** its ability to reproduce rapidly.
- **D** its ability to fly.

EXERCISE 8 DANGER LURKS

The Richter Scale is a 10-point scale used to measure the amount of energy released in an earthquake. Small earth movements, say 3 on the scale are common and hardly felt. An earthquake greater than 8 on the scale is both rare and highly destructive. The only earthquake to cause loss of life in Australia (measuring 5. 5) occurred in Newcastle on 28 December, 1989, when the Newcastle Workers' Club collapsed killing six people.

Earthquakes are the vibrations set off when parts of the Earth's crust move against each other. Although we feel that the Earth is solid, and therefore still, it really isn't. The Earth's crust is made up of about a dozen huge blocks and several smaller ones which are constantly on the move. Like a gigantic mobile jigsaw they move slowly in response to currents coming from deep within the molten interior of the Earth. As these moving pieces rub or scrape against each other vibrations are set off. When the movement is sudden or jerky the result is an earthquake.

" Throughout the day the streets of the city echoed to the wail of sirens as rescue vehicles carried the dead and injured to hospital. A dark cloud of smoke and dust rose from the rubble of fallen buildings and the fires. The streets were littered with shattered glass and great chunks of bricks and concrete. The city looked as though it had been hit by a bomb." **(From Nature the Annihilator, G. Wilson).**

Sound familiar? Well no, it's not a description of the tragedy of New York's World Trade Centre, which occurred on September 11, 2001, it is an account of the earthquake that struck Mexico City on September19, 1983. One of the largest ever recorded, it was responsible for the death of altogether, counting people who had heart attacks or died later from their injuries, 4 200 people.

The earthquake only lasted for 3 minutes but its effects were devastating. In the Central Business District one hundred multi-storey buildings were destroyed – hotels, office and apartment towers, churches, schools, and medical and government buildings. The quake occurred at 7.19 a.m. An hour later and these blocks would have been packed with employees.

The Cocos Plate is a crustal plate lying off the western coast of Mexico. This small plate is in the process of slowly sliding underneath the much larger North American Plate, but its edge of contact, or fault line, is uneven. From time to time over the centuries uneven bumps on the Cocos Plate have caused it to stick. While the plate is stuck, no movement takes place but great pressure is built up. When finally the force towards movement overcomes friction, the Cocos Plate lurches forward, and enormous shock waves are generated bringing death and misery to surrounding areas. This is exactly what happened in1983. The Cocos Plate moved forward a metre along its whole 450-kilometre edge and the subsequent earthquake measured 7.8 on the Richter scale.

44 The Richter Scale is

A a graphic method of recording earthquakes. **B** a method for measuring Earth movements.
C a record of earthquakes kept in Germany. **D** Both 'A' and 'B'.

45 In its effects, the devastation caused by the Mexican earthquake was like

A a computer simulator. **B** the effects of a gigantic mobile jigsaw.
C a bomb blast. **D** the tragedy at the World Trade centre.

46 What causes the Earth to quake?

A The fact that the Earth is not solid. **B** The sudden movement of crustal plates.
C The loss of flexibility in the Earth's crust. **D** Volcanic disturbances.

47 Why are so many serious earthquakes generated along the Cocos fault?

A Its zone of contact is uneven. **B** It is in a tropical area.
C It is difficult to tell. **D** Two plates are moving apart there.

48 The casualties in Mexico would have been higher

A had the time of the occurrence been later. **B** had the time of the occurrence been earlier.
C if the gas lines had been ruptured. **D** if the water supply had been cut off.

49 In Australia, large earthquakes such as the Mexico one,

A are frequent. **B** are infrequent. **C** are predictable. **D** have not occurred.

50 A point of fracture in the Earth's crust is called a

A block. **B** fault. **C** bump. **D** plate.

THE LAVA TUBES OF UNDARA

EXERCISE 1

Inside one of the Tubes

Undara the sleeping giant, awoke. Welling up from deep inside the crust of the Earth, it threw flaming fountains of molten rock and gas thundering into the darkened sky. Wave after wave of fiery, molten lava slid down the trembling sides of the rapidly building volcano, spreading across the land and incinerating all in its path. Searching fingers of lava found their way into old river systems and began to race outwards in long tubes down the ancient watercourses. At the surface, where the lava was in contact with the atmosphere, it cooled and hardened, but underneath the lava was still boiling hot and the liquid lava continued to flow. The fiery liquid was insulated by the hardened lava outside and so was able to travel incredible distances - over 90 kilometres to the north and over 160 kilometres to the north-west.

Finally the eruption slowed and stopped, but still the lava in the tubes kept flowing on from the lower ends, like water from a hose that has been disconnected from the tap. Long hollow pipes of lava were left in the creek beds – the Undara Lava Tubes of Queensland had been born!

In time, the tubes, which were lower than the surrounding land, became partly covered with sediment and vegetation grew over them. As more time passed, where the lava was thin, parts of the tube roof collapsed. As still more time elapsed the climate became dry, and the collapsed depressions were the only places where a kind of rainforest vegetation could grow. These collapsed, sunken sections of the tubes became conspicuous because of their dense dark-green rainforest-like vegetation that was so different from the surrounding open woodland. And so they were noticed by people, first by Aborigines, who avoided them, and then by European explorers and finally by people who, realising their tourist potential, began to develop them.

1 What was Undara?
- **A** A sleeping giant.
- **B** A dormant volcano.
- **C** A lava pipe.
- **D** A watercourse.

2 The lava flows
- **A** travelled incredible distances.
- **B** occupied old watercourse channels.
- **C** cooled first on the outside.
- **D** All of the preceding.

3 When the eruption stopped, the lava flow
- **A** ceased abruptly.
- **B** ran out of the pipes like water from a hose.
- **C** reversed its direction.
- **D** became unmanageable.

4 The collapsed sections can be recognised today because the microclimate
- **A** has formed large holes.
- **B** has made the river beds sandy
- **C** attracted Aboriginal settlement.
- **D** caused a different vegetation to grow.

5 The Lava Tubes are likely to become
- **A** a danger to passing traffic.
- **B** a major tourist attraction.
- **C** closed to the public.
- **D** no longer visible.

THE WRECK OF THE SIRIUS

EXERCISE 2

The wreck of the Sirius

On 17 March 1790 the Sirius was wrecked on a coral reef close inshore on the southern side of Norfolk Island. It was Captain Hunter's first trip to the island and he did not have the detailed knowledge that Commandant King had of the island's treacherous shores. Earlier Hunter had managed to offload part of his cargo of convicts on the more dangerous eastern side of Norfolk Island, but had been prevented from unloading the remaining convicts and precious provisions, by bad weather. For three days Hunter stood his ship out to sea waiting for the weather to improve. Finally an effort was made to land the remaining cargo in Sydney Bay. The first boats containing provisions had just begun the short trip to shore across the shallow coral reef present on the southern side of the island, when to his dismay, Hunter felt the wind suddenly change from west to south.

Horrified onlookers on shore saw the ship lift, then be caught by the strong rip between the smaller Phillip and Nepean Islands. Sirius began to drift relentlessly towards the reef located closer inshore. Hunter immediately gave orders for the anchor to be dropped, but before the cable could be brought to bear to check it, the ship struck the reef. The on-shore wind blew harder and as it increased so the waves grew quickly in size. The side of the ship was breached and the vessel began to take water.

On board the stricken ship, Hunter ordered the masts to be cut away and pushed overboard to lighten the ship, meanwhile instructing his sailors to try to haul the Sirius forward using the anchor cable. It was no use. As the day wore on the sea rose, but the tide fell wedging the Sirius ever more firmly on the reef. There was great danger of the ship breaking in two, so Commandant King onshore gave the order for the ship to be abandoned and every effort was then bent towards salvaging whatever was possible from the ship. A line was floated ashore tied to an empty keg and a 7 inch rope hawser pulled across with a wooden heart attached, by which means people could be transferred. All floatable things were thrown overboard to be carried ashore by the waves.

The wreck site as it is today.

6 In the passage the word 'breached' means

- **A** twisted.
- **B** holed.
- **C** grounded.
- **D** supported.

7 When the Sirius began to drift towards the reef, Hunter's first move was to

- **A** cut off the masts and rigging.
- **B** throw the floatable provisions overboard.
- **C** drop the anchor.
- **D** haul the ship forward manually.

8 **The masts were cut away in an attempt to**
- **A** allow the ship to be steered better.
- **B** bring the anchor to bear.
- **C** lighten the ship.
- **D** make it easier to unload the remaining cargo.

9 **Hunter stood his ship out to sea because**
- **A** the convicts were mutinous.
- **B** it was safer there while waiting.
- **C** King advised him to.
- **D** the wind was from the south.

10 **In the passage the word 'relentlessly' means**
- **A** alternately.
- **B** strongly.
- **C** definitely.
- **D** slowly but surely.

READING TEST 6

HOME BAKED BREAD

EXERCISE 3

DIRECTIONS

1. Sieve contents of flour pack and place in bowl. Add contents of yeast sachet.
2. Add approximately 300 ml of tepid water sufficient to make a soft but dry dough.
3. Beat for 5 minutes with a wooden spoon until the dough is uniformly smooth.
4. Turn dough onto a floured board and knead for 15-20 minutes.
5. Return the kneaded mixture to the bowl and cover with a clean, dry cloth, then place in a warm position to rise for half an hour.
6. When dough has approximately doubled in size repeat the kneading process for a further 5 minutes.
7. Shape the dough and place in a large, greased tin. Cover with a cloth again and allow to double in size once more, (30 minutes usually)
8. Knead the dough one more time, this time by folding towards you then pushing away with the palm of your hand. Turn the dough a quarter of a turn each time you knead.
9. When the dough feels firm and elastic and no longer sticky, shape and place in baking tin.
10. Bake in a pre-heated oven (190° C) for 30-40 minutes.
11. When cooked turn out loaf onto wooden board. If ready, crust will be hard and loaf will sound hollow when flicked with finger. If not completely ready return to oven minus tin for a further 5 minutes to harden crust.
12. Cool the loaf on a wire rack before storing.

11 **The flour should be**
- **A** placed straight into the bowl with the yeast.
- **B** mixed with the yeast then sieved.
- **C** made first into a watery dough.
- **D** sieved before being combined with yeast.

12 **To cause the mixture to rise properly,**
- **A** the flour must have yeast added.
- **B** the dough must be beaten with a wooden spoon.
- **C** tepid water must be added to the flour.
- **D** All of the preceding.

13 **When the dough is firm, rubbery, and has lost its stickiness**
- **A** it is ready for kneading.
- **B** it is ready for baking.
- **C** it should be floured and kneaded.
- **D** it should be aired on a board.

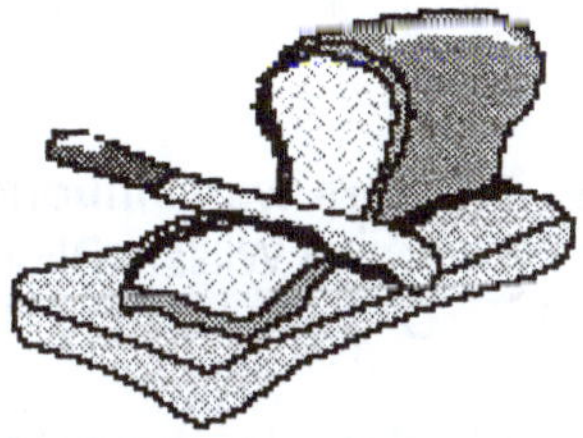

14 **Cooking in the way described recommends**
- **A** any part of the process to be 'skipped'.
- **B** the loaf to be returned to the oven if not fully cooked.
- **C** sampling with a wooden skewer.
- **D** flavouring to be added at the end.

15 **After the dough has been taken out of the bowl for the second time, it should be**
- **A** floured then baked.
- **B** covered with a warm cloth.
- **C** kneaded again for a short time.
- **D** shaped and left to rise once more.

MATTHEW FLINDERS

EXERCISE 4

When Captain Cook met his death in February 1779 at Hawaii, there lived in the village of Donington, Lincolnshire, a boy of five. He, like James Cook before him, was to win fame by his own endeavours as the leading explorer, navigator, marine surveyor and map-maker of his day. His name was Matthew Flinders.

Flinders was the son, grandson and great grandson of country physicians of Flemish extraction, and was educated at Donington parish school and at Horbling grammar school a few miles away. It was here that he studied Latin and Greek and gained a grounding in mathematics which subsequently enabled him to master the science of navigation.'

(-Australia's Heritage Paul Hamlyn Pty Ltd 1970)

It was supposed that Flinders would follow the family profession, but, after he had read Defoe's *Robinson Crusoe* as a lad, he announced that he meant to go to sea and no amount of argument would shake his determination. He wanted to sail in "uncharted seas" and he was determined not to be among the "unnoticed middle order of mankind". He confessed " I burned to have adventures of my own."

At the age of 14, Flinders joined the Navy and served as a midshipman on the *Bellerophon,* the greatest warship of the time, and participated in The Battle of Brest. His experiences on board this ship however confirmed his belief that his destiny lay outside the normal run of naval duties. When the chance came for him to travel with Captain John Hunter (later Governor) to the colony of New South Wales in 1796, it was too good an opportunity to miss.

The next five years of Flinders's life were the most productive. With George Bass he circumnavigated Van Diemen's Land, discovered Bass Strait and charted most of the coast south of Sydney. In the leaky, unseaworthy ship *Investigator* he circumnavigated Australia, keeping meticulous records all the while. On his way back to England in 1803 on another leaky ship, the *Cumberland,* Flinders was forced to put in to the French Island of Mauritius. Here he found to his dismay that France and England were again at war. The French Governor Decaen thought that Flinders might be a spy and so detained him on the island for six and a half years. Decaen confiscated Flinders' records of his voyages and sent them to France. Fortunately Flinders had sent a duplicate set of his charts to England by another ship and so he was eventually able to publish an account of his "Voyage to Terra Australis". Flinders' health, never good, was damaged by his long stay at Mauritius and he died at the young age of 40. Sadly, as he lay dying, unconscious and unaware, the first copy of his book was placed beside him.

Matthew Flinders

16 Flinders was influenced in his decision to become a sailor

- **A** by William Bligh's exploits on the Bounty.
- **B** by his desire to learn to navigate.
- **C** when he read Defoe's book.
- **D** by his teachers at the parish school.

17 Flinders, in character,

- **A** was unusually lazy for an explorer.
- **B** was determined and resourceful.
- **C** was prone to take chances.
- **D** was pleasant but forgetful.

18 Flinder's ability at mathematics enabled him
- **A** to become an accomplished navigator and map maker.
- **B** to become a determined explorer.
- **C** to become a well-liked commander.
- **D** to escape from Mauritius.

19 Flinders' most productive time as an explorer was
- **A** when he sailed with Cook.
- **B** when he served on 'Bellerophon'.
- **C** during his early years in the colony.
- **D** after he left Mauritius.

20 Which description best suits Flinders?
- **A** Talented seaman who died too soon.
- **B** Talented seaman whose obstinacy caused his own downfall.
- **C** Cook's most talented pupil.
- **D** A lifelong friend of Governor Hunter.

21 The decision by Flinders to send a set of charts to England on another ship could be described as
- **A** unnecessary.
- **B** selfish.
- **C** prudent.
- **D** stressful.

22 In the text the word 'detained' means
- **A** entertained.
- **B** defended.
- **C** punished.
- **D** imprisoned.

23 In the text the word 'meticulous' means
- **A** precise.
- **B** obvious
- **C** superficial.
- **D** descriptive.

READING TEST 6

BELIEVE IT OR NOT - MUSCLES

EXERCISE 5

We all know that muscles are the workers of the body; our bodies have over 600 of them. They are made up of tight bunches of long, stringy fibres. But did you know that these workers can turn to fat? When we start exercising a lot, our muscles grow thicker and stronger, then, when we stop exercising, these same muscles shrink and grow weaker. We might expect this to happen. How is it then that some muscles turn to fat without shrinking? Well the people who have been exercising a lot are also used to eating a lot, and when they stop exercising, you guessed it, they tend to eat the same amount. The extra energy is stored as fat in the muscle fibres.

24 When we exercise, our muscles
- A turn thicker and stronger.
- **B** begin to store energy.
- C shrink and grow weaker.
- **D** lose weight.

25 When we stop exercising we may grow fat because
- **A** we eat more than we need to.
- **B** our diet is inappropriate.
- **C** diet is a personal thing.
- **D** the muscle cells automatically grow larger.

26 Which description best fits our muscles?
- **A** Short stringy fibres crisscrossing a cheese-like layer of fatty substance.
- **B** Loose groups of cells gathered in the middle.
- **C** Elastic bands stretched inside a plastic tube.
- **D** Pieces of string wound around a bottle.

HOT AIR

EXERCISE 6

On the 25th July, 1868, Mr F.W. Birmingham, a surveyor, experienced a vision as he walked through Parramatta Park, near Sydney. It involved heads floating towards him and subsequently he observed an 'ark' moving along the same path as he, and landing some distance ahead. A disembodied voice spoke to him asking him if he wished to enter and inspect the ark. Mr Birmingham, once he had recovered from his initial shock, replied that he would most gladly accompany the spirit. He was 'floated' to the object, which was triangular in shape. A second more-transparent spirit spoke to him inside the Ark. Of a neutral grey tint and in the general shape of a man, it was dressed in a frock coat as was usual for the time.

Mr Birmingham was shown around the ark, after which the spirit disappeared and he fell into his normal sleeping state. Waking next morning in his bed he was deeply impressed by his vision of the night, so much so that he published a book entitled, *A Machine To Go Through The Air*.

Almost a hundred and fifty years later we can only wonder if this was the first recorded visit by an unidentified flying object to visit Australia, or whether Mr Birmingham was perhaps, for various possible reasons, in an unstable state of mind. We can be certain however that the first recorded flight of a hot air balloon took place in Paris, France, in June 1783. Some eleven metres in diameter, the balloon belonging to the Montgolfier brothers was inflated over a fire of straw and rags. Watchers were spellbound as the hot air forced the balloon to rise majestically skywards. Later that year the Montgolfiers inaugurated the first passenger flight by reinflating their balloon in the presence of King Louis XVI and Queen Marie Antoinette. Beneath the canopy, a cage was suspended containing a sheep, a rooster and a duck. The King inspected every part of the 'aerostatic' machine including the means whereby it was inflated. The Queen was so entranced that she ordered that the flying sheep be installed in her private zoo after its airborne adventure. In those troubled times of privation when many were starving, we can be less certain about the fate of the rooster and the duck.

Balloons in Parramatta Park

Back in Australia, two Australian air adventurers, John Allen and Thomas Gale, in January 1871, managed to get their balloon airborne, strangely enough in the same place where Mr Birmingham had witnessed his vision. Their flight, unfortunately, came to a sticky end in the mud of the Parramatta River. In 1890 Miss Van Tassell made Australian balloon history when she ascended to a height of two kilometres above Newcastle and parachuted down. Not only did she make her ascents solo, but she was without the comparative safety of a basket, using instead a trapeze bar - at times hanging by her feet upside down!

27 Why was Mr Birmingham slow to reply to the spirit?

- **A** He was considering the offer.
- **B** He really did not want to go.
- **C** He didn't want the responsibility.
- **D** He was too shocked to reply at first.

28 The second spirit was

- **A** full-bodied and more solid than the first.
- **B** dressed in the clothes of the time.
- **C** not very co-operative.
- **D** full-bodied and brightly coloured.

29 **Nowadays we would view Mr Birmingham's account as**
- **A** improbable.
- **B** substantial.
- **C** superficial.
- **D** sensible.

30 **The second flight of the Montgolfiers' balloon was unusual because**
- **A** it contained animals as well as people.
- **B** the Queen decided to fly as well.
- **C** it had a cage of animals suspended beneath the canopy.
- **D** the King was asked to supervise the inflation.

31 **Miss van Tassels' exploits were historic because**
- **A** she flew so high over Newcastle.
- **B** she performed trapeze acts while flying.
- **C** she flew solo.
- **D** All of the preceding.

32 **The flight by Gale and Allen**
- **A** was highly successful.
- **B** was successful but had an unfortunate ending.
- **C** took place in Sydney's Domain.
- **D** was a complete failure.

33 **From the text, the word 'privation' means**
- **A** belonging to the army.
- **B** to be arrested many times.
- **C** lacking the necessities of life.
- **D** to be deprived of one's privacy.

READING TEST 6

THE HAMMOCK

EXERCISE 7

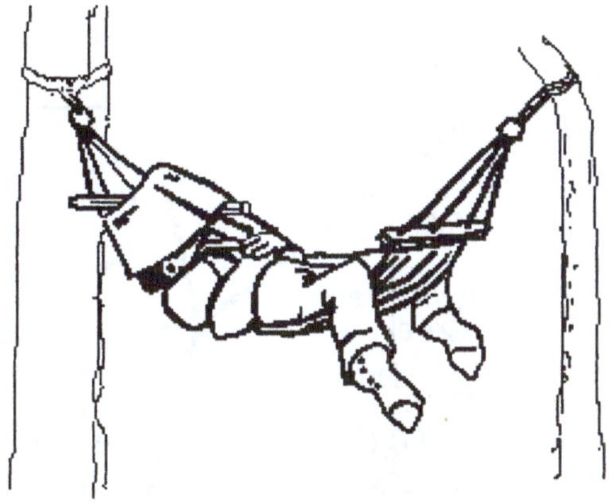

Hammocks are difficult to climb into but once in, they are also hard to fall out of. But do you know the origin of the word hammock?

Well the hammock was invented by the Indians of South America. Their word for the hammock was 'hamaca'. Easy to make, the Indians used it for resting and sleeping in the forest. The early Spanish explorers and settlers thought that it was such a good way to sleep in the hot climate (and remember houses were in short supply) that they quickly borrowed the idea. The idea next spread to sailing ships and the military and of course it didn't take long for 'hamaca' to be changed into the word 'hammock' that is used today.

34 **The Indians used to sleep and rest in hammocks because**
- **A** they were easy to make.
- **B** they knew how to climb into them.
- **C** they were cool to use.
- **D** All of the preceding.

35 **The idea of the hammock was**
- **A** borrowed from the Spanish.
- **B** quickly used by the early explorers and settlers.
- **C** not taken up for some time.
- **D** used first by the sailors.

36 **The sailors probably liked the hammock because**
- **A** they were made of rope.
- **B** they could see through the net.
- **C** they would not fall out of them in rough weather.
- **D** they were provided free in the ships.

37 **The word 'hammock' is**
- **A** a corruption of an Indian word.
- **B** originally a word used to mean 'a small hill'.
- **C** a corruption of the word for climate.
- **D** originally a word meaning 'house'.

BOMBADERRY CREEK

EXERCISE 8

Located only 2 km north of Nowra, New South Wales, is Bombaderry Creek Walk. Turn off the Princes Highway into Narang Rd and leave your car at the first car park that you encounter. Avoid the lower car park because of the danger of vandals interfering with your car. Take your tuckerbox, thermos and camera and you are ready to set off. Proceed along the way indicated by the signs, to the escarpment.

At the cliff edge you can look down on the weir that was built in 1938 for the town's water supply. Ignore the sign saying 'Weir Walk' and follow the track saying 'East Walk'; you will cross below the weir on your return trip. As you walk along the cliff top you will notice a typical dry eucalypt forest with grevillias, flannel flowers, tea tree and banksias, but soon your first descent will take you into rain forest species growing in the shade of the huge overhanging cliffs. The sandstone gorge that you are now in was formed some 240 million years ago. Continue on past mossy gullies, orchid covered cliffs and water worn caves until you reach your first real obstruction where a massive section of the cliff has fallen into the creek. Scrambling around this impressive feature, walk on until you reach a sign saying 'She-Oak Crossing'. Here you turn to cross the creek on two wooden bridges below a massive casuarina (she-oak) tree. This is a good spot to 'have a cuppa' or eat an apple because by now you have been walking for about an hour and a half.

The return walk on the western side duplicates the eastern side except that now you have some really strange tree formations to look at. In two places the giant eucalyptus maculata trees (spotted gums) have attached themselves to the side of the cliff and one particularly big one has grown across the path like a huge elephant's foot. If you look across you will get a good view of the rock fall that you had to climb over before. The track finally reaches a point where some steep steps lead back up to the top of the cliffs. You will come to a boggy stretch (but the path is dry). Here the ecosystem changes and you may be lucky enough to see a special kind of frog and a special kind of butterfly that only lives in such wet areas. Another lookout is located opposite your very first viewing point because you are nearly back to the start of the walk. Descend to the creek once more and cross it on stepping-stones then climb back up to your car.

The walk, graded as moderate by the Parks and Wildlife Service, is one of the best short walks you will ever go on because of the interesting geological features to be seen, the abundance of bird life and the variety of ecosystems present. Best of all, even though it is so close to town, very few people seem to know about it.

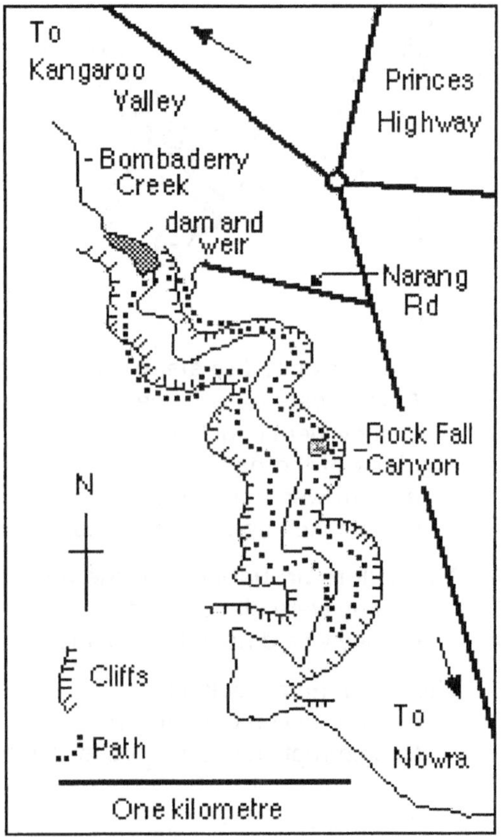

38 The Bombaderry Walk
- **A** follows the course of a creek.
- **B** is a popular walk.
- **C** can be completed in less than two hours at a normal walking pace.
- **D** is graded as difficult.

39 An escarpment is a(n)
- **A** gorge.
- **B** line of cliffs.
- **C** cave formation.
- **D** overhang.

40 The section of fallen cliff is
- **A** on the western side.
- **B** on the eastern side.
- **C** impassable.
- **D** continuous.

41 The return path travels
- **A** along a disused train line.
- **B** by the Camellia Gardens.
- **C** across the top of the weir.
- **D** across the creek on stepping- stones.

42 **The Bombaderry Walk is**
A well signposted.
B poorly signposted.
C very time-consuming.
D a sunny walk.

43 **You should leave your car at the top car park because**
A it is closer to the road.
B it is closer to the Walk.
C of the danger of vandalism.
D It has the best facilities.

44 **From the passage you should conclude that an ecosystem is**
A a water feature. B a set of life conditions. C a eucalyptus tree. D a regulated path.

45 **The walk is a memorable one because of**
A its strange tree formations.
B the interesting geology.
C the variety of its ecosystems.
D All of the above.

READING TEST 6

ANDY'S GONE WITH CATTLE

EXERCISE 9

Our Andy's gone with cattle now –
Our hearts are out of order –
With drought he's gone to battle now
Across the Queensland border.

He's left us in dejection now;
Our thoughts with him are roving;
It's dull on this selection now,
Since Andy went a-droving.

Who shall wear the cheerful face
In times when things are slackest?
And who shall whistle round the place
When Fortune frowns her blackest?

Oh who shall cheek the squatter now
When he comes round us snarling?
His tongue is growing hotter now
Since Andy crossed the Darling.

Oh may the showers in torrents fall,
And all the tanks run over;
And may the grass grow green and tall
In pathways of the drover;

And may good angels send the rain
On desert stretches sandy;
And when the summer comes again
God grant 'twill bring us Andy.

Henry Lawson *

46 **Why were the people's hearts 'out of order'?**
A Andy had taken all the cattle.
B Andy had gone to Queensland droving.
C The squatter was annoying them.
D It was a time of drought.

47 **Andy would be missed because**
A he did most of the work.
B he was never down hearted.
C he handled the cattle.
D they were having a bad time.

48 **Why would the squatter's tongue be growing hotter?**
A He was an unpleasant person.
B The squatters hated the farmers on the selections.
C He was demanding money.
D He knew that Andy was away.

49 **From the passage, a tank is most likely a word for a**
A river. B creek. C dam. D bottle.

50 **In the last two verses of the poem, the poet is**
A praying for good rains along the drover's track.
B praying that there will be enough grass for Andy's cattle.
C praying for Andy's safe return.
D All the preceding.

* Henry Lawson was the most famous poet and story-teller of Australia's pioneering days.

BLOODY BRIDGE

EXERCISE 1

Bloody Bridge as it is today.

Of all the terrible legends of Norfolk Island, this is perhaps the most famous. But legend it is. It concerns the construction of the stone bridge in Music valley just beyond the old convict cemetery. The story goes like this.

In the time of the second convict settlement of Norfolk Island in 1825, a detachment of convicts was engaged in the construction of a stone bridge across the creek in Music Valley at the eastern end of the Island. The overseer was a particularly brutal one and he taunted the convicts until they rebelled. One of the convicts struck the guard from behind with a rock from the bridge, killing him instantly. The convicts knew that they would be hung if found out, but what to do with the body? The solution was to wall up the body of the unfortunate guard in the half-finished bridge. When the overseer was found to be missing at the change of guard time, the convicts said that he had gone down to the beach for a swim; it being a hot day, the inference being that he may have drowned. A search failed to find the guard so the convicts were questioned more closely. All was going well until a suspicious red stain was seen to be weeping from between the hurriedly placed rocks.

The body of course was soon discovered, and after a swift trial the convicts were found guilty of murder. They were executed the very next day. They were buried in a common grave, outside the consecrated ground of the cemetery, called, to the present, 'Murderers Mound'. In the winter of 2001, a series of high tides combined with bad weather washed human bones from the area onto the small beach at the end of the cemetery, thus adding credibility to the story today.

1 The murdered officer was
- **A** unhappy with his service at Norfolk island.
- **B** unlucky to be murdered the way he was.
- **C** disliked for his extreme cruelty.
- **D** drowned while swimming.

2 The convicts sought to hide the body
- **A** by taunting the guard.
- **B** by pretending to work on the bridge.
- **C** because they knew the penalty for murder.
- **D** None of the previous.

3 The murderers were betrayed by
- **A** other convicts.
- **B** the small amount of work done.
- **C** the tell-tale bloodstain.
- **D** the hollow sound of the bridge.

4 The story is made more believable by
- **A** the trial documents.
- **B** the eye-witness accounts.
- **C** the commandant's records.
- **D** the exposure of human bones much later.

5 In the passage the word 'taunted' means
- **A** punished.
- **B** satisfied.
- **C** provoked.
- **D** bribed.

6 In the passage the word 'weeping' means
- **A** seeping.
- **B** crying.
- **C** running.
- **D** disfiguring.

7 An 'inference' is a
- **A** suggestion.
- **B** precedence.
- **C** certainty.
- **D** qualification.

8 A 'legend' is
- **A** a disturbance.
- **B** a lengthy book.
- **C** a popular myth.
- **D** a truthful account.

PECULIAR PIKAS

EXERCISE 2

Imagine a tiny, busy creature the size of a small bird, that looks like a rabbit, has small round ears, a loud call, and spends most of the day scurrying around collecting grass, flowers, herbs and any other vegetation it can find. You are thinking of the Canadian pika. Actually the pika is a strange but endearing kind of alpine rock rabbit that occupy dens deep inside the talus slopes that accumulate at the foot of steep mountains high up in the Canadian Rocky Mountains. When a new road is pushed through the mountains the pikas say, 'thank you very much,' and soon colonise the rock fills of the cuttings and culverts.

Unlike most other rabbits, the pika is most active in the daylight hours. Even so, because it is so tiny and its coat resembles the rocks and rubble of its surroundings, this small creature is seldom seen by most hikers. Its presence is more often betrayed by the loud braying beep that it gives as an alarm warning to other pikas. The call is followed by acceleration underground.

Since pikas do not hibernate, they must store food for the winter period. As a consequence during the brief summer period they are extremely busy gathering all sorts of vegetation. They lay out the material that they collect on bare rocks for drying by the Sun. When their harvest is well-enough cured, it is added to the piles of hay in caves deep inside their boulder homes.

A Pika. Note the small rounded ears.

When winter covers the alpine world in deep snow, these little bundles of life are snug and warm below. Running back and forth between their caches, they traverse well-worn routes with hardly a glimmer of light. Cross-country skiers slide along unaware of the drama below. Spring, when the snow is well and truly melting, is the time for birthing, and female pikas have three or four babies at this time. Their main predator is the weasel but pikas are extremely quick movers and therefore hard to catch.

8 Curing the vegetation by the Sun
- **A** makes it easier to share.
- **B** makes it more digestible.
- **C** makes it easier to handle.
- **D** enables it to be stored for long periods.

9 Pikas are seldom seen
- **A** only because they are small.
- **B** only because they are well camouflaged.
- **C** because they are small and well camouflaged.
- **D** because they are very quiet.

10 Pikas differ from most other wild creatures because
- **A** they are nocturnal.
- **B** they are extremely energetic.
- **C** they store their food.
- **D** they are most active in daylight.

11 Pikas are
- **A** herbivorous.
- **B** carnivorous.
- **C** omnivorous.
- **D** destructive.

12 Pikas can be best described as
- **A** mischievous.
- **B** meddlesome.
- **C** energetic.
- **D** frenzied.

13 A 'cache' is
- **A** a den.
- **B** a hiding place.
- **C** a storage place.
- **D** an underground track.

14 You know when there are pikas about because
- **A** they stand up like a gophers.
- **B** they sound a warning call.
- **C** they thump the ground like other rabbits.
- **D** of their numerous hills on the ground.

H.M.S. BELLEROPHON

EXERCISE 3

An old painting of Bellerophon lying in Plymouth Harbour.

On June 1st 1815 an attempt was made by the French to break the blockade of Europe imposed by the British navy. France under Napoleon had already conquered most of Europe but was short of food. A convoy of American grain ships escorted by a fleet of French warships attempted to penetrate the blockade and unload at the French port of Brest. The convoy was intercepted however by the British fleet commanded by Admiral Howe. A great naval engagement ensued and for many hours the battle raged. Although some of the grain ships managed to limp into harbour, eventually the British emerged as victors inflicting heavy losses on the French.

One of the British warships participating in the battle was *Bellerophon*. With 74 guns, *Bellerophon*, the flagship of the Fleet, was possibly the finest warship afloat at the time. The ship was in the thick of the battle for some hours, taking a bad battering, and her casualties included the captain, Rear Admiral Pasley, who lost a leg to a cannon shot. On board *Bellerophon* at the time was a young officer, scarcely more than a boy, acting as Aide-de-Camp to the Admiral. His name was Matthew Flinders.

In between bouts of destruction caused by French broadsides and the noise and chaos of the *Bellerophon's* own guns being fired as the battle raged back and forth, Flinders was able to find time to jot down notes on the course of the battle for the Admiral. This was one of his official duties. The description in his journal, copied up at the end of the battle, runs to 40 pages and is regarded by naval historians as the best account of this most famous battle. From it they are able to judge exactly the course of the engagement.

Flinders survived the 'Battle of the Glorious First' and, at a later date of course, became quite famous in different way as a navigator and explorer, although still serving as an officer in the Royal Navy. The *Bellerophon* too lived on to carry out at least one more famous voyage when she carried Napoleon from France to Portsmouth before he was transported as a prisoner to the Island of St Helena in the Atlantic Ocean.

15 Why was Bellerophon special?
A It had 74 guns. **B** It was a fine ship. **C** It was Howe's flagship. **D** All of the preceding.

16 What is a blockade?
A The forced isolation of an area by land or sea.
B A naval engagement involving warships.
B The rapid firing of a ship's guns.
D The final stage of a war.

17 The Battle of Brest became known as
A the Brest Blockade.
B the Battle of the Glorious First.
B the Convoy Conflict.
D Howe's Triumph.

18 What was the purpose of the English naval actions?
A to capture Napoleon.
B to defeat the French fleet.
C to cause the French to fight among themselves.
D to starve the French into submission.

19 **Why was Flinders' journal so important?**
- **A** It caused Flinders to be promoted.
- **B** It saved him from being wounded.
- **C** It provided an accurate account of the battle.
- **D** None of the preceding.

20 **Bellerophon later became famous as**
- **A** the Royal Transport ship.
- **B** a floating prison.
- **C** the ship that took charge of Napoleon.
- **D** Flinders' exploration ship.

21 **After the Battle of Brest, Flinders**
- **A** went on to become famous as a writer.
- **B** reassessed his role in the navy.
- **C** left the navy to become an explorer.
- **D** became Aide-de-Camp to the Admiral.

FLOATING AND PAINFUL

READING TEST 7

EXERCISE 4

Have you ever been stung by a blue bottle? If you have, you will know all about an extremely painful experience. Each year on New South Wales beaches, when the north-easterly sea breezes coincide with the hot summer weather, many bathers are stung by these floating, blue, poison factories.

Strangely, each blue bottle is not a single animal. It is made up of a colony of four separate, but interconnected animals; all are dependent on each other and cannot live apart. The topmost, most visible creature to us, is the semi-transparent, blue sail which provides flotation to the other parts. In a school of blue bottles, half the sails face one way, and the rest are at 90° to that as a protection against an adverse wind blowing the whole school onto a beach.

Underneath the blue float are the other animals - some are concerned with reproduction, some trumpet-shaped ones with eating and digestion, and others, those with the long tentacles, sting and paralyse small sea animals to provide food. To the unwary human swimmer, the metre long stinging tentacles can be a prelude to a burning sensation, or at worst, nausea and vomiting, severe muscle pain and even breathing difficulty.

The best treatment for blue bottle sting is to apply an ice pack for five to fifteen minutes. Vinegar, which is often recommended, is only useful for jellyfish stings. If a tentacle, or part of one, is still attached, it should be washed off gently with salt water. Do not use fresh water as this will activate the tentacle to inject more poison. Scratching the sting only serves to make it feel worse, and can lead to infection.

Scientists are still mystified by the life cycle of the blue bottle. They have no idea how the separate animals come to live together. So next time you poke a blue bottle that has been stranded on the beach with a stick just to make it pop, spare a thought for this oddity of Nature.

22 **Blue bottles are most troublesome on New South Wales beaches**
- **A** in the spring.
- **B** when sea breezes and warm weather coincide.
- **C** in all seasons.
- **D** in the evening.

23 **The blue bottle is unusual because**
- **A** it has a flotation chamber.
- **B** it is semi-transparent.
- **C** it is dangerous to humans.
- **D** it is not a single animal.

24 **When treating a blue bottle sting it is**
- **A** advisable to use an ice pack.
- **B** not advisable to use fresh water.
- **C** useless to swab with vinegar.
- **D** All the preceding.

25 **The angle of the blue floats in relation to the body parts**
- **A** is a natural safety device for the blue bottle.
- **B** allows it to float better.
- **C** changes as the day wears on.
- **D** makes it semi-transparent.

26 **When you are swimming on the beach it is wise to**
- **A** take blue bottle sting repellent with you.
- **B** be cautious when nor-east winds are blowing.
- **C** stay close to the shore.
- **D** take a thermos of cold water with you.

LIGHTHOUSES

EXERCISE 5

Greenway's lighthouse at South Head had to be supported with iron bands.

The early sailing ships were always at the mercy of the wind and sea, and captains were never quite sure exactly where they were after the long journey across the southern Indian Ocean. Moreover, landfall would often occur at night, so it is little wonder that in the days of sail, shipping disasters were common around the Australian coast. In the 1840s a flurry of construction occurred to remedy the situation. Prior to then, there were only a handful of navigation lights to guide ships along Australia's vast 20 000 kilometre coastline.

The very first navigation light was an iron basket filled with burning coals and held aloft on a tripod. It was located on South Head, Sydney, during the 1790s. Hardly a reliable guide for the narrow entrance to Port Jackson, it was replaced in 1816 by Australia's first lighthouse. Designed by the convict architect, Francis Greenway, the light from its 23 metre tower could be seen 40 kilometres out to sea. This stone lighthouse lasted until 1866 when it became unstable and had to be strapped with iron. A new lighthouse was built behind it.

Australia's most westerly lighthouse is on Dirk Hartog Island, Western Australia, while the most easterly is at Byron Bay, NSW. The most southerly lighthouse is at Matsuyker Island off the coast of Tasmania, and the most northerly lights the way on Booby Island, famous for its sea birds in Torres Strait. Also in the north is the lightship, Carpentaria, stationed 275 kilometres west of Thursday Island.

Each lighthouse has its own signalling code, and the frequency and duration of light flashes given out enable shipping to identify the lighthouse, and therefore the ship's position. Most of the isolated lighthouses are now fully automatic and light-keeping is not the lonely occupation it once was.

The lighthouse at Cape Otway. Cape Otway juts out into the sea at the western approach to Bass Strait – a region notoriously dangerous for shipping even today.

27 In the early days of sail there were many wrecks on the southern Australian coast because

A land fall was often not made in daylight.
B lights were weak or non-existent.
C ships had to go where wind and currents took them.
D All of the preceding.

28 The phrase 'prior to then' means

A after that time.
B before that.
C because of that.
D possibly.

29 The first lighthouse made by Greenway

A was located inside Sydney Harbour.
B had to be replaced after 50 years of service.
C was an iron basket filled with coals.
D guarded the entrance to Port Phillip.

30 The Cape Otway light was installed
- **A** to guard the entrance to Port Phillip.
- **B** to show the way into Melbourne.
- **C** to signal the narrowing of Bass Strait.
- **D** to show the narrow entrance to the Derwent River.

31 As a ship's captain, to understand the system of lighthouses around Australia you would need
- **A** only a map.
- **B** only a code book.
- **C** a map and a code book.
- **D** a two way radio.

32 Dirk Hartog Island is an island
- **A** off the coast of Queensland.
- **B** off the coast of Western Australia.
- **C** south of Tasmania.
- **D** off the west coast of Victoria.

33 From the passage find phrases that mean
- **A** a bustle of activity.
- **B** an untrustworthy beacon.

34 'Lighthouse keeping is not the lonely occupation it once was' Why is this so?
- **A** There are more lighthouses and keepers than there used to be.
- **B** The most isolated lighthouses are automated and don't need keepers.
- **C** The public (tourists) are allowed to visit the lights these days.
- **D** Modern navigation techniques these days make them redundant.

READING TEST 7

ANDY'S RETURN

EXERCISE 6

Andy's Return

With pannikins all rusty,
And billy burnt and black,
And clothes all torn and dusty,
That scarcely hide his back;
With sun-cracked saddle leather,
And knotted green-hide rein,
His face burnt brown with weather,
Our Andy's home again.

His unkempt hair is faded
With sleeping in the wet;
He's looking old and jaded;
But he is hearty yet.
With eyes sunk in their sockets –
But merry as of yore;
With big cheques in his pockets,
Our Andy's home once more!

Old Uncle's bright and cheerful;
He wears a smiling face;
And Aunty's never tearful
Now Andy's round the place.
Old Blutcher barks for gladness;
He broke his rusty chain,
And leapt in joyous madness
When Andy came again.

Henry Lawson

35 It is evident that
- **A** Uncle was disappointed with the amount of money Andy had brought back with him.
- **B** Andy was looking extremely well after his long trip.
- **C** Andy was no longer the cheerful person he once was.
- **D** None of the preceding.

36 The word 'unkempt" probably means
- **A** blonde.
- **B** uncared for.
- **C** curly.
- **D** silky.

37 What does "as of yore" mean?
- **A** Having sunken eyes.
- **B** As he used to be.
- **C** As often as possible.
- **D** Being fond of jokes.

38 Why would the family have been relieved ?
- **A** Andy had brought all his gear back with him.
- **B** Uncle was bright and cheerful again.
- **C** Andy had not spent his wages.
- **D** Aunty wasn't tearful any more.

DEPARTMENT DIRECTORY

EXERCISE 7

Ground Floor • You are here	Second Floor
Ladies' wear and accessories	China and glassware
Perfumes and cosmetics	Sporting goods
Records and cassettes	Photography
Computers	Electrical appliances
Mobile Phones	Car accessories
Men's wear	Camping gear
Books and stationery	Gardening
Snack food	
First Floor	**Third Floor**
Children' s wear	Curtains and blinds
Toys	Floor coverings
Baby wear	Outdoor furniture
Knitting	Furniture and bedding
Haberdashery	Tools
Manchester	Pool accessories
Ladies' and men's shoes	**Fourth Floor**
Travel Bureau	Restaurant
Passport photos	Accounts
Luggage	Rest rooms
	Public phones

39 Which floor would you go to if you wanted to buy a writing pad?

A Ground Floor. **B** First Floor.
C Second Floor. **D** Third Floor. **E** Fourth floor.

40 Why do think bedding is on the Third Floor, not the Ground Floor ?

A It belongs with the furniture. **B** Not many shoppers require this item often.

C It is handy to the floor coverings. **D** Beds and mattresses are too heavy to carry.

41 Which one of these would you *not* be likely to find on the Second Floor?

A Food blenders. **B** Sleeping bag.
C Venetian blinds. **D** Tripod for a camera.

42 Records and cassettes are on the Ground Floor because

A they can be heard from the street. **B** they can be more easily supervised.
C they take up so much room. **D** they are a popular item.

43 Why are Travel, Passport Photos and Luggage on the same floor?

A For customer convenience. **B** So that customers will buy on impulse.
C They make the floor look more attractive. **D** To allow you to charge these expensive items.

44 If you wanted to make a payment on a lay-by, which floor would you go to?

A First Floor. **B** Third Floor.
C Second Floor. **D** Fourth Floor. **E** Ground Floor.

45 If you wanted a quick bite to eat, where would you go?

A Ground Floor. **B** First Floor. **C** Second Floor. **D** Fourth Floor.

CORAL

EXERCISE 8

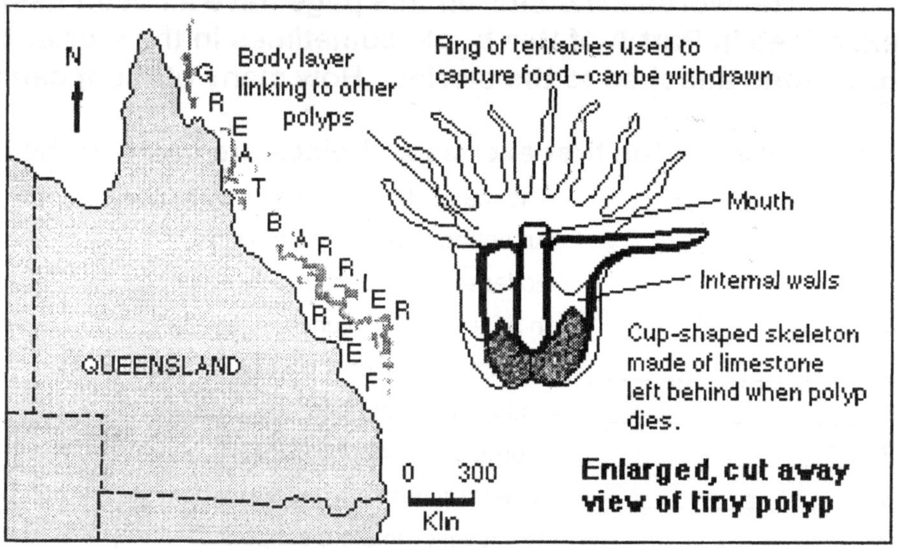

The Great Barrier Reef stretches for 2000 kilometres along the Queensland coast. It is not only the largest coral reef complex in the world, but it is the biggest construction of any kind made by living animals; nothing made by humans comes close to being as large and extensive. Approximately 2500 separate reefs make up the Great Barrier Reef; combined they would cover an area twice the size of England.

The structures of the Great Barrier Reef have been built by countless millions of minute animals called 'polyps'. Each of these minute, soft-bodied animals builds an exceedingly small, cup-like home of corallite (lime) to live in and to give it support and protection. These limestone apartments are joined together in huge clusters like blocks of flats – sometimes tall and pointed, and sometimes low and spreading.

To thrive, coral polyps need a constant environment of warm water that is clear and shallow with enough movement to carry plankton, the even-smaller floating animal food, to the non-moving polyps.

The shallow continental shelf off the Queensland coast, particularly along the outer edge, provides ideal conditions for the tiny coral animals.

46` The Great Barrier Reef is located

A off the coast of New South Wales.
B off the coast of Queensland.
C in central Australia.
D off the coast of Northern Territory.

47 Corallite is a form of

A limestone.
B animal bones.
C water current.
D sandstone.

48 To thrive, the coral polyps need

A moving water to bring a food supply.
B warm, clear water without sediment
C shallow depth of sea.
D All of the preceding

49 Coral polyps are linked to their neighbours by

A muscular material.
B corallite.
C pointed tentacles.
D internal walls.

50 In the passage, the word 'minute' means

A growing for a short time.
B single-celled.
C tiny.
D joined in clusters.

REVISION READING TEST – Part A

The words asked for on this page have all been used in the comprehension exercises in Part A of this book, sometimes in the stories and sometimes in the questions attached to the stories. How many of them can you recall?

Definitions. (In the first exercise, choices are given in the box.)

1 ____________________ The mass of rock brought down by a glacier.
2 ____________________ An unhappy or sorry condition.
3 ____________________ To lessen or reduce the severity of.
4 ____________________ In an ancient and unchanged state.
5 ____________________ Uncaring or insensitive to a situation.
6 ____________________ Unduly confident and arrogant.
7 ____________________ A deduction or conclusion.
8 ____________________ A general term for pests and noxious animals.
9 ____________________ To dispel or make disappear.
10 ____________________ A dirty and unruly appearance.
11 ____________________ A record of happenings.
12 ____________________ Neat and orderly in habits.

Choices:
presumptuous dissipate vermin journal
mitigate inference pristine plight
meticulous oblivious unkempt moraine

Choose the word which best defines each of the following:

13 **solitary** : standing, reclusive, aggressive, indisposed. ....
14 **truncated**: broken, elongated, chiselled, shortened. ....
15 **apt**: similar, consequential, appropriate, sequential. ....
16 **relentless**: alternate, unyielding, definite, strong. ....
17 **legend**: souvenir, collection, sample, myth. ....
18 **sturdy**: robust, immortal, vigorous, dense. ....
19 **impending**: imminent, terminating, swallowing, tearing. ....
20 **notorious** exceptional, impressive, infamous, unconscious. ....
21 **masticate**: lubricate, chew, sample, swallow. ....
22 **regenerate**: improve, retrain, renew, compare. ....
23 **prior:** later, earlier, punctual, repeated. ....
24 **ambience:** adjacent, veil, cover, surroundings. ....
25 **humidity :** aridity, moisture, danger, ecosystem. ....
26 **vulnerable:** warlike, simple, susceptible, critical. ....
27 **arable:** dry, cultivable, open, poor. ....
28 **idle:** useful, useless, unused, statuesque. ....
29 **ferocious:** fierce, fanciful, cruel, steady. ....
30 **contingent:** brutal, taunt, suspicious, detachment. ....

CONTENTS - PART B

WONDERS OF THE WORLD

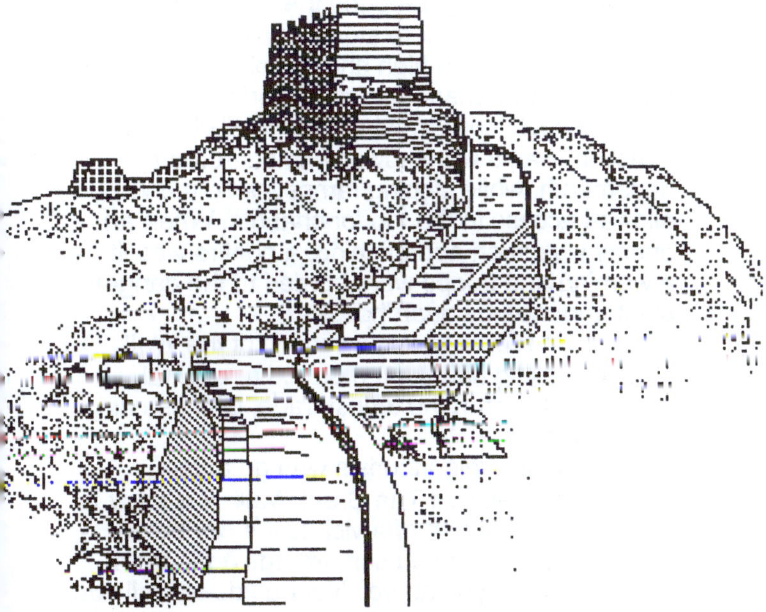

THE GREAT WALL OF CHINA

EXERCISE 1

READING TEST 1

'You're not a hero until you have climbed to the top of the Great Wall.'
Old Chinese Saying.

Well, just at that moment Peng Li didn't feel like much of a hero. It was 6 a.m., just before sunrise, and he was standing on the topmost point of a section of the wall about 75 kilometres north of Peking (nowadays called Beijing). An icy wind was swirling over the battlements and Peng Li was cold. He was so cold he had even forgotten how tired he was. And he still had another two hours of guard duty to do! It was spring, but the cold wind had come down from the still-frozen wastes of Siberia far to the north. The wind blew up the face of the Wall and seemed to go over him, under him, and even right through him. It reached under his iron and leather helmet and his moustache was stiff with frost from his breath. Suddenly Peng Li's aching cold was forgotten because he heard a sound - a sound where there shouldn't have been a sound - a sound like a rock being dislodged followed by a muffled curse.

Straining his eyes through the mist and gloom of the weak light, Peng Li saw what he hoped he would never see, a band of perhaps fifty armed men, a ferocious-looking lot, creeping up the side of the mountain. Shouting the alarm, he struck the massive bronze gong kept in the corner of the tower, then ran to the great cauldron where the supply of oil was kept. His hands were cold and numb causing him to fumble as he tried to ladle oil onto the pile of wood and twigs at the bottom of the bonfire. The brigands, realising they had been seen, began to charge up the steep slope as fast as they could. . . . .

At the time of the first Ch'in Emperor (221 B.C.), China was divided into seven States. Each of these States had built walls and fortresses for defence against the many warlike nomadic tribes to the north. After unifying China in a series of bloody wars, Ch'in began the task of joining up the many pieces of previous walls to form the 'Great Wall' that would stretch right across the north, a distance of some 2400 kilometres. Millions of peasant farmers, about 1/5 of the total population of China, were drafted to work for long periods on the immense task. They were forced to abandon their families and farms and many died as a result of the hard labour, poor food and bitterly cold northern winters. Peasants from the south who were used to warmer weather just didn't stand a chance in their thin cotton clothing. They died in their thousands. Those who died working on The Great Wall were buried in it and became part of the foundations. One old Chinese poem tells the story of a poor, peasant woman who went to The Great Wall to search for the body of her husband. Her cries of sorrow, so the tale goes, were so moving that the section where he was buried fell down.

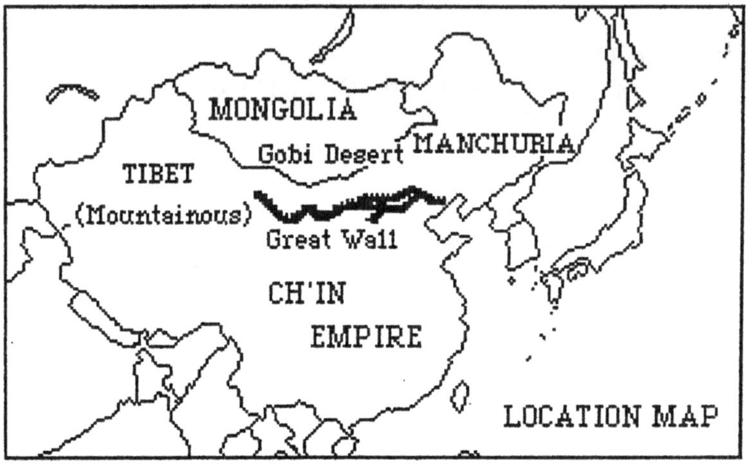

The Great Wall is said to be the only man-made feature visible from space. It is estimated that the earth and stone used in its construction would build a wall 5 metres high and one metre wide, right around the world. In the eastern sections, where stone was plentiful, it was about seven metres high and 6 metres wide, wide enough for two chariots to race along side by side. At each 'corner', where the Wall changed direction, was a watchtower with guardrooms underneath, while sloping ramps inside the Wall allowed access to the top for chariots. When an enemy was seen approaching, a bonfire was lit as a warning and troops were hurried to the danger point from nearby guardhouses.

In recent times, a section of the Wall north of Beijing has been restored to original standards to catch the tourist trade, Chinese as well as foreign.

Most foreign tourists who go to the Chinese capital, visit The Great Wall. It is easy to arrange a trip as part of a visit to the city before you go to China, or you can arrange a trip from any hotel when you arrive. Your guide will tell you that you have to climb up to see the magnificent view north into Manchuria from the peaks on either side of the valley. There isn't much to see in the valley bottom which is crowded with people and stalls selling souvenirs, and anyway you want to be a 'hero', so off you go. The western side of the valley is harder to climb than the eastern side. Of course you will decide to take the hard way because there are not quite so many people and you want to show how fit you are. You actually walk on the upper, fighting level of the Wall itself. The steps are quite steep, and each step is very high. Before long you are thinking that maybe the other side would have been better for you.

When you arrive at the topmost tower you need to take deep breaths but then you can look down. You can imagine what it would have been like to stand guard, like Peng Li, as the wind whistled up (and it seems it always does) from the cold, northern plains of Manchuria and Mongolia. To the north, the land slopes away towards far-off plains, while to the south, the valleys lead back towards Beijing.

The section of the Wall on which you are standing is built on a ridge; most of the Wall is built that way for obvious reasons. It is possible to walk out much further along the Wall, past the area that has been repaired, but the surface is crumbly and dangerous. Besides, you have to get back in time to purchase, proudly, your "I Climbed the Great Wall" (and lived) T-shirt. Unfortunately the steps going down on the way back will seem even steeper!

And just what did happen to Peng Li? Well no one really knows. The attack by the armed raiding party was just one of the many thousands that occurred along The Great Wall through the centuries, but for the sake of our story

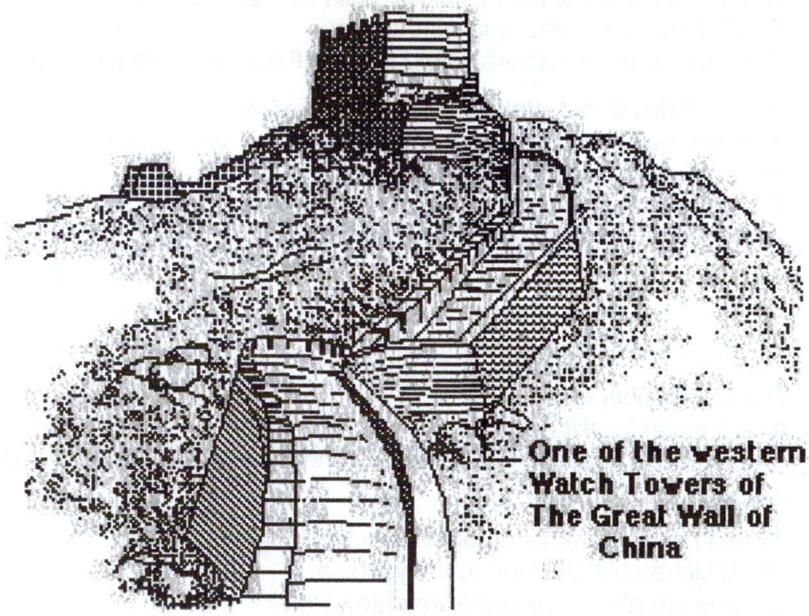

One of the western Watch Towers of The Great Wall of China

we'll say that the attack was easily repelled. The bandits had hoped to slip quietly through, unnoticed, to rob and pillage in the richer, and warmer, southern valleys.

Fighting warned and well-armed soldiers was not really on their most-wanted list of things to do. The soldiers, alerted by Peng Li and protected by the bastions on the Wall, were able to fire their arrows down onto the marauders who ran fleeing down the mountain. Peng Li was given promotion for his watchfulness and quick reaction. He was put in charge of the watchtower - but on his next watch duty he was cold again!

Choose the correct/best answer to complete the following sentences.

1 **The first Ch'in Emperor's idea was to**
- **A** get the marauding nomads to unite.
- **B** begin a series of costly wars.
- **C** join up existing walls and fortresses.
- **D** divide the land into States.

2 **In the text the word 'drafted' means**
- **A** forced.
- **B** accommodated.
- **C** surrendered.
- **D** abandoned.

3 **The oil was kept in the cauldron**
- **A** to oil the chariot wheels.
- **B** to pour on the attackers.
- **C** to light a signal fire.
- **D** to keep the soldiers warm.

4 **A suitable word in the passage for 'marauding' would be**
- **A** plundering.
- **B** objecting.
- **C** ridding.
- **D** compensating.

5 **From the passage, we can assume that workers who died**
- **A** had a funeral paid for by the Emperor.
- **B** came only from the south.
- **C** caused parts of the wall to fall down.
- **D** formed part of the foundations of the Wall.

6 **The Great Wall was built to follow the ridges**
- **A** so that the Emperor could be seen as all-powerful.
- **B** so that the Emperor's soldiers could be easily seen.
- **C** because there was less wind there.
- **D** so that enemy soldiers would find it difficult to approach unseen.

7 **Parts of the Great Wall have been restored**
- **A** because China does not have very good relations with Russia to the north.
- **B** because it gives the Chinese Communists something to boast about.
- **C** as an attraction for tourists, especially foreigners.
- **D** because most people find it hard to climb the Wall.

8 **In desert areas the Great Wall did not need to be as high because**
- **A** there was often a lack of suitable stone.
- **B** the desert itself was a protection.
- **C** the sand was constantly moving.
- **D** the enemy tribes there were smaller.

9 **The Great Wall is**
- **A** a popular tourist destination.
- **B** said to be visible from the Moon.
- **C** usually approached through the Chinese capital, Beijing.
- **D** All of the above.

10 **The Ch'in Emperor**
- **A** did not achieve his ambition to unify China.
- **B** achieved his ambition to unify China.
- **C** was not able to build the watchtowers.
- **D** was not a good planner because he could not fulfill his plan.

11 **Peng Li's "bandits" were hoping to**
- **A** attack the sleeping guards.
- **B** get through to the rich south, unnoticed.
- **C** rob the people of the northern plains.
- **D** stop Peng Li being promoted.

12 **The climate on the northern part of the wall could be best described as**
- **A** mild.
- **B** warmer than in the south.
- **C** harsh.
- **D** good for building.

From the passage find words that mean:

- **13** projecting part of a fortification
- **14** a courageous person
- **15** a poor farm worker
- **16** a large vessel for boiling
- **17** an inclined plane joining different levels
- **18** without feeling

THE MYSTERIOUS MOAI

EXERCISE 2

READING TEST 1

The huge stone statues stand half-buried, gazing uneasily across the grassy slopes of the ancient volcano to the ocean, or lie face-up to stare vacantly at the empty blue sky. They are the mysterious moai of Easter Island.

Easter Island is tiny, an insignificant speck lost in the vastness of the southern Pacific Ocean. A mere 80 kilometres around, it is further from any land than any other place on earth. Yet at one time it was the home of around 30 000 native people. How did these people find their way to the island, what were their mysterious moai used for, and how were the moai made?

The moai (pronounced mo- eye) vary in size from 2 metres to 21 metres in height. They have elongated, square faces with heavy brows, prominent nose, small mouth, thin lips and jutting chins. Eyes were made from white coral and obsidian (a kind of black volcanic glass). There were two distinct types of moai; the earlier type with long ears made by the first inhabitants, and those with short ears representing later arrivals on the Island.

The moai were carved face-up in a horizontal position. A trench was cut in the rock around each figure, then it was hoisted up while the detail of the back was carved. The moai had to be dragged from the construction quarry on log rollers to their village site, a difficult task as most moai weighed many tonnes. The extinct Rano

Raraku volcano in the centre of the island provided the hard, black, basalt rock from which the moai were made. The hats or topknots that some of the figures had, were found in another crater.

Originally set up on stone platforms, called ahu, at the edge of the sea facing inland toward a village, the moai were the focus of the religious ceremonies of the village. After the death of a respected person (male or female it made no difference) a moai would be constructed because it was thought that the spirit of the ancestor would inhabit the moai to watch over and protect the village. When wars broke out between rival tribes on the island, each would try to destroy the other's moai to show their dominance. Because so much importance was attached to the moai as protectors, loss of the moai belonging to a village would cause the villagers to lose the will to fight.

The slopes of Rano Ranaku are littered with moai in various stages of completion, for an interruption to moai construction took place suddenly in the second half of the 17th century. At that time population pressure on the island was extreme. There were just too many people for the food supply and other resources. The once plentiful hickory trees were almost completely removed to make houses and canoes. Finally a disastrous series of bloody wars took place between the Long Ears and the Short Ears. Work on new moai ceased and most of the existing moai were toppled from their pedestals and destroyed. Prior to the wars, 600 magnificent moai sat deliberately watching upon their ahus; when the wars came, over 300 were left deserted in various stages of construction.

The alarming drop in population that occurred due to warfare was exacerbated by the arrival, soon after, of Christian missionaries. Unfortunately the European missionaries brought new problems for the Islanders. Many diseases came with them; diseases like measles and chicken pox, from which the Europeans were largely immune, became deadly killers to the isolated people of Easter Island. With the Europeans came slavery too. The overall result of war, disease and slavery was disastrous. Unbelievably in the space of two decades the native population of Easter Island was reduced from about 30 000 to only 120 people and the ancient culture of the people had been destroyed.

The moai never were completed. The only moai that can be seen standing on a proper ahu in Easter Island today are those that have been restored in the last 50 years. One particularly fierce set was rebuilt by the archaeologist Thor Heyerdahl who proved that the island could have been reached by people from South America. He sailed his reed boat *Kon-Tiki* from Peru to Easter Island in 1947. The actor Kevin Costner made a film about the moai wars, rebuilding some of the villages and their moai out of plastic in the process.

Today Easter Island is part of Chile and the population has recovered to about 3000 people, but these are mostly of mixed descent. Trans-Pacific jets land at Easter Island on their way from Australia to Chile and many tourists break their journey, either going to or coming from the mainland of South America, to see the moai. Easter Island is an interesting place to visit. Little trace of the ruined villages now exists but there are still plenty of the half-finished stone moai gazing vacantly down from the slopes towards the sea. Enough to cause any tourist to stop and wonder just a little.

Circle the best answer to complete the sentences.

19 The moai were placed facing the village

A to provide work for the new arrivals. **B** to satisfy the tribal elders.
C so that they could protect the villages. **D** to warn of approaching danger.

20 Rival tribes tried to destroy their enemies' moai so that

A they could use the moai to bargain with.
B their enemies would lose their will to fight.
C their enemies would not be able to attract tourists.
D the spirits would be satisfied.

21 In the passage the word 'exacerbated' means

A improved. **B** alarmed. **B** reduced. **D** made worse.

22 On the Island there were once many trees, but there are few today. The passage tells us that the reason for this was

A the severe climate. **B** extreme population pressure.
C volcanic explosions. **D** catastrophic bushfires.

A Moai standing on an Ahu

23 Thor Heyerdahl set out to prove that

A ocean currents were stronger in the Pacific Ocean than the Atlantic.
B the original inhabitants could have come from South America.
C the Easter Islanders made reed boats better than any other Islanders.
D the Easter Islanders had sailed to South America.

24 Wars broke out because

A there were too many people for the size of the island.
B the Long Ears hated the Short Ears.
C the Short Ears took over the moai quarries.
D the European missionaries caused trouble.

25 For the inhabitants of Easter Island, the arrival of the missionaries was

A beneficial. **B** unimportant.
C despicable. **D** calamitous.

26 A word describing the plight of the Islanders towards the end of the 17th century would be

A decimated. **B** expanding. . **C** cooperative **D** saved.

State whether the following statements are True (T) or False (F).

27 The moai were constructed whenever a famous person died. ( )
28 They were set up facing out to sea to protect and warn of danger. ( )
29 Some of the moai had imposing hats or topknots. ( )
30 Heyerdahl's theory about the Islander's origins was disproved. ( )
31 The riddle of the moai's construction has never been solved. ( )
32 The Easter Islanders succumbed to European diseases. ( )
33 An ahu was a stone platform. ( )
34 The wars were caused basically by extreme population pressure. ( )
35 Kevin Costner built some magnificent stone moai for a film. ( )
36 The red volcanic stone for the moai hats came from the volcano Rano Raraku. ( )
37 The differing waves of native arrivals on Easter Island could be distinguished by their facial features. ( )
38 Today there are about 3000 pure-blood islanders living on Easter Island. ( )
39 The ruined villages have been rebuilt as tourist attractions. ( )

From your reading of the story of Easter Island you should be able to fill in the blanks in the passage below with a suitable word. The first letter of a suitable word has been given for you.

Despite the good intentions of **40 m**................, the story of Easter Island and its inhabitants is a **41 s**............... one. It is a story of **42 w**............... between races of similar ethnicity, caused by **43 e**............ population, and **44 d**.............. brought in by outsiders. It is a story too of **45 d**.............. by other races more technically **46 a**............... .

From the passage find words that mean:

47 protected or free from
48 a person who studies ancient relics
49 showing no signs of thought or expression
50 base or support for a column or statue

THE WORLD'S GREATEST EXPLOSION

EXERCISE 1 READING TEST 2

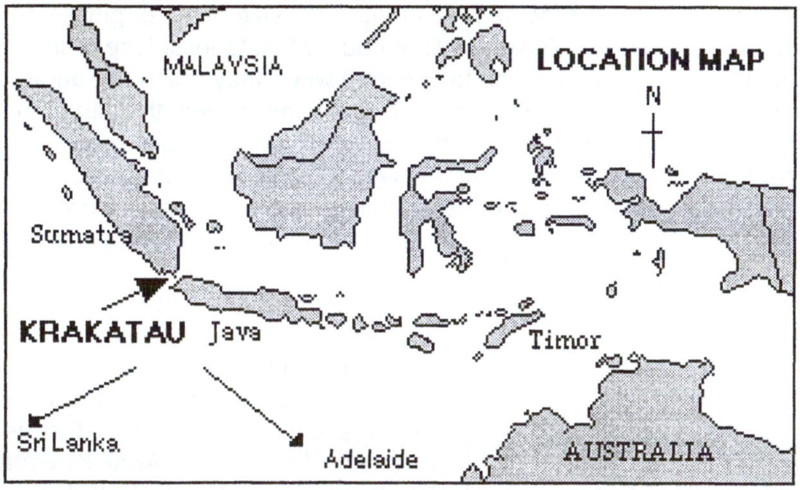

People are fascinated by volcanoes. Some people are even crazy enough to descend into the craters of volcanoes to study them while they are erupting. Some have died because they went too close to an eruption. But no one would have been able to study the eruption of Krakatau in1883 too closely because it was the greatest explosion in living history.

On 27th August 1883 the island of Krakatau, located in the narrow Sunda Strait between Sumatra and Java, disintegrated in a series of massive explosions. It was the largest noise in recorded history and it was heard as far away as Adelaide in South Australia and Sri Lanka on the other side of the Indian Ocean. The tsunamis, which were generated by the volcanic activity, spread outwards from Krakatau. Pounding inland, mountainous 40-metre waves and towering walls of water destroyed the Sunda Strait area, drowning more than 36 000 people in the coastal villages there. Many of the drowned were washed back into the ocean by the returning waves, and ships' captains who were first on the scene, reported sailing through sea that was 'choked with bodies'.

An estimated 21 cubic kilometres of earth, ash and magma was ejected into the air, and the cloud of gas and dust, all that was left of Krakatau, circled the Earth several times causing strange 'blue suns' and 'orange moons' in the Northern hemisphere. In Europe, lower-than- average temperatures were recorded as the circling ash and dust in the atmosphere partially blocked the heat of the Sun.

In North America, brilliant sunsets and low average temperatures were recorded for as long as three years after the Krakatau eruption. So brilliant were the sunsets that in parts of the United States, fire brigades were called out when embarrassed firemen mistook the glow of the red fires for bushfires. In the seas off Batavia (now the capital of Indonesia called Jakarta), fisherman were able to scoop up 'dizzy' fish that had been affected by the vibration and pressure changes in the ocean caused by the explosion 100 kilometres to the east.

According to the Javanese Book of Kings, an even larger explosion had taken place on the same site in 410 A.D. Then, a large volcano called 'Ancient Krakatau', an island 11 km in diameter and 2 km high, blew up. Only three small parts of this Ancient Krakatau were left standing on the rim of a new, huge collapsed crater. These were the islands of Panjang, Setang and Rakata. In the years that followed Rakata grew in size and joined with two new volcanoes that appeared inside the old caldera. This new island was the Krakatau that exploded in 1883. After the 1883 eruption, there was a hole in the sea floor where the new Krakatau had been. It was 200 metres deep and covered 28 square kilometres of the sea floor; it was the empty belly of the Krakatau volcano. The nearby islands of Setang and Panjung had disappeared too, but in a different way. They were buried with ash and pumice (a light volcanic rock) over 30 metres deep. A month later the surfaces of these islands were too hot to stand on in bare feet.

The original Krakatau Island ceased to exist in1883, but our story continues. In 1927 volcanic activity began again in the sea over the submerged Krakatau caldera. Again a series of submarine explosions took place and three new islands were born. These, being made of ash, were quickly washed away by the sea, but then a fourth island emerged. This last island was made of lava and so remained. The new island grew and grew earning the name 'Anak Krakatau' meaning 'Child of Krakatau' in the Indonesian language.

Anak Krakatau survived a fairly turbulent childhood, having major eruptions in 1952 and 1972, and went on to become an unruly teenager. Although it is fairly safe to visit Anak Krakatau today it is, nevertheless, an active volcano and deserves respect. To land on Anak Krakatau you must approach from the north where the island's only beach is located. The sand is black and littered with pumice. In front of you then is a fairly steep climb, 800 metres to the outer crater. The ash-and-pumice slope is black too and absorbs a tremendous amount of heat from the tropical sun (pumice is a light volcanic rock). There is no shelter from the sun so it is best to finish your climb before ten o'clock; the few trees on the island are near the water's edge.

From the top of the outer rim, the view is spectacular and when you look across at the remains of Panjang, Setang and Rakata, you can get some idea of the huge size of the original explosion of Krakatau. Most tourists lose their inclination to continue when they reach the outer rim because the climb to the inner cone, the site of the 1972 eruption, is over very steep, loose material. If you attempt the second climb you can expect to be nauseated by clouds of sulphurous gas or hot steam depending on the whim of the volcano.

In 1995 the cone of Anak Krakatau was 195 metres high and measured 2 kilometres in diameter. Anak Krakatau continues to erupt, on average, every seven years. Because of its scientific interest, Anak Krakatau has been included in Ujong Kulon National Park. Biologists are able to use the slopes of the volcano as a natural laboratory to study the way in which plants and animals are able to colonise its uninviting slopes.

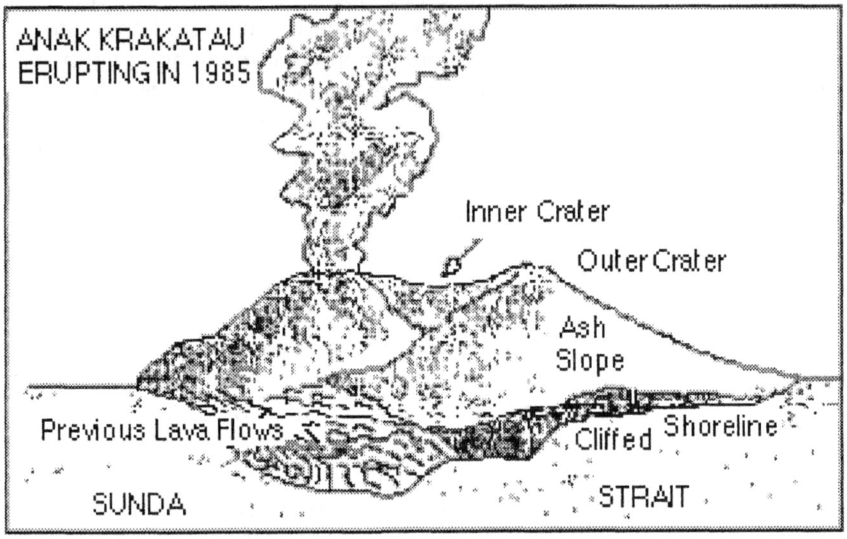

Choose the best answers to complete the following sentences:

1 **Krakatau is located**
A west of Australia. **B** north-west of Australia.
C north-east of Australia. **D** east of Australia.

2 **A tsunami is a**
A tidal wave. **B** volcanic explosion.
C type of coastal ship. **D** small island.

3 **The firemen were embarrassed because**
A it was so late at night. **B** the fires were not very hot.
C they were not really fires. **D** the fires had gone out.

4 **The original volcano was called**
A Anak Krakatau. **B** Panjang.
C Krakatau. **D** Ancient Krakatau.

5 **The ash slope on Anak Krakatau becomes hot because**
A the black sand absorbs heat from the Sun . **B** the volcano keeps erupting.
C the volcano is active. **D** it takes a long time to cool down.

6 **Anak Krakatau can only be approached by sea from the north because**
A elsewhere the currents are too strong. **B** the rest of the island has cliffs and lava flows.
C the inner crater is active and erupting. **D** the gas is too sulphurous.

7 **In the passage 'depending on the whim of the volcano' means**
A 'whatever it feels like doing'. **B** 'every day'.
C 'to let off steam'. **D** 'to make you feel ill'.

8 **In the passage it states that Anak Krakatau has become an unruly teenager. This means that**
- **A** its activity is quiet and predictable.
- **B** it is active and unpredictable.
- **C** the eruptions are devastating.
- **D** it is no longer safe to visit.

9 **Anak Krakatau could be described today as being**
- **A** extinct.
- **B** dormant.
- **C** active.
- **D** ancient.

10 **The Sunda Strait is between**
- **A** Java and Malaysia.
- **B** Java and Borneo.
- **C** Sumatra and Java.
- **D** Australia and Java.

11 **Anak Krakatau has become a natural laboratory for**
- **A** the investigation of dormant volcanoes.
- **B** the re-establishment of natural vegetation.
- **C** the tolerance of sea birds to sulphur in salt water.
- **D** the re-emergence of the tourist industry after a volcanic explosion.

Find words in the passage that mean

12 collapsed crater
13 thrown out
14 light volcanic rock
15 impulse or urge
16 underwater
17 child of
18 refuge
19 feeling violently ill
20 hill made by a volcano
21 re-establish

MULU NATIONAL PARK

EXERCISE 2

READING TEST 2

Nothing can prepare you for the Mulu Caves. I mean you know that they are big because a lot of people have told you that they are. But they are seriously big. Try seven times the size of St Paul's Cathedral in London, or, if that doesn't impress you, bigger than 50 jumbo jets put wingtip to wingtip - and that's just the first cave!

The Mulu caves are in Sarawak, a country in the northern part of the large Island of Borneo, part of the Mulu National Park. The last Ice Age did not penetrate the depths of Mulu that is near the Equator, and so the Caves are surrounded, and protected, by some of the most primitive, untouched forests on Earth - hence the National Park.

Reaching Mulu is not as difficult as it once was. Travel to Mulu nowadays can be by small plane, but previously access was only by a long and tiring trip by local boat. Since you would only be visiting the Caves in the dry season this often meant that you would have to get out and help push the

The Boardwalk in Mulu Park Is home to millions of small bats

boat, a glorified canoe really, up over shallow rapids. When you reach the edge of the Park your cut feet and hands are forgotten, because there is a wonderful boardwalk constructed over the floor of the rainforest, but it is a fair distance to walk, about five kilometres. The boardwalk meanders in and out of the trees and sometimes through them - they are so big. But not as big as the Caves themselves! Deer Cave, the largest, is home to an estimated three million wrinkle-lip bats. Your visit will have been timed to coincide with the bats dusk feeding flight, surely one of the world's greatest natural wonders. This is what you have come to see.

Every evening the bats form up in long spirals inside the cave. Each spiral bat colony, of perhaps a thousand or more, waits its turn to exit from the cave through the relatively small opening. Each bat seems to know the order and time without any squabbling, although the whistling and beating of tens of thousands of wings is deafening. The small bat has a wing spread only of about 10 centimetres, but the noise produced by the tiny wings beating, magnified by the number of bats flying is overpowering – almost as overpowering as the smell in the Cave - the excreta of three million bats can produce a smell that is, to say the least, challenging to the olfactory organ. The boardwalk in fact is built right across the floor of the Cave, it would be impossible to walk through the cave because of the guano deposits left by the bats.

Once you have marvelled at the way in which the bats form up inside the cave entrance and start to fly off, there is just enough time left to walk quickly back to the nearby observation platform at the Ranger Station. There you can watch the patterns made by the bats against the darkening night sky. The serried ranks of bats writhe and turn in black snake-like spirals high above as they head off in colonies to their favourite feeding grounds in forests many kilometres away. It is not too much of a stretch of the imagination to view each black, living ribbon as a great black snake slithering off into the forest.

When it is finally too dark to watch, then comes the long walk back. If you have been really naughty however and delayed until is quite dark, you will be treated to another of Mulu's great natural wonders - its fireflies. These tiny but wonderful will-of-the wisp insects will light your way, flitting in and out of the dark, menacing forms of the tree trunks. No doubt you will get into trouble from your guide and the rest of the party for being back late. They will have been waiting anxiously in case you have had an accident in the dark, and there is still the river trip by canoe to a tourist lodge a few kilometres downstream. This can be quite exciting in the dark. But the firefly display is worth any number of complaints.

22 The overpowering noise was produced by

A the bats chattering.
B the bats squealing and squeaking.
C the bats' wings.
D the large number of tourists.

23 Before going out, the bats use the entrance to Deer Cave as

A a safety refuge.
B a marshalling area.
C a place to talk to other bats.
D hunting area.

24 The Mulu forests contain primitive trees because

A the Ice Age did not reach there.
B the region has been remote and hard to reach until quite recently.
C they are part of a protected national Park.
D All of the above.

25 Why should you visit the Caves in the dry season?

A In the wet season it rains fairly continuously.
B The Caves are too wet and the ground very muddy.
C The river quickly becomes too high in the wet season.
D All the above.

26 Why is dusk the best time to see the bats?

A It takes so long to get there.
B The Rangers have other duties in the day time.
C The bats begin to fly out to feed then.
D The bats are returning then after feeding in the forest.

27 When they are setting out, the bats fly
A in pairs. B in rectangular formation.
C in spirals. D close to the ground.

28 Why should you not delay the return trip?
A The river will have to be negotiated in the dark.
B Fireflies are a common sight in the area.
C The guide will go without you.
D There are many more bats to see at the river.

THE STONE JUMPERS OF NIAS

EXERCISE 3

READING TEST 2

In most parts of the world, old cultures and customs have disappeared before the relentless march of Western civilisation, but on Nias, a small island 140 km by 50 km off the western coast of Sumatra, remnants of an old Stone Age civilisation remain as they were centuries ago.

The black, stone villages of remote southern Nias stand at the head of long flights of stone stairs guarded by high stone entranceways. Inside, the houses are wooden but they are aligned on either side of a long central street paved with the same black flagging used on the stairways. Each house sits touching its neighbour on a platform of huge wooden piles and beams fitted together without nail or screws. Being hilly country, the hilltop villages overlook one another. The long black lines of the streets, framed by the dark thatch roofs of the houses, resemble strange dark reptiles basking in the tropical sun. The mammoth forest trees used to construct the ancient houses have long since disappeared so that now when a fire occurs, (always a risk with the ultra dry timber), the old houses cannot be rebuilt. Gaps in the lines indicate where fires have occurred.

On Nias the interiors of the houses are basically the same. Each has a long room overhanging the central street where the family can sit, cool and unobserved, to watch the goings-on of the day. Sections of the roof over the family room can be raised and it is a common sight to see the day's washing spread out on the straw around the propped-up opening. Access to the elevated living floor of the buildings is by narrow stairway.

The grandest house in the village is of course is that of the local King or Chief. It stands usually on a veritable forest of tree trunks in the centre of the stone street. In front of the each King's house is a circle of stone blocks, some carved in the shape of chairs, used in past times by the elders of the village when discussing policies or settling disputes. Funerary tablets (still present) were placed at the front of the King's house to display the corpses of important villagers. Many of the ancient chair stones are finely etched to aid in the calculation of religious events and record the passing of the seasons.

In the southern villages, near to the council circle located in the central square of the village, old 'jumping stones' can be found. The jumping stones were really flat-topped pyramids two metres high built of roughly-hewn stone blocks. In olden times young men, as part of their physical preparation as warriors and to prove themselves ready for marriage, had to hurdle these high stone pyramids. Not so long ago the warriors of Nias were headhunters. They believed that the bridge to the land of the dead was guarded by a huge cat. This animalt took great delight in pushing off anyone who had not made his mark in life by taking the head of an enemy. The pyramids of the jumping stones represented the walls of enemy villages where the heads were to be found and where manhood could be proved; hence the importance of the ritual feat of stone-jumping.

For their trial the would-be warriors had nothing to assist them but a small launching stone about 30 cm high and a patch of unpaved earth to land on. As they jumped they had to further show their agility by twisting to face the way they came. They were allowed only two attempts in an eighteen-month time period to prove that they were strong enough and skilled enough to join the village war parties. Bamboo spikes were added to the top of the pyramid to make the jump more realistic (and more hazardous!). Today, for a consideration, some villages will stop their normal activities and give a display of ancient ceremonies, war dances, and singing, culminating in a jumping exhibition by some of the young village men.

Nowadays the winds of change have reached Nias just as they have reached most other parts of Indonesia. Encouraged by the Government as a way of unifying the far-flung and diverse parts of the nation, the family rooms in the houses have television sets. Young men's thoughts no longer turn to stone-jumping, except as a way of earning the necessary tourist dollars to allow them to take part in more modern dreams. One such dream is shared by an increasing number of young Australians who have become tired of Bali - the dream of riding the long, even waves of the southern beaches of Nias island has become a much more exciting prospect. For any young aspiring board riders who might be reading this, Nias has excellent waves (or so the Coca-Cola people think in one of their ads) but it is difficult part of the world to reach. To reach Nias you first have to get to Sumatra (the city of Medan is one starting point there), then fly by small plane to the island or go by slow, local boat. The journey across Nias to the south, where the villages and the waves are, is a nightmare crammed into a local bus.

But there is more to Nias than just catching a wave. In southern Nias the adventurous tourist can step backwards in time and catch a glimpse of bygone times. In the shade of the ornately carved overhangs the people carry out the tasks of everyday life as they have done for generations while dogs, pigs and chickens, wandering at will searching for scraps, complete the illusion.

How good is your memory? Can you answer these questions without referring to the text?

29 How did stone-jumping originate?

30 Why is the landing difficult?

31 Where is the jumping stone located?

32 How many attempts were allowed? In what time frame?

33 How was the jump made to be more realistic?

Choose the best answer to complete the following sentences:

34 In the olden days, the villages were built

A in a valley. **B** on a hill top.
C by a river. **D** on the side of a hill.

35 Some people argue that in the long run tourism will be good for the people of Nias because
- **A** the government will make large money grants to the islanders.
- **B** it will keep the young men fit and healthy.
- **C** there are no jumping stones left to practise on.
- **D** it will give them a reason to keep their customs and culture alive.

36 In Nias, and throughout Indonesia, the Government has supplied television sets to out-of-the-way villages
- **A** as a way of unifying the nation.
- **B** to provide entertainment.
- **C** to promote tourism.
- **D** to sell various items.

37 The most serious physical threat to the villages these days is
- **A** the use of modern machinery.
- **B** fire breaking out.
- **C** invasion by a neighbouring community.
- **D** American tourists.

38 On Nias one experiences the illusion of
- **A** completing a difficult journey.
- **B** eating tropical fruits.
- **C** stepping backwards in time.
- **D** country medicine.

39 What does 'for a consideration' mean?
- **A** When TV cameras are present.
- **B** For a cash payment.
- **C** If there are enough tourists.
- **D** Being given enough time to prepare.

40 What does' Nowadays the winds of change have reached Nias' mean?
- **A** The government is encouraging young people to leave Nias.
- **B** Nias is resisting change.
- **C** The government is now supplying TV sets to the villages.
- **D** Things are beginning to change in Nias.

Find words in the passage that mean:

41 unstoppable

42 an adjective used to indicate 'realness' or 'truth'

43 enjoying the warmth of

44 having a design cut into it

45 ending in

46 ambitious

47 bringing together

48 dangerous

Copper-green Phillip
With a beak like a hawk,
perches on his pedestal
and will not talk
to the stuttering starlings
fluttering around
or the crumb-seeking pigeons
patterning the ground;
and though, daylong,
bird calls to bird,
copper-green Phillip
says never a word.

Lex Banning

CAPTAIN ARTHUR PHILLIP AND THE BIRDS

EXERCISE 4 READING TEST 2

49 Phillip was speechless because he
- **A** was tired of the silly birds.
- **B** had a bad stutter.
- **C** was made of bronze.
- **D** was on a pedestal.

50 What was it that caused the patterning on the ground?
- **A** The bird calls.
- **B** Birds looking for crumbs.
- **C** The shadow of the pedestal
- **D** The copper-green colours.

THE RUINED TEMPLE OF TA PROHM

EXERCISE 1 READING TEST 3

In the space of few seconds we were transported into a world of mystery - a world of menacing strangler trees, fallen masonry, collapsed corridors and sunken paths. "It's like Harrison Ford and the Temple of Doom," said someone in a low voice and there was a murmur of agreement. Cameras clicked and one of the party began to sketch a huge fig tree that had *eaten* a temple with its roots. "If the tree were removed," explained Mina our guide, seeing the sketch, "the temple would collapse, so we leave it the way it is."

Inside the temple and its many smaller buildings, it was cooler. Huge fig trees with interlocking branches hid the sun, and in the dim light we could see their swollen and twisted roots. We had spent the day exploring temple after temple. In one place we would admire the finely carved figures on the wall panels, in the next we marvelled at the absolutely immense faces which formed some of the walls. We had climbed, explored, wondered and perspired (it was very hot by this time) until the temples had all begun to look the same. But now it was a relief to enter a cooler, dimmer world.

It was strange inside the temple, even a little scary. Seeds spread by birds had dropped onto the temple roofs and walls. Some had sprouted and sent down roots into cracks between the sandstone blocks of the floors and corridors. On reaching the soil underneath, the tree roots grew and expanded forcing the walls apart and causing the roof to fall down in parts. The result was a jumble of fallen blocks, tree roots and dim corridors. On the ground beautiful carved panels and statues, many broken, were mixed with mosses and creepers, and it was upsetting to see tourists walking on some of the delicate panels that were strewn about.

The Khmer people originally came overland from India to Cambodia around the 1st Century A.D. They spread southwards and were the main cultural force in Cambodia for over a thousand years. Located in the north-west of present-day Cambodia, in its hey-day Angkor Thom was the centre of the Khmer Empire. Scattered inside the walls of the huge, ancient city of Angkor Thom are hundreds of wats or temples, including Angkor Wat, the largest stone building ever built. Ta Prohm is just one of the many ruined, but still beautiful, temples of this great capital. The city was enclosed by a massive wall and there were moats, causeways, and reservoirs, all built by hand.

The entrance to the temple of Ta Prohm

In 1431, Siamese people from Burma captured the city. The palaces of the Khmer Kings, which had been mostly built of wood were burned and destroyed; only the stone temples and religious buildings survived. The city was abandoned and left to the jungle. Soon most of the walls were covered by the quick-growing, tropical vegetation. Vines and creepers twined around the ornate stone walls, and in a short time, the city was forgotten.

In 1860, Angkor Thom was discovered by a Frenchman, Henri Mouhot, but it was not until the middle 1900s that serious attempts to uncover and restore the temples were made. In the last 100 years there have been many expeditions to Angkor Thom and many attempts to save and restore the crumbling temples. Because of its great size and the cost factor, even today many of Angkor's sites have not been uncovered.

1 **Ta Prohm could be best described as**
A a well-restored temple.
B a ruined, but still beautiful, temple.
C a magnificent, ancient palace.
D the world's largest stone temple.

2 **It is unlikely that Angkor Thom will ever be completely restored because**
A the temples look better in a jungle setting.
B the cost, given the size of the compound, would be prohibitive.
C no-one has the skill to restore them today.
D most of the temples have already been robbed.

3 **Ta Prohm reminded the tourists of the 'Temple of Doom' because**
A it was gloomy and menacing.
B it was difficult to gain entry.
C it was difficult to walk inside.
D the temple was so beautiful.

4 **The roof had fallen in parts because**
A the Siamese had destroyed it.
B there were no walls to support it.
C the wooden buildings had been burnt.
D tree roots had forced the walls apart.

5 **The city of Angkor Thom was abandoned because**
A the water supply had begun to diminish.
B it had been destroyed by invaders.
C the jungle had quickly taken over.
D there were too many temples to restore.

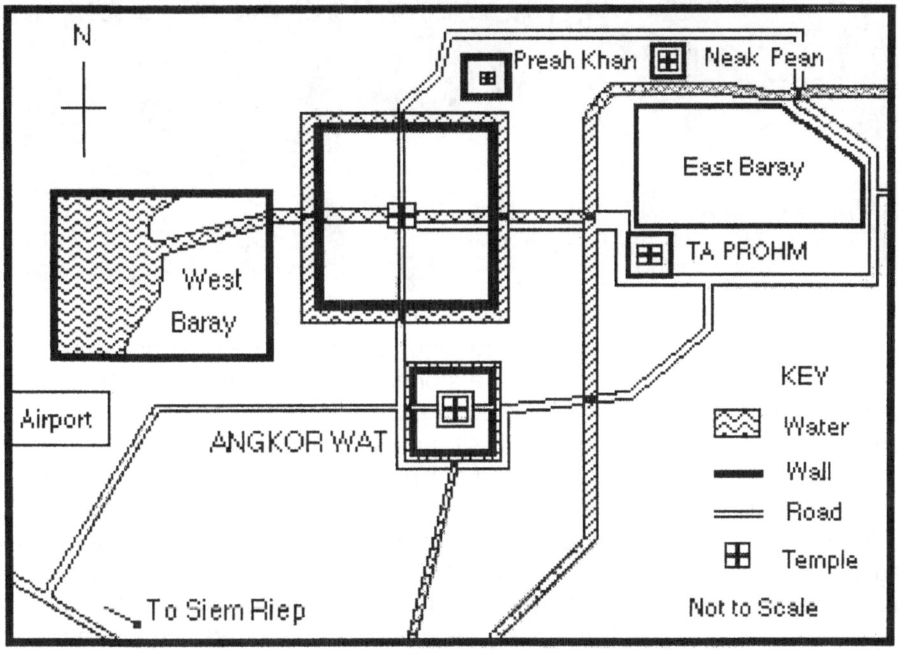

6 **The tourist was upset because**
A the people were walking on the carvings.
B the temple had been allowed to fall into disrepair.
C the trees had begun to invade the central square.
D the guide was not sympathetic.

7 **A 'Wat' is**
A a moat.
B a causeway.
C a temple.
D a palace.

8 **The word 'menacing' means**
A ominous.
B unfortunate.
C collapsing.
D dangerous

9 **From Angkor Thom, the city of Siem Riep is to the**
A south. B north. C east. D west.

10 **The Cambodian word 'Baray' probably means**
A river.
B aerodrome.
C roadway.
D reservoir.

THE WORLD'S LARGEST STONE BUILDING

EXERCISE 2 **READING TEST 3**

We had struggled out to the bus in the darkness, the idea being to watch the sunrise over Angkor Wat and get some pictures of reflections in the water of the moat. Now we were huddled at the western entrance gate looking along the causeway towards the temple. The sky was just beginning to lighten behind the Wat. In the distance we could see some twinkling lights and faintly hear the tinkle of bells emanating from the darkened temple. As the first faint rays of streaked the horizon we noticed that the lights were getting closer, but it was still difficult to see against the lightening sky. Then, out of the gloom, came a procession of Buddhist monks. It was an awe- inspiring sight, one that we hadn't expected. The monks, over two hundred of them, had been to dawn prayers in the temple. Walking in twos they passed silently by, except for the swish of their yellow robes and slap of their open sandals. As you can guess though, there were quite a few extra clicks and flashes from our cameras. . . . . . .

Most visitors approach Angkor Wat through the doorway of the western entrance. The view that suddenly appears is one of the most impressive sights anywhere in the world. The five towers of the Wat loom at the end of a raised causeway (bridge) made of huge flagstones and edged with a stone wall. There are nagas (snake-like dragons) at each end.

The temple of Angkor Wat is the masterpiece of Khmer architecture. Not only is it the largest of all the Khmer monuments, it is the largest stone building in the world. The amount of stone used to build it exceeds that of the largest of the Egyptian pyramids. Like the other Wats in Cambodia, it is completely covered with the most amazing carvings, but, unlike the pyramids, it was a temple made for everyday use. Although located just outside the ancient city of Angkor Thom, Angkor Wat is almost city in itself. It covers an area 1 km long by 800 metres wide, surrounded by a moat almost 200 metres wide and with an outer wall outside the moat.

Angkor Wat has five towers that are placed on the topmost of three stone galleries or levels. The lower gallery of the Wat is surrounded by a pillared half-gallery. The walls of the half-gallery are almost a kilometre in length and covered from floor to ceiling with carved scenes from the great Hindu stories and legends. They form the longest continuous stone carving ever made.

The five towers of Angkor Wat represent the five mountains that form the abode of the Hindu gods. The tallest central tower is 65 metres above ground level; quite a steep and dangerous climb on narrow stone steps that have been worn smooth by the millions of bare feet that have passed over them. Over 1700 *apsaras* (heavenly dancers) adorn the walls of the temples, as well as *simhas* (lions), *makaras* (sea monsters), *kalas* (faces) and *nagas* (snakes). There are carvings of warriors in battle, courtiers and musicians at the royal court, and of course slaves and ordinary people, all paying homage to the king.

. . . . . .

We were due to leave Siem Reap the next morning, but that afternoon we climbed to another temple located on a hill about two kilometres away from Angkor Wat. It was more like a mountain than a hill but we bravely refused an expensive ride on elephants to the top. Once up we joined other tourists that were watching to photograph the last rays of the sun catching the magnificent temple towers of Angkor Wat that glistened in the sea of green on the plain below. The trip down to the bus in the dark was a bit of stumble, but the climb had been worth it. As we climbed aboard the bus to go to the airport I looked across to where some of the towers in Angkor Thom were visible poking through the trees and I thought back to the apologetic words of our guide Mina:

"Alas, it is such a great pity. Many of the statues and panels have been removed. Some have been taken to museums in Siem Reap and Phnom Penh but many of them have been stolen. They cut off their heads and hands and sell them to dealers across the border in Thailand. The dealers in Thailand then sell them to collectors in Western countries. It is a sad sight and a source of great shame to all Cambodians."

And it was true. I thought about the long causeway over the moat surrounding the city of Angkor Thom that we had seen the day before. It was lined with twin rows of statues, gods on the left and demons on the right. On each side the sets of massive stone figures were joined by a huge stone snake forming a stone balustrade. Unfortunately on this railing the heads of many of the huge sculptures were missing; stolen. It was indeed a sad sight to see these huge, beheaded, stone statues. We were later to find other examples inside the temples of Angkor Thom where whole figures, weighing over a tonne, had been lifted off their pedestals and carted away in the night by organised gangs of thieves. It is to be hoped that The Cambodian Government will gain the upper hand in its fight against the temple vandals because Angkor Thom and neighbouring Angkor Wat are probably the greatest of all remaining religious temple sites in the world.

Choose the best answer to the following questions:

11 In what way was Angkor Wat different to the pyramids?

A Only kings were buried there. **B** The temperature remained constant.
C It was made for the people to use. **D** Only monks could use it.

12 The steps at Angkor Wat are treacherous because they are

A worn and steep. **B** smooth. **C** narrow. **D** All the preceding.

13 Why did the people on the bus go early to Angkor Wat?

A To see the sunrise. **B** To see the monk's procession.
C To see the reflections. **D** To see the sunrise and photograph reflections.

14 Why are Angkor Wat's five towers important to Cambodians?

A They have a deep religious significance.
B They hold the frame of the building together and provide unity.
C The monks pray there.
D They are so old.

15 Where is the world's longest continuous stone carving?

A Around the third gallery. **B** Around the five towers.
C Around the half-gallery. **D** On the ceiling.

16 Why was Mina apologetic?

A The statues had no heads. **B** He was ashamed of his fellow Cambodians.
C He did not like the Western dealers. **D** The statues had been stolen that night.

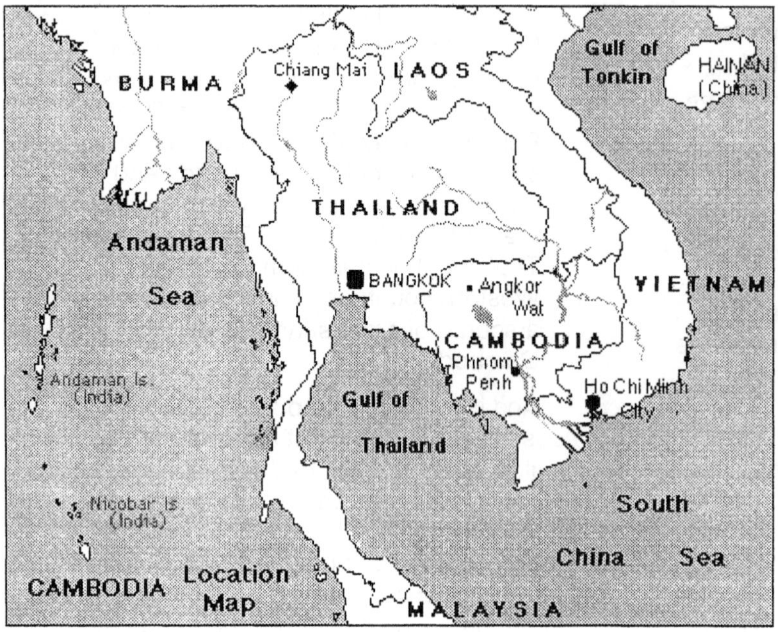

Location Map South-east Asia

17 Why was the monk's procession so awe-inspiring?

A They had such bright orange robes.

B They appeared silently out of the dark.

C They walked in single file.

D They rang small bells as they walked.

18 From the passage, what is a 'causeway'?

A A bridge. **B** A path.

C A moat. **D** An entrance.

19 Who according to Mina buy the statues?

A Tourists. **B** Museums only.

C Robbers and conservators.

D Museums and collectors.

20 What was the saddest sight of all?

A The old elephants. **B** The headless statues.

C The beggars on the steps . **D** The gloomy procession of monks.

21 What is a balustrade ?

A A causeway. **B** A kind of railing. **C** A fence. **D** A wall.

22 Why is Angkor Wat such an impressive sight when first seen?

A It is the world's largest stone building.

B The Buddhist monks in their orange robes create a colourful sight.

C You see it suddenly through an archway.

D It looks so cool and refreshing after all the heat.

Find the word in the passage that means

23 coming from **24** home or living place **25** tribute or respect

26 evil spirits **27** open balcony or level **28** people who ruin or damage

THE COLOSSEUM

EXERCISE 3

READING TEST 3

The Colosseum of Rome was the greatest arena ever built in the ancient world. Not quite circular in shape it measured 183 metres long by 152 metres wide and rose to a height of 56 metres. The great open-air theatre was begun by the Emperor Vespasian in 72 A.D. and completed eight years later in the reign of the Emperor Titus. Its opening celebrations lasted for 100 days and included, as the Roman poet Martial tells us, the killing of an 'enormous number of wild animals and gladiators'. The Colosseum was originally called the Flavian Amphitheatre after the Emperor Flavian. Later it took its popular name from a large (colossal) 35-metre statue of the Emperor Nero, which once stood nearby.

From the start, the Colosseum was a wonder of engineering. It was constructed on the site of an artificial lake that had been made for the pleasure of the Emperor Nero. But before that, the

THE COLOSSEUM

EXERCISE 3

READING TEST 3

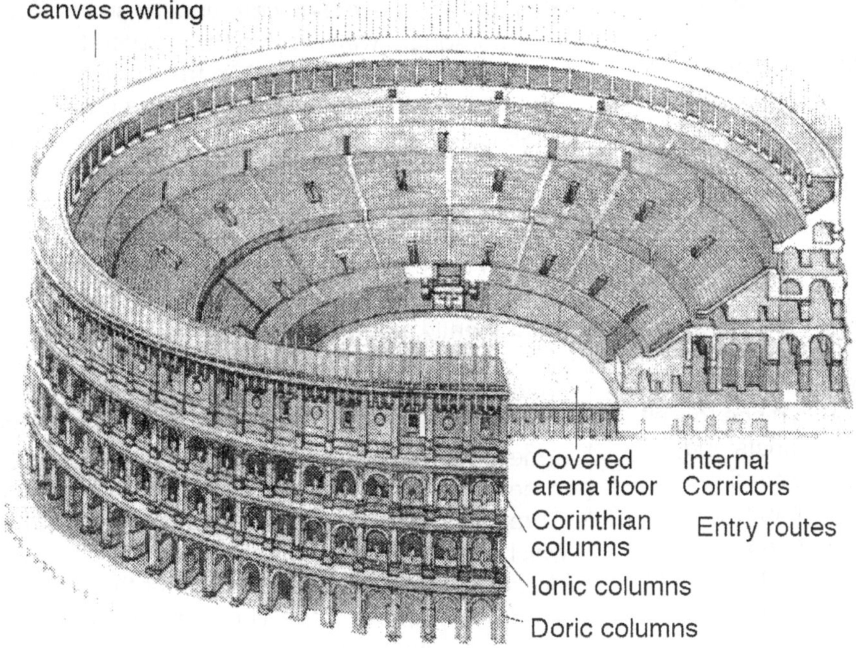

(senators and other important people) surrounded him and usually there were representatives of foreign countries in their national dress - all adding to the colour of the scene. Behind the nobility, the second or middle level, was for the ordinary Roman citizens. Farthest away, going upwards, was an area for the lowest class of citizens, while at the very top there was a terrace that provided standing room.

When filled, it is estimated that the Colosseum could hold up to 80 000 people. There was an official called a *designator* whose job it was to see that the classes kept to their 'designated' areas. Access to the seating was easy as there were no less than 160 entrances. Passageways conducted the audience to the outside, so that the crowd could leave without trouble when the games were over.

site had been a swamp, not a good place for any sort of big building even today. The Romans however filled the lake with concrete to form the Colosseum's foundations. (Concrete by the way was a Roman invention). In 1864 rumours of treasure buried beneath the Colosseum gained the attention of Pope Pius IX. He gave permission for a treasure hunt to be carried out. Alas, the engineer charged with excavating under the Colosseum didn't find any treasure - but he was astounded (and annoyed) by the amount of good, hard, Roman concrete that he found instead.

Viewed from the outside, the Colosseum had three levels, each one with 80 arches separated by pillars and half-columns. A fourth level at the top had a solid wall containing holes into which poles were placed to support a leather canopy. The canopy, which could be stretched across the whole amphitheatre on sunny days, was controlled by sailors who were familiar with sails and rigging. These were especially chosen for the job from the Roman fleet at Micenum. It is said that on a windy day, the noise made by the flapping of the leather canopy, sounded like thunder.

Inside, the amphitheatre had three main seating levels. At the bottom, closest to the action, was the podium. This was for the Roman nobility. On a raised platform on the podium sat the Emperor wearing his royal robes. Officials

When someone mentions the Colosseum most people just think "Oh yes, the Colosseum, that's where the gladiators fought," or, "That's where the Christians were thrown to the lions." They don't think much about it, but really the Colosseum was a place of terrible savagery. From all over the Roman Empire wild animals were trapped and brought to the Colosseum. From Nero's time onwards the early Christians were thrown into the arena with lions and tigers that had been purposely starved to make them savage. Sometimes criminals were put into the arena and made to kill each other. All died just to please the mob of bloodthirsty spectators and help maintain the popularity of whatever Emperor happened to be in power. Over the long period of time that the Colosseum operated it is known that some animal species were exterminated (made extinct) in areas of the Empire just to keep the Roman masses happy.

The surface of the arena was made of sand placed over a wooden platform. Beneath it there were cages with lifts, which could release wild beasts into the arena, and an elaborate system of tunnels along which gladiators, prisoners and criminals passed. The arena could even be made waterproof and was sometimes used to stage mock sea battles, complete with boats and soldiers! Crocodiles were often hunted from boats and on foot in the shallow water.

The last games in the Colosseum were held in 523 AD and around this time the Colosseum began to be used for bull fighting.

By the Middle Ages from, about 750 AD to 1450 AD, the Colosseum had fallen into disrepair. Apart from the occasional play or pageant, it became a hiding place for thieves, robbers, and witches. Great lumps of the white travertine stone used to build the gigantic amphitheatre were carried off to construct many of the streets and churches of Rome that are famous today. Around about the early 18th century, the Colosseum became fashionable as a place to visit and admire, especially by moonlight. Tourists and painters from other European countries visited the ruins, which were thought to be very 'romantic'. Historians and archaeologists have excavated underneath the floor area of the Colosseum and have built up a very complete picture of the building in the time of its greatness.

Today the Colosseum is a matter of concern to archaeologists and historians because it stands like an island in a river of Roman traffic. Its side is broken where stolen stone has been taken, and its rock faces are shaken by vibrations and pitted by exhaust fumes. But the Colosseum battles on. It features on every tourist pamphlet and on every postcard stand. It is the most photographed ruin in the world!

Gladiatorial contests were first staged at funerals as a sign of the wealth of the person who had died. By the time of the Emperors they were the main part of the blood sports that took place at the Colosseum. Gladiators were mostly slaves or criminals and their lives were usually short. If a gladiator fought well in his combat, even though he lost, the crowd might save him from death. The Emperor would judge the mood of the crowd. If the noble ladies waved their handkerchiefs he would signal to the victorious gladiator. For the loser, *thumbs up* meant life, while *thumbs down* meant death. Sometimes a great fighter might live long enough to be awarded a 'wooden sword' by the crowd. He then could retire from the arena permanently, but this was rare.

The gladiators lived in 'schools' and were specially fed and trained in every way of fighting, with all kinds of weapons. 'Retiarius', were lightly armed with nets and a particularly nasty spear with three points called a trident. The heavily armed 'Thracian' gladiators wore beautiful bronze helmets, which were locked on with twist keys. Unfortunately these made it hard for the gladiator to see. Vital parts of the Thracian gladiator's body, like the stomach, were unprotected so often they were no match for the lightly-clad, and therefore speedy, net and spear men. Mostly the gladiators fought to the death.

Are the following statements True (T) or False (F)?

29 The word 'colosseum' is derived from the Roman word for large. ( )

30 The rumours of treasure buried underneath the arena were just that, rumours. ( )

31 The Designator's task was to seat the various classes of spectators correctly. ( )

32 A leather canopy covered the entrance to animal cages. ( )

33 On occasions the arena was made waterproof. ( )

34 One advantage of the Colosseum was the preservation of animal species for use in the arena. ( )

35 Specialists such as archaeologists are worried by the effect of vehicle emissions on the remaining stone. ( )

36 During the Middle Ages the Colosseum was used to stage moonlight play performances. ( )

37 The colosseum superstructure was built mainly of concrete. ( )

38 On sunny days, sailors were a common sight in and around the Colosseum. ( )

39 The Emperors used the games in the Colosseum as a means of keeping the Roman citizens satisfied with their lives. ( )

40 When the games were over the citizens had to fight their way to the exit. ( )

41 The use of gladiators at the games had its origins in a much earlier funeral custom. ( )

42 The Thracian gladiators often triumphed over the heavily-armed net men. ( )

43 The Colosseum was built on the site of a swamp. ( )

From the passage find words that mean:

44 made extinct **45** where combats took place

46 brochure **47** moveable roof

48 on-lookers, watchers

49 currently popular

50 round or oval building with tiered seating and central open space.

FLYING STONE GEESE

The Big Wild Goose Pagoda

Pagodas are tower-shaped religious buildings with many storeys. The first pagodas were built in India and had many sides. The Indian style of pagoda was spread throughout Asia by Buddhist monks.

The Chinese however made changes in the building style. Their pagodas traditionally have eight sides and wide eaves that turn upward. They are usually built of brick, porcelain or glazed tiles and have wooden, spiral staircases or steep ladders inside leading to the higher floors. Each floor is smaller than the one below. The Big Wild Goose Pagoda in Xian (China) shown in the drawing was built in 652 A.D. to house scrolls containing Buddhist Scriptures brought all the way from India. It stands 65 metres tall with 7 storeys - it had 14, but an aeroplane flew into the side of the Pagoda during World War II almost demolishing it. The Big Wild Goose Pagoda was later restored but lost its top floors. Nearby there is also a Small Wild Goose Pagoda with 15 storeys built in A.D. 707 that is 45 metres high. Both pagodas are in use today by Buddhist monks.

Japanese pagodas are usually made of wood as are many of the pagodas of Burma and Nepal. The Nepalese pagodas are great in size and the wood used in them is decorated with intricate carvings. In Tibet pagodas are made of bricks and stone because of a lack of wood. Of all the pagodas the Indian are perhaps the grandest because they are covered in porcelain and ceramic figures.

The tallest and largest pagoda in the world however is the gold-encrusted Shwe Dagon. Standing on an artificial hill 58 metres above sea level and soaring another 99.4 metres into the sky it dominates the Yangon (Rangoon) skyline. It is a golden beacon to the people of Myanmar (Burma). Begun over 2500 years ago to enshrine 8 hairs from the fourth Buddha, and other relics from the time of the third Buddha, the pagoda has been rebuilt and enlarged seven times. Its present form dates back to 1769 when an earthquake brought down the top or *hti* of the pagoda. The fallen hti still lies beside the pagoda on the marble plinth (platform) on which the pagoda is built. The marble of the plinth extends outwards from the pagoda to form a great encompassing square, and it is pleasant on awarm night to wander bare-footed around the great edifice on its cool surface.

The present top, donated by King Mindon in 1871, consists of three parts; a golden umbrella made of seven gold-plated rings; a golden weather vane encrusted with 1100 diamonds and 1383 precious stones; and a diamond orb that is studded with diamonds, 4351 to be exact. A single large diamond weighing 76 carats tops the globe-shaped orb. Underneath the hti, a further 29 metres of the pagoda is gold-plated, while the remainder is covered in gold paint.

The Small Wild Goose Pagoda

The Shwe Dagon is more than just a pagoda though. It occupies 5.6 hectares and is surrounded by countless smaller temples, pagodas and shrines for worship. Many of these smaller temples, over shadowed as they are, would be worthy of a visit in their own right.

As is common in Asia, Shwe Dagon is the focus for a number of religious festivals throughout the year. Then the pagoda comes alive. Quite apart from the bright orange robes of the monks, the platform becomes a riot of colour because the ceremonies often include people dressed in traditional costume.

Finally a word of warning if you visit the Shwe Dagon on your own. The central stupa (spire) of Shwe Dagon is circular, very large and surrounded by a great number smaller temples. These temples no doubt are easily differentiated by the people of Yangon, but to Western eyes they look very much alike. The exits down long marble staircases are similar too, so it is easy to mistake the way you came in and get lost. And don't forget, you won't be able to ask where you are!

Choose the best answer to the following questions:

1 Where did the pagoda building style originate?

A Burma. **B** China. **C** Japan. **D** India.

2 How does one get from one floor to another in Chinese pagodas?

A By a special lift. **B** Only by ladders.
C By wooden staircases or ladders.
D By baskets with pulleys.

3 Why does the Big Wild Goose Pagoda have less storeys than the Small Wild Goose Pagoda?

A The Emperor had it dismantled.
B The plans were lost.
C The plans were misinterpreted.
D An accident occurred.

4 Why are the pagodas in Tibet built the way they are?

A There are many skilled stone masons.
B There is a plentiful supply of clay.
C The country is above the tree line.
D Tiles give a better appearance.

5 How is it that pagodas are found right throughout Asia?

A The style was spread by a religious order.
B They were built by the same person.
C The Chinese Emperor was envious.
D So that they could be easily seen.

6 Why is the Shwe Dagon a golden beacon to the people of Yangon?

A It has other temples around it. **B** It is made of gold and dominates the skyline.
C It is the focus of festivals. **D** It is the religious focus of the people.

7 Why has the Shwe Dagon been rebuilt so often?

A Each king has wanted to show his importance. **B** The area is unstable geologically.
C The spire is too thin for the weight of the orb. **D** The Buddhists required it.

8 Why is it easy to get lost at Shwe Dagon?

A The central stupa is circular. **B** It is surrounded by many, similar temples.
C The entrances and exits all look the same. **D** All of the preceding.

9 At night it is pleasant to wander around the great pagoda bare-footed because

A it is such a long way to walk. **B** the marble is cool and soothing.
C the sandals that are issued are usually too small. **D** None of the preceding.

10 In the passage the 'over-shadowed as they are' refers to the way in which

A the larger temple blocks the Sun. **B** the smaller temples are not worth visiting.
C Shwe Dagon detracts from their appearance. **D** Shwe Dagon has too much gold on it.

Choose words from the text that mean:

11 religious writings **12** centre of attention **13** foundation platform
14 finely detailed **15** enclose in a special container **16** ancient holy remains

INTERMENT IN TORAJA

EXERCISE 2

READING TEST 4

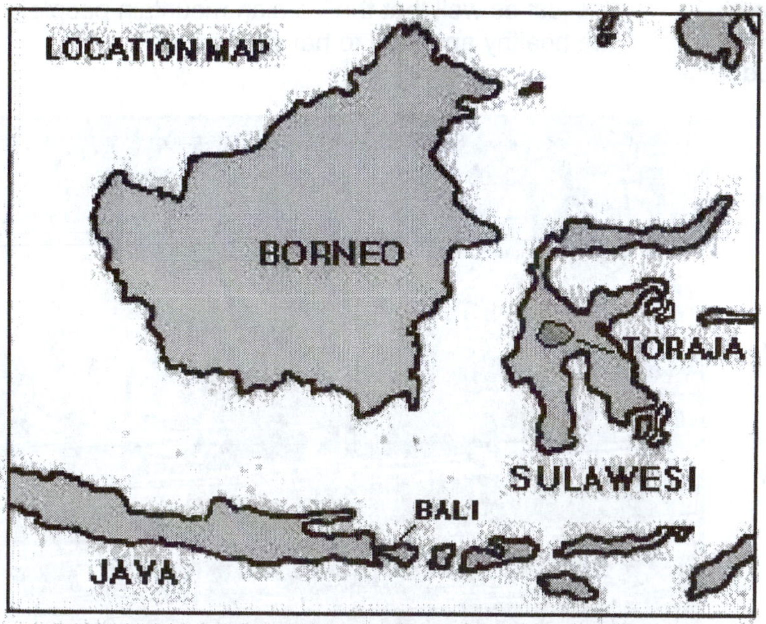

Sulawesi is one of the larger islands of Indonesia.

How would you like to be buried (dead of course) in the side of a cliff with a hollowed-out tree trunk as a coffin? You would have your wife or husband drop a cat (live of course) over the cliff as a sign of grief, and you would have an effigy of you set up outside on a balcony to keep watch over your grave. If this sort of thing appeals to you, you should go to live with the Torajans. To the Torajans, death is the most important part of life. It's true. They spend the whole of their lives saving up to have a wonderful funeral when they die!

When a funeral takes place in Torajaland all the neighbouring villages attend and special bamboo houses and viewing places, painted red and decorated with red ribbons, are built to accommodate the guests. Over a thousand people may attend so it may be necessary to build perhaps a hundred and fifty bamboo houses. These must be paid for by the near relatives. Everyone brings offerings, but the close relatives bring expensive gifts of pigs and buffaloes. The value of each gift is very carefully recorded because the relatives' share of the deceased's estate depends on the value of the animals that they bring with them. The live animals are tied up or laid out in front of the deceased's family for counting. As you can imagine a hundred or so squealing pigs with the odd chicken or two can make a fair bit of noise! The length of the funeral ceremony depends upon the standing of the dead person in the village - for an important person it may last for several days. On the first days the visitors pay their respects to the family – it takes that long for everyone to arrive and be presented. During this time the body is kept in a special raised house with open sides where large photographs of the deceased are displayed. On day three there is feasting, singing and dancing and, of course, much talking as villagers catch up with the gossip from other villages. The animals are slaughtered during this time to feed the people present. Surplus meat is divided up between the villages in a fair way. Toraja buffaloes are not worked in the fields but are specially tended by children and young men so as to be fat for killing. During the funeral season special pig and buffalo markets are held at the end of each week.

On day five the body may be taken in its coffin on a special bier, shaped like a boat with a roof, to the vault in the cliff, and the villagers begin to return home. The funeral 'boat' is left at the cave site so that the spirit of the dead person cannot hide inside the bier and unknowingly be brought back to the village. The body of the deceased person is carefully placed in a cave that has been chiseled into a limestone cliff overlooking the valley of the bereaved village. Soon after the burial a new figure is added to an existing row of statues lined up on a balcony outside the tomb. These life-size figures represent the people buried inside the tomb and have a variety of life-like poses. Some have walking sticks, some are waving and some have their hands to their eyes as if to keep out the sun. It is the job of the ancestors, whose spirit then lives in the statues, to watch over the village. Young children who die under the age of two however are not buried in the way just described. They are placed in a cavity hollowed out in the trunk of a large tree. The tree bark soon grows over the cavity and the Torajans believe their spirit then becomes part of the tree and lives forever. Several may be buried in the one large tree.

Because of the great expense of Torajan funerals - the animals killed may be worth as much as $A400 000 - a body may be kept in the house of the nearest relative for long periods until the funeral can be afforded - in some cases, years. The body is not regarded as dead but just "sick" and is offered food three times a day. The body is kept warm with a fire by night. In the old days, fluids were drained from the bodies by means of small bamboo tubes and kept in jars for the later burial – altogether a rather smelly business. Thankfully today the Indonesian Government insists that formalin be used as a body preservative.

At first the Indonesian Government tried to discourage the whole Torajan burial tradition because of its cost and because it was so different to any other burial culture in Indonesia, or anywhere else in the world for that matter. A large tax was placed on animals purchased for funeral ceremonies, but then the Government realised the enormous tourist potential of the strange burial traditions.

An airstrip was built so that rich tourists, usually American, could fly into Toraja rather than take the long and bumpy bus trip to the region. Visitors lucky enough to witness a traditional Torajan funeral (someone has to die after all) have also to bring a gift to the relatives of the deceased. This fortunate custom, for the Government, has become yet another way of tapping into some of the wealth of the visiting tourists.

Despite the cost there never seems to a shortage of extravagant burials in Toraja. They are held during the dry season when village workloads are low and the weather is good, so that a funeral every week or so is not unusual. As the years pass the funerals become more and more costly as the villages continue to vie with each other. If Village A cannot at least match the funeral held by Village B, it reflects badly on the people of Village A. Perhaps it is just as well that the Torajan mountain people are healthy and tend to have long lives!

The effigies in a cliff face

Toraja is set high in the mountains of an isolated part of the island of Sulawesi and although the area has been opened up in recent years, the Torajan people live much the way they always have.

The Torajans like to have two sets of customs in case one fails - they are Christians now but believe that their elaborate funerals keep their ancestors happy, so that they in turn will make life more bearable for those who are still earthbound.

Choose the best answer to the following questions.

17 Toraja belongs to which nation?

A Malaysia. **B** Kalimantan. **C** Suluwesi. **D** Indonesia.

18 Why do most burials take place in the dry season?

A That is when there is much work to do in the fields.
B The weather is cold at that time of year.
C That is the time when most tourists are around.
D The villagers have more spare time and the weather is good.

19 Why are the bodies sometimes not buried for long periods?

A Often the family cannot afford the cost of the funeral.
B It is the custom.
C The more important the person is, the longer the wait.
D It takes time to make a cave.

20 Why do the close relatives bring so many expensive animals as gifts?
- **A** It is a matter of pride.
- **B** It is expected of them.
- **C** The law requires it.
- **D** They get a larger share of the estate.

21 What is the proper way for a husband or wife to show grief?
- **A** Bring many pigs or buffaloes to the funeral.
- **B** Wear some article of clothing belonging to the dead person.
- **C** Throw a cat off the highest cliff.
- **D** Carry the coffin to the cave.

22 Compared to the other Islands of Indonesia, Sulawesi is
- **A** relatively large.
- **B** relatively small.
- **C** insignificant.
- **D** typical.

23 Why is there always a ready supply of buffaloes for the ceremonies?
- **A** They are expensive.
- **B** They are specially bred for the purpose.
- **C** The children look after them.
- **D** The villagers regard it as essential.

24 Why do the villages try to outdo each other with their funerals?
- **A** They like to have the time off to gossip.
- **B** They like feasting and festivals.
- **C** They lose 'face' if they don't.
- **D** It will be their turn sooner or later.

25 Why did the Government try to discourage the Torajan burial custom?
- **A** The tourists were too much of a nuisance.
- **B** The Torajans were converted to Christianity.
- **C** There were not enough animals, particularly buffaloes.
- **D** They were too costly and time wasting.

26 Why do you think the Torajan burial customs continue even though the people are now Christian?
- **A** Torajaland is so isolated and cut off from the world.
- **B** The Torajans perhaps do not believe the promises of Christianity.
- **C** Most would prefer to have a new system.
- **D** The people make a lot of money from the tourists.

27 Which of these statements best describes the Torajans' life and beliefs?
- **A** Their ancestors are present with them all the time.
- **B** Music and festivals are the most important aspects of living.
- **C** The Torajans are able to adapt to change easily.
- **D** They are subject to close control by the central Government.

28 The length of the funeral ceremony depends upon
- **A** the time of year.
- **B** the number of animals brought by the relatives.
- **C** the amount of money contributed by the neighbouring villages.
- **D** the importance of the deceased.

Find words in the passage that mean:

29 a statue made in the likeness of
30 wastefully elaborate
31 a moveable coffin stand
32 to compete with

Burial caves cut into the cliff face.

THE LEANING TOWER OF PISA

EXERCISE 3 READING TEST 4

"*Chiao* Marco. Do you know what the crowd's all about?"

"*Chiao* Enrico. Yes, they're here to see *Professore* Galileo carry out one of his famous experiments."

"What's that madman going to do this time ?"

"Today he's going to prove that a ball weighing1 kilo falls just as fast through the air, as one weighing 10 kilos. Look he's getting ready to roll the weight off the edge of the balcony now."

"Quick Marco, let's get a bit closer. My money's on the heavy ball, what do you think?"

Pushing through the crowd Marco and Enrico gazed up at the famous professor. Surrounded by serious-faced timekeepers and observers from the University of Padua, an equally serious Galileo prepared to roll the two weights down an inclined ramp jutting out from the seventh floor of the Tower of Pisa. At the foot of the Tower more observers and timekeepers had taken up their positions near the expected point of impact.

The roar of anticipation, which went up as the two balls appeared over the edge, quickly changed into gasps of amazement as the two weights crashed down. They gasped, not because Marco and Enrico got too close to the landing zone, and had been hit by the weights, but because the weights arrived at exactly the same moment!

History records that Professor Galileo of the city of Pisa, did roll two balls of different weight from a height to prove that the force of gravity was constant, no matter what the weight of the falling object was. It is not certain whether Galileo used the Tower of Pisa for his famous experiment. It is generally accepted that he did because it would have been a good place for the experiment. In those days a higher, more-convenient building would have been hard to find.

Pisa is in northern Italy about 75 kilometres west of Florence. The city's main claim to fame is its leaning building. The building is wonderful, but it is not the most wonderful ever built. There are many other far more beautiful or historically important old buildings in Italy. For example, the church just next to it, the Duomo, (for which the Leaning Tower is really just the bell tower), is one of the most beautiful in Italy. But, because of its lean, the Leaning Tower is one of the best-known buildings in the world – certainly the best-known in Italy. The biggest wonder is that it is still there. Its story is almost as strange as the way it looks.

Galileo

The Leaning Tower is circular in shape and stands 55 metres high. Its walls are 4 metres thick at the base and about 2 metres thick at the top. It has 8 floors or storeys. Semi-circular arches supported by 15 columns surround the basement storey. The storeys above, called arcades, have 30 columns each, except for the eighth storey, where the bells are, which has only 12 columns.

In Galileo's time the Tower of Pisa did not have quite the lean that it has today but it had some. Architects first noticed that the tower had begun to list when the building was only 10 metres high. And the Leaning Tower took an incredibly long time to finish - would you believe nearly 200 years, from 1174 to 1350! Needless to say the church architect who designed it, a person called Bonanno, wasn't around to see its completion. They tried to correct the problem of the lean as building went on, but, as the building grew higher it also grew heavier, and so the leaning increased. That is why if you look at the tower closely, it doesn't look quite right, especially at the top.

The Leaning Tower's lean has been caused by subsidence - the Tower is made of heavy Italian marble, too heavy for the soft alluvial land on which it stands - but the main cause of its lean has been its poor foundations. The original foundations were only 3 metres deep. They were shallow, did not reach down to underlying bedrock, and were only as wide as the basement level walls, so the whole tower is like a giant stick which has been poked into soft ground. As time has passed the ground under the Tower has gradually, given way, more on one side than the other, causing the tower to lean. By 1859, when the Leaning Tower was measured accurately, it was 4.7 metres out of perpendicular. In 1910 the lean had increased to 5.01 metres.

Pisa's Tower acts like a magnet to tourists. The Italian Government, realising its importance as a tourist attraction, has tried a number of schemes to stabilise it. The whole area around the tower has been drained and concrete has been pumped under the weak side. The rate of increase in the lean has been slowed almost to zero but despite all efforts it still increases slightly each year. For safety reasons the 294-step climb to the top of the tower, over worn, sloping steps, is no longer permitted.

STOP PRESS

"It started with a few creaks and groans and a low rumbling sound. Then the building began to tremble, like the muscles on the leg of a runner who was coming last in the marathon at the Sydney Olympics, and showing symptoms of extreme fatigue. Then it began to move, in slow motion at first, but with gradually increasing speed. Pieces of marble and plaster, like flakes of snow in a snowstorm, began to shed from the walls, followed by segments from the external columns. Gathering speed the whole height of the building seemed to collapse in on itself and, with a great roar, it came down. On the rooftop the flag gained new life for an instant giving one last flutter before it too disappeared into the jumble of falling masonry. Slower than the noise, a great cloud of dust rose up and spread out in a circle around the stricken Tower as it began to settle. Finally all was quiet."

Just kidding. It really didn't happen as described in the '**STOP PRESS**'. Well it might have happened that way. Well actually it may not happen that way, even though the Leaning Tower of Pisa now leans at an angle of 16° to the perpendicular. In 1910 the angle was 11°. By 1995 the slope had been stabilised at 1.5 cm per year but on September 15, 1995 the lean of the tower increased by 5 centimetres in one night causing great fears for its ability to stay upright! Latest news is that engineers think that they solved the tower's problem. Instead of trying to strengthen the low side, as has been done previously, attempts are now being made to weaken the foundations of the high side. The method seems to be working because in 2000 the lean of the Tower actually began to reverse. Meanwhile though, if you plan on visiting the Leaning Tower of Pisa, I think you had best not leave it too long before you make your trip. And while you are there, make sure you listen carefully for any creaking or rumbling noises and don't stand on the low side!

Choose the best answer to complete the following sentences:

33 Galileo's gravity experiment proved that

A the heavier ball would reach the ground first.
B the lighter ball would not fall as fast.
C both balls would reach the ground at the same time.
D there was no such thing as gravity.

Post script
Galileo was born near Pisa, on February 15, 1564 and died near Florence, on January 8, 1642. His many inventions and discoveries in mathematics, physics and astronomy often brought him into conflict with the generally held views of the time, especially those of leading churchmen, with regard to the position of the Earth in the Universe. As we know now of course, Galileo was right, but for many years Galileo had to keep to himself to avoid persecution by the Church.

34 The Leaning Tower's problem is caused mainly by

A too many tourists
B shallow foundations.
C no attention to details.
D the weight of the Duomo.

35 The Leaning Tower could be best compared to

A a magnet.
B a garden stake
C a wedding cake.
D a paddle pop.

36 The Leaning Tower is

A the most beautiful building in northern Italy.
B more beautiful than the Duomo.
C the most important building in Rome.
D simply a bell tower.

37 Bonanno didn't see the completion of the building because

A he was overseas. **B** he was fired.
C he was dead. **D** he was designing another building.

38 The 'stop press' section is an attempt at

A confusion. **B** subterfuge. **C** humour. **D** sarcasm.

39 A word used in the passage to mean 'lean' is

A thin. **B** sink. **C** stabilise. **D** list.

40 The hopeful message of the 'stop press' section is that

A you should not stand too close to buildings where material might fall.
B one day the Leaning Tower will lean too far and fall.
C masonry can be very dusty.
D modern engineering can solve any problem.

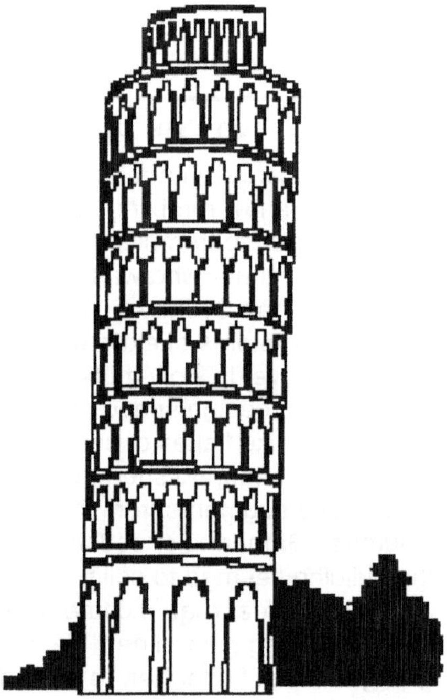

41 The discoveries made by Galileo

A brought him great riches.
B caused him to be burned as a wizard.
C brought him into conflict with religious leaders.
D made him the most popular man in Rome.

42 Galileo's relations with the Church in Rome could best be described as

A precocious. **B** cordial.
C straightforward. **D** None of the preceding.

43 A 'post script' is

A material that has been sent by mail.
B additional material added later to a letter or article.
C extra material that the author would like to use but cannot.
D None of the preceding.

44 Galileo's inventive genius

A was limited to the field of mathematics.
B was very wide-ranging.
C was limited to the field of astronomy.
D was only concerned with gravity.

45 Which of these proverbs could be well applied to the Leaning Tower?

A Too many cooks spoil the broth.
B Don't count your chickens before they hatch.
C Don't burn your bridges behind you.
D People in glass houses shouldn't throw stones.
E If at first you don't succeed, try, try ,and try again.

Find words in the passage that mean:

46 to make secure and maintain at a certain level
47 vertical
48 the settling of soil
49 footings for a building
50 harassment or pursuit with enmity

THE DRAGONS OF KOMODO

EXERCISE 1 READING TEST 5

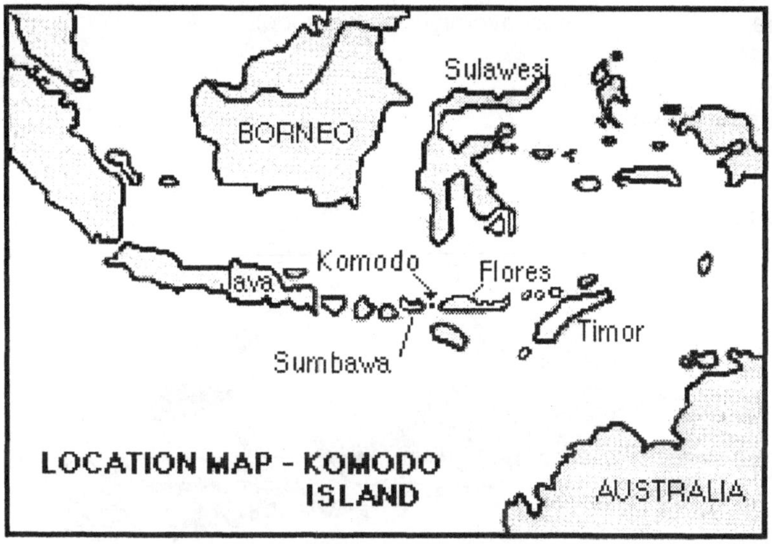

If you intend to walk around on the Island of Komodo you had better take a guide with you, because Komodo is the home of the largest and most dangerous lizard in the world, the Komodo Dragon. The 3 metre, 130 kg Komodo Dragons are not relics of the age of the dinosaurs, they are modern, efficient reptiles. Like all monitor lizards, they have ear openings, tapered heads, eyes with eyelids and round pupils, massive bodies and legs each with five claws. A leathery skin covered with small hard scales finishes off their ensemble. Their claws are razor sharp and they have serrated teeth, toxic saliva, and a very powerful tail. All in all not your average garden variety pet.

The Island itself is not a very attractive place either. Part of Indonesia, it is a dry and desolate place formed from the rocky rim of an old, collapsed volcanic crater. The giant lizards are its only claim to fame. Why the lizards are found there, and on the nearby islands of Rinca and Padar and the coastal tip of Flores, is not known, for they could live quite well in any warm, fairly dry climate.

The Komodos live in burrows and, being diurnal animals, are only seen during daylight hours. Their favourite pastime, apart from soaking up the sun, is eating, and their menu is varied. It consists of deer (their favourite), birds, and even other smaller brother and sister Komodos. At times their diet has been known to include the children of villagers (there is a fishing village on the Island), and the occasional unwary tourist who has ventured too close to take pictures. Their method of hunting is the essence of simplicity and laziness. They lie motionless alongside a bush track, where, looking like a log, they just grab a leg of a passing victim or knock it over with a swing of their powerful tail. Their strong gastric juices enable them to digest every part of their prey, hair, horns, hoofs and bones!

Komodo Dragons are sexually mature at around 7 years of age and it is thought that they live for over 50 years. The females lay from 15 to 30 eggs that take 9 months to hatch. The young must fend for themselves and spend at least 5 years living in trees on the Island catching birds, frogs and insects. They must do this because of the older lizards. Mature Dragons are good swimmers and are often seen swimming in the sea where their tail action resembles that of crocodiles.

A National Park has been established on Komodo, and it is easy enough to see the Dragons because they are fed regularly by staff at established places. When a tourist pays for a goat, it is slaughtered and its carcass thrown down into a dry creek bed. While the tourists view from the safety of an elevated, fenced enclosure, the Dragons, huge and lumbering, climb over one another in their haste to get at the goat. Quietly, save for an occasional deep grunt, within 10 minutes, every part has been eaten.

Oh, and I forgot to warn you. Getting to Komodo is quite a trip by small boat across open sea, unless of course you are rich enough to travel on one of the luxury tourist ships. Actually the water journey between Flores and Komodo can be hazardous for small boats due to the differing levels between the Pacific and Indian Oceans in this area. Small boat owners will only travel across in daylight.

And if you survive the sea voyage, and the Dragons, there are a lot of cobras (yes that's right cobras) so it really is essential to have a good guide with a long forked stick - the longer the better. The Komodos are hard to see and extremely dangerous and, well, the cobras can be anywhere. Don't be foolish and try to be the sun-tanned Aussie - wear strong shoes and trousers or jeans of some sort, for that little extra bit of peace of mind.

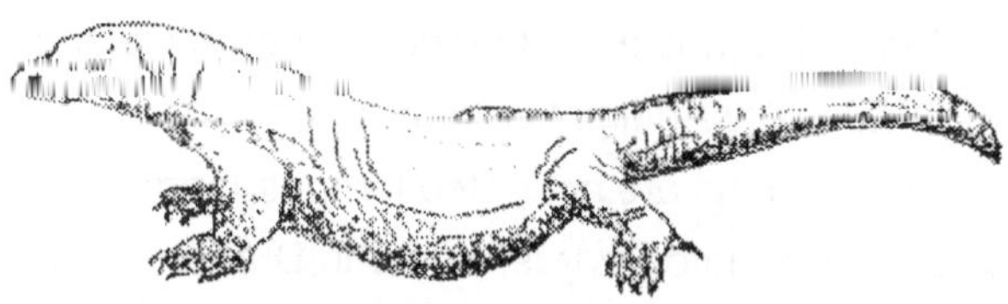

To get to Komodo you have to catch a ferry from Flores or Sumbawa Islands, or hire a boat. Either way the trip is long and uncomfortable. Because the Dragons are more active in the heat of the day, this will mean a very early start around 3 a.m. for a 10 o'clock appointment with the Dragons. Don't forget you have to return to the island that you came from because you can't stay overnight on Komodo.

1 **The crossing to Komodo is dangerous because**
- **A** the boats are only small.
- **B** there are many rips and whirlpools.
- **C** it is usually dark when tourists set out.
- **D** All of the preceding.

2 **The strangest thing about Komodo Dragons is that they**
- **A** resemble other lizards.
- **B** are able to swim well.
- **C** are so large.
- **D.** have evolved in only a very small area.

3 **The most important safety rule is to**
- **A** have a good pair of strong walking shoes.
- **B** make sure you have a strong, long stick.
- **C** wear jeans or other long trousers.
- **D** have a local guide with a long stick.

4 **A 10 o'clock appointment is necessary so as to**
- **A** avoid the heat of the day.
- **B** see the smaller Komodos while they are still on the ground.
- **C** correspond with the Dragons' most active time.
- **D** make sure that you get a guide.

Are the following statements True (T) or False (F)?

5 The Dragons' method of hunting is by patience rather than by stealth. (   )

6 The fact that Komodo Dragons are 'modern efficient lizards' means that they would thrive in an area like The Northern Territory. (   )

7 Because they are so dangerous, tourists cannot be assured of a good view of the Dragons. (   )

8 Komodo Dragons have a smooth unblemished skin. (   )

9 The Komodo Dragons are both carnivorous and cannibalistic. (   )

10 For safety young Komodo Dragons must live in the trees for some years. (   )

11 Being nocturnal, the Komodo Dragons are most active at night. (   )

12 The Komodo Dragons are not the only dangerous animals on Komodo Island. (   )

13 Komodo Dragons are found in numerous locations throughout the Indonesian Archipelago. (   )

14 Boatmen like to make the trip from Flores to Komodo at night when the sea is calmer. (   )

15 Komodo Island is part of an active volcano. (   )

16 Komodo Dragons are not as dangerous as their name might suggest. (   )

17 Some Dragons are found on the nearby Island of Flores. (   )

18 Dragons are diurnal creatures. (   )

19 The Dragons are not noted for their longevity. (   )

20 Like all monitor lizards, Komodo Dragons do not have an external ear opening. (   )

ANOTHER OPERA HOUSE

EXERCISE 2

READING TEST

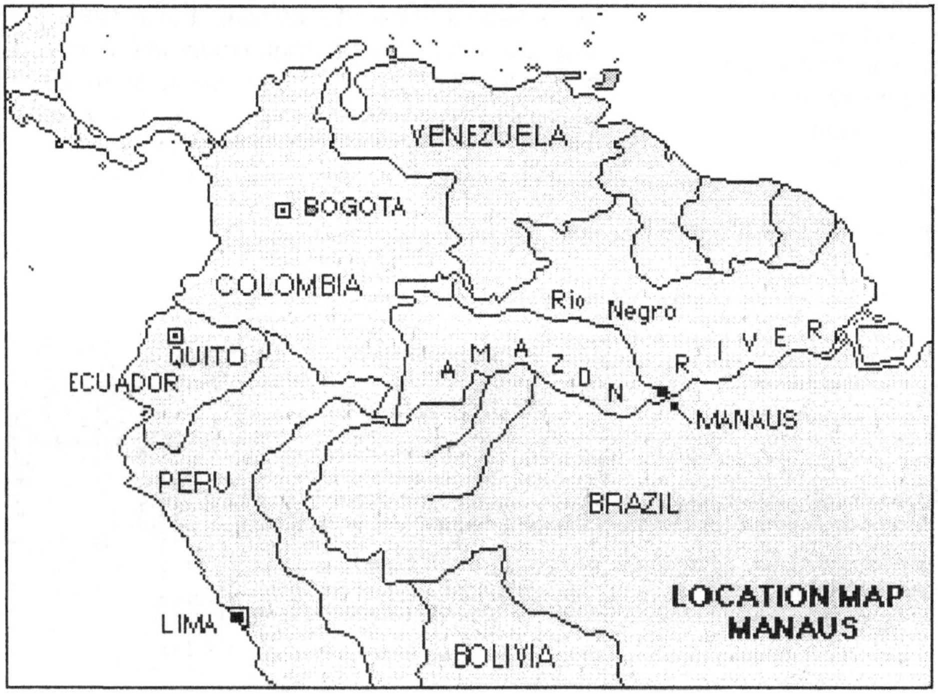

The people of Sydney think that they have the most spectacular and unusual opera house in the world. And maybe they have. But let's think for a moment about another opera house, the Opera House at Manaus in Brazil.

Eduardo Ribeiro was a rich man, very rich in fact. He was also a man who loved music, so he decided to build an Opera House. Now you might think this was unusual, but not that unusual, because, after all, Ribeiro was very rich. What was most unusual however, was the fact that Ribeiro's Opera House was to be built in Manaus - on the banks of the Amazon River, close to the Equator and 1450 kilometres from the sea. You should also realise that the materials for the ornate marble-and-tile building would have to be brought many thousands of kilometres from Europe.

Added to all of this, the whole Amazon Region is one of the wettest areas of the world and the climate can be easily described in three words - hot, wet, and steamy. You would find the climate decidedly unpleasant and, everything considered, you would have to agree that Manaus was a strange place to choose to build an Opera House. But that is just what Ribeiro did.

Eduardo Ribeiro had made his money from rubber. Between 1850 and 1910 nearly all of the world's supply of latex rubber came from Brazil. At that time the demand for rubber was enormous – cars began using petrol in the mid-1880s and John Dunlop had invented the pneumatic (air-filled) tyre in 1888. Great fortunes were made until it was found that the rubber tree would grow in other tropical areas. Legend has it that Henry Wickham,of Brazil smuggled a few seeds out inside a walking stick, but the truth is that in 1875 Wickham managed to charter a special ship to carry no less than 70 000 seeds of the tree to the Royal Botanic Gardens in England. The young rubber trees that grew from these seeds were sent around the world, and by 1910 the Brazilian rubber monopoly was broken – but not before Ribeiro had amassed his fortune.

Ribeiro was determined that his Opera House would rival anything in the world, so material and artists were brought in from Europe to make the beautiful building that we see today. On the outside of the building, the dome is covered with 36 000 decorated ceramic tiles painted green and yellow, the national colours of Brazil. Made in the shape of a harp, the central nave can seat 640 people. Surrounding it are 3 floors with box seats with, on the first floor, a box for the President. The stage curtain is the magnificent painting "Meeting of the Waters", originally done in Paris by Crispim Amaral. This curtain rises vertically so as not to damage the painting. Around the ceiling of the auditorium are painted scenes depicting music, dance, and drama. The central gold chandelier descends to the level of the seats for cleaning purposes and the changing of light bulbs. Above this chandelier, in the middle of the roof, there is a painting imitating the view of someone standing beneath the Eiffel Tower.

On the first floor of the building, at the front but not inside the auditorium, is a large room called The Noble Room. We would call it a ballroom. The floor of this room is of small wooden pieces, called parquetry, so finely made that it was fitted together without nails or glue. In Ribeiro's day this room was used for balls and receptions or as a place where Ribeiro and his friends would go to strut and talk between acts or after the performance. Around the side of this hall is a gallery where people could, and still do, sit to watch the 'goings on' of the rich and famous.

The Theatre itself is lavishly decorated, with beautiful carved chairs for seating, plush red upholstery and gilded columns. Inside the auditorium, at the top of each column, are modelled masks of many of the famous operatic composers; such as Mozart, Rossini, Beethoven and so on. Outside, the theatre is bounded by wide streets and is set off at the front by a large mosaic square that matches the white facing of the building.

Some of the most famous singers in the world sang in the opening season of Ribeiro's Opera House, including the famous tenor Enrico Caruso and Australia's Dame Nellie Melba. When the rubber boom collapsed the theatre too went into a decline. It fell into disrepair, but in 1965 it was restored by the Brazilian Government at a cost of $A12 million. It is too costly to stage an opera season at Manaus these days although it is used for pop performances and symphony concerts. And of course it is a great tourist attraction.

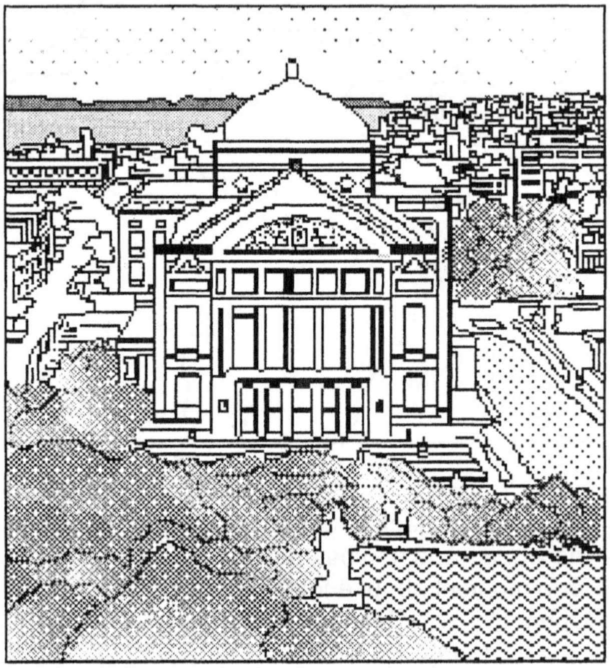

The Wonderful Opera House at Manaus

21 What was unusual about Ribeiro's choice of site for an opera House.?
- **A** It was so far from anywhere.
- **B** There were few materials available.
- **C** The climate was unpleasant.
- **D** All of the above.

22 From the passage, what do you think a 'monopoly' is?
- **A** A group of rubber plantation owners.
- **B** People who have control over the supply of a commodity.
- **C** People who sell but never buy.
- **D** A secret group of workers.

23 Why were the tiles green and gold?
- **A** They represent the Amazon rainforest.
- **B** They fitted on the rounded dome.
- **C** They are the national colours of Brazil.
- **D** They were made of baked porcelain.

24 Why is it necessary to raise the curtain vertically the way they do?
- **A** The sight of the curtain rising is very impressive.
- **B** To stop the paint cracking.
- **C** The stage is small and it gives more room that way.
- **D** It gives the impression of the meeting of the two rivers.

25 What is parquetry?
- **A** The name given to a kind of dance floor.
- **B** The name for a gallery overlooking a ballroom.
- **C** Any kind of wooden flooring.
- **D** Flooring made of wooden blocks.

26 What happened when the rubber boom collapsed?
- **A** The Opera House was restored.
- **B** The Opera House was neglected.
- **C** The Opera House changed from oil to cheaper electric heating.
- **D** Melba and Caruso had to support the Opera House.

Choose words from the passage that mean:

27 covered in gold paint
28 pattern made from glass, stone or tiles
29 a light fitting having many lights or candles
30 material coverings or hangings
31 showing or representing art
32 made like new

EXERCISE 3 THE TAJ MAHAL READING TEST 5

The Taj Mahal, arguably the world's greatest monument

"'Empire has no sweetness, life itself has no relish for me now'."

So it is said, mourned Sha Jahan over the death of his wife, Mumtaz. 'Mumtaz Mahal' was the name of the beautiful Queen of the last great Mughal Emperor, Sha Jahan. Her name meant 'Chosen One of the Palace' and Mumtaz was the Emperor's favourite. Sha Jahan had a number of wives, but she was the closest to Sha Jahan's heart. Unfortunately, in 1637, a short eighteen months after Sha Jahan was proclaimed Emperor, and just when she could have expected a life of comfort and splendour, Mumtaz suddenly died.

Sha Jahan had been on one of his military campaigns, and he had taken Mumtaz with him because he could not bear to be away from her.

Overcome with grief at her sudden death (she was 37 years of age) Shah Jahan decided to erect a fitting monument to her memory. And so the world's most famous building was begun.

The name itself, 'Taj Mahal', comes from Mumtaz's name, because, right from the start, it was her building. An open site on a bend in the River Yamuna near Agra, India, the central city of the Mughal Empire, was chosen for the great building. The task was enormous and it took 20 000 skilled workmen and master craftsmen 22 years to create the lonely palace for the dead Mumtaz. It also took 40 million rupees, a great fortune in those days. Over 1000 elephants were used to transport the white marble all the way from Rajasthan in north-western India. Elephants were also needed to work the pulleys necessary to lift the great blocks of marble into place. In the town of Mumtazabad, which sprang up near the site of the building, children played amidst the clatter of metal tools shaping the huge, gleaming slabs of marble.

The entrance gate to the Taj Mahal was made of red sandstone, a favourite building material of the Mughal emperors. It still stands, and, massive as it is, as you pass through it you are overcome by the even greater size of the colossal, domed mausoleum that appears in front of you.

For its foundation the Taj Mahal is set upon an immense, patterned plinth containing many thousands of tonnes of sandstone. The plinth is overlaid by white marble and a double marble staircase leads to it from the surrounding formal gardens and water ponds. The central dome is flanked by ornate minarets (prayer towers) located one at each corner of the plinth. These are sloped slightly outwards so that, if an earthquake were to occur, they could fall without injuring the main building.

The marble walls and towers of the Taj Mahal are inlaid with verses from the Koran, the Holy Book of the Moslems. The inscriptions on upper levels of the building are larger than at ground level so as to give the appearance of a uniform size of writing - no detail of construction was small enough to be overlooked. Inside the single central chamber are two false tombs protected by an elaborate, fret-worked marble screen inlaid with thousands of semi-precious stones. Mumtaz and later Sha Jahan were laid to rest in a vault immediately below. Today visitors are allowed into all parts of the building, but must take off their shoes or wear specially- made slippers so as not to desecrate the holy place.

The story of Sha Jahan's lost love is sad enough but more is to come. Eventually Sha Jahan grew tired of Agra and moved his capital city to Shajahanabad, (now Old Delhi), where he continued to reign wisely and well. Sha Jahan's health was good but unfortunately he had a fanatical son, named Aurangzeb, by another wife. Aurangzeb was desperate to become Emperor. He could not wait for Sha Jahan to die of old age, but he could not bring himself to murder his father. Instead he imprisoned Sha Jahan in a wing of the Red Fort in Agra. The rooms chosen by Aurangzeb for his father's prison were located at the top of the furthest corner of the Red Fort - they just happened to be directly opposite the Taj Mahal, about 5 kilometres away. Sadly, for the last seven years of his life Sha Jahan could only sit and stare at the Taj Mahal rising serenely from the mustard fields and mud-walled villages on the other side of the Yamuna River. At least, each time he looked at the gleaming white building shimmering in the heat haze rising from the river, he could dream of the love of his life, Mumtaz.

Choose the best answer to the following

33 The name 'Taj Mahal' comes from

- **A** a town in India.
- **B** the name of Aurangzeb's wife.
- **C** the name of Sha Jahan's wife.
- **D** the Red Fort in Agra.

34 Sha Jahan took Mumtaz with him on a military campaign because

- **A** she liked to travel.
- **B** she was ill.
- **C** she came from that village.
- **D** he did not want to be without her.

35 The site on the Yumuna River would have been chosen because

- **A** there was water nearby.
- **B** the marble was close by.
- **C** Mumtaz's health was poor.
- **D** the building would have been easily seen.

36 The writing was larger at the top

- **A** so that it all looked the same size from below.
- **B** so that it all looked the same size from above.
- **C** because the text from the Koran was holy.
- **D** to make it easier to read.

37 The minarets were sloped the way they were

- **A** so that the prayers from the priests would carry further.
- **B** to minimise damage from earthquakes.
- **C** to make people wonder all the more at the magnificent building.
- **D** to enhance the appearance of the building.

38 The word 'Mumtazabad' means

- **A** a mustard field.
- **B** a skilled worker.
- **C** Mumtaz's monument.
- **D** the city of Mumtaz.

39 In the quotation at the beginning of the passage, the word 'relish' means

- **A** sweetness.
- **B** enjoyment.
- **C** bitterness.
- **D** power.

40 From the passage we can tell that a plinth is

- **A** a kind of base.
- **B** a tool for working marble.
- **C** the most common form of building material in those days.
- **D** a very hard form of marble.

41 The story is particularly sad because

A Aurungzeb was so cruel.
B Sha Jahan could no longer see Mumtaz.
C Sha Jahan could see his favourite wife's mausoleum in the distance.
D Sha Jahan knew that his son had imprisoned him.

Are the following statements True (T) or False (F)?

42 Mumtaz was Aurangzeb's mother. ( )

43 Sha Jahan was murdered. ( )

44 The Taj Mahal has a reflection pool in front of it. ( )

45 The ashes of Sha Jahan were scattered in the Yumuna River. ( )

46 A minaret is a prayer tower. ( )

Find words in the passage that mean:

47 regretted deeply the loss of
48 having extreme beliefs
49 a series of battles
50 a building housing a tomb or tombs

LOST CITY OF THE INCAS

EXERCISE 1

READING TEST 6

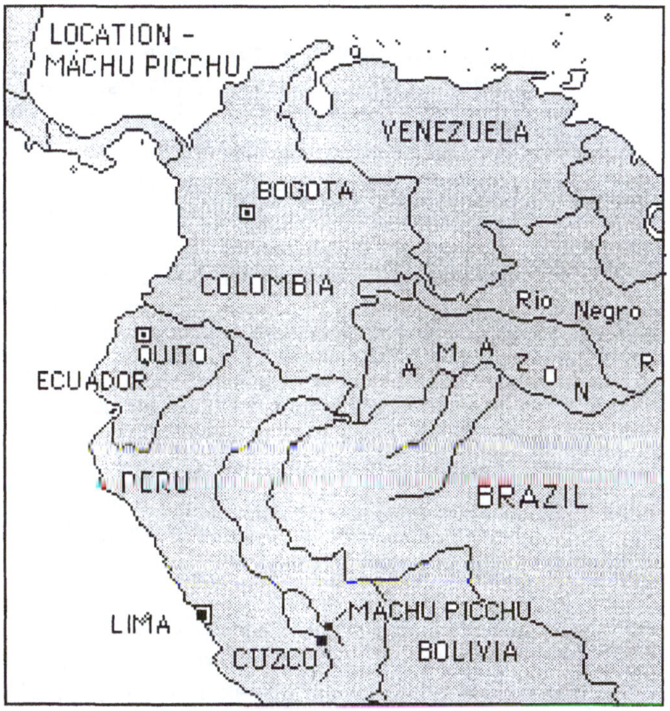

Hiram Bingham was cold and wet. In fact Hiram Bingham was very cold and very wet. His heart was thumping too because he had just climbed a huge cliff, but Hiram Bingham didn't care. It was the greatest moment of his life. He stumbled through the last of the thickets and undergrowth at the top of a steep mountain in the Peruvian Andes and there it was, Machu Picchu, the lost city of the Incas. Although the surrounding forest had reclaimed some of the site, the outline of stone houses, great stone staircases, paved streets; terraces and wonderful, circular temples could be dimly seen through the mist that swirled in gusts across the mountain top. In his mind's eye he had seen the city a thousand times, but the reality was a thousand times better than his imagination.

Bingham had been searching for the hidden city of the Inca King, Manco, on and off, for over 20 years. Careful study of ancient documents had led Bingham to believe that the hidden city did exist. After years of fruitless searching however, he was about to give up on his latest expedition and return to his occupation as a history lecturer in the United States. But when Bingham gazed upon the magnificent stone buildings that appeared magically out of the mist he knew that his search was over and he had found the final hiding place of the Incas. The date was July 24, 1911. That fateful morning, Doctor Bingham's companions had preferred to stay in the warmth of their tent rather than scale the steep cliffs above the river on such a cold and rainy day. Besides they had heard stories of ancient ruins before. And so it was that Bingham was left to climb alone.

Why did Machu Picchu remain hidden for so long? Well the words 'Machu Picchu' (pronounced mach-oo pich-oo) mean 'old hilltop'. And that's just what Machu Picchu was, a hilltop. Sited on the top of a granite hill it was hidden on three sides by vertical cliffs overlooking the narrow, winding gorge of the Urumbamba River, a tributary of the far-off Amazon.

Machu Picchu could only be reached with great difficulty. It could be approached by a paved trail built midway up the side of the vertical cliffs surrounding it, but this trail contained a number of bridges built into the sides of the cliffs. Tree trunks that could be easily removed in an emergency spanned the bridges. A second hidden track led over the mountains behind Machu Picchu through dense forest. Then of course there was the gorge of the wild Urumbamba River that was impassable for most of the year. On the only side where a difficult approach was possible a high, stone wall had been built, and if there was one thing the Incas knew how to do, it was to build stone walls. Above the wall, large boulders had been positioned to roll down on an advancing enemy and further up the slope, secondary walls completed the internal defences. On the nearby Huayna Picchu ("New Hilltop') a watchtower was permanently maintained to warn of enemies approaching. This was reached by a steep stone staircase constructed around and, by tunnel, through the mountain. Machu Picchu was in fact a stone fortress perched upon a hilltop deep in the forests of the Andes.

Machu Picchu with Huayana Picchu in the background

The Incas were a race of people living in the western foothills of the Andes Mountains in South America. They were Sun-Worshippers and at its peak around 1000 A.D. their civilisation stretched from southern Chile to Ecuador. Some think that Machu Picchu was the original starting point of the Inca civilisation, begun over 1000 years ago by priests who went to the isolated mountain top to be closer to the Sun. It is thought that, as the Sun Religion spread to areas with better climate and soils for farming, the old city of Machu Picchu was forgotten, except by a few of the Sun Priests.

In 1536 Manco Inca, the last of the Inca kings, was in fear of his life at the hands of the Spanish. The old forgotten city of Machu Picchu offered the perfect hiding place. Taking what remained of the Inca nobility (priests and members of the Royal Family) Manco disappeared. The city and the fate of the last Incas remained hidden until the arrival of Hiram Bingham.

Today, inside the city walls of Machu Picchu, the astounded traveller sees an amazing collection of stone temples, palaces, houses, tombs, plazas, public squares, gaols, wells, baths, altars for sacrifices, and scientific observation points. You can if you wish sit in the gaol and think of the poor prisoners that were held there. The gaol was a small square surrounded by stone seats set into stone walls. The prisoners were made to sit in the seats and put their arms through holes made in the stone walls on each side of their body. Their hands were then tied on the outside. Even the children of Machu Picchu were catered for with polished stone slippery dips. Rather too hard on the clothes though these days!

All the buildings of the city and their various parts are constructed of the native stone of the mountain ledge. All are packed on top of each other and connected by curving stone stairways, for the site is really very small. The house roofs were made of wood and straw that have of course rotted away, but some have been restored to show what the houses were like. Narrow terraces both inside and outside the walls were used for growing potatoes and corn so that the city was fairly self-sufficient. Even the watchtower on Huayana Picchu had its own vegetable terraces. The Incas knew all about earthquakes and each wall in the city was sloped inward at 13° to the perpendicular, which also happens to be the latitude of the site (the Inca priests were Sun-Worshippers remember and were able to make accurate observations of the Sun). For additional strength, each stone was locked into its neighbour in an irregular pattern, without mortar, but so tightly that a razor blade cannot be inserted even today. At Machu Picchu in a wilderness of thick forests, roaring rivers, vertical mountains and swirling mists, King Manco, the earthly representative of the Sun God, ruled with his priests and faithful followers from 1536 to 1572. The Spanish never found his lost city, but Machu Picchu became the tomb as well as the cradle of the Inca civilisation. It seems that the city just 'died out' - mysteriously, the cemetery when excavated yielded 184 female bodies and only 36 males.

If you are touring in South America, a visit to Machu Picchu is a must. Machu Picchu is in Peru and you get there by going first to Cuzco, the large capital city of the Incas, then by narrow switchback railway along the Urumbamba Gorge. (The Urumbamba River is one of the headwaters of the mighty Amazon River.) Stay overnight at the hotel right at Machu Picchu so that you can properly explore the city. If you are energetic, you can try the three-day overland hike to Machu Picchu from Cuzco but be careful of robbers. At least don't be like Hiram's companions; the sight of Machu Picchu on the mountain is magic and well worth the trouble of getting out of bed.

1 Hiram's companions did not accompany him because
- **A** they thought the climb was too hard.
- **B** they claimed it was too wet and cold.
- **C** they had heard stories about the lost city before.
- **D** All of the above.

2 How was the city protected on the weakest side ?
- **A** With tree trunks that could be removed.
- **B** With stone walls and boulders.
- **C** By thickets and undergrowth hiding the trail.
- **D** By vertical cliffs above the wild river.

3 Why was the location of the city forgotten?
- **A** The Incas found better farming areas.
- **B** The priests wanted to observe the Sun better.
- **C** The city contained too much gold for safety.
- **D** The maps were hidden by Manco.

4 Why were the terraces constructed?
- **A** The Incas were farmers and needed land.
- **B** The Incas needed level land for their stone houses.
- **C** So that the city could feed itself in time of need.
- **D** The soldiers needed to be kept occupied.

5 The houses were made earthquake proof by
- **A** the use of strong mortar in the joints.
- **B** sloping the walls at 13°.
- **C** smoothing the walls with sharp blades.
- **D** making the walls of light material.

6 What do you think 'became the tomb as well as the cradle' means?
- **A** Incas lived and died at Machu Picchu.
- **B** When the old priests died, no one knew where Machu Picchu was.
- **C** The cemetery when excavated only had a few bodies in it.
- **D** The Inca civilisation started and ended there.

Are the following statements True (T) or False (F)?

7 Bingham's discovery that particular day was just a lucky chance ( )

8 In 1536 Manco Inca was killed by the Spanish at Machu Picchu. ( )

9 The Inca civilisation reached its peak about 1000 years ago. ( )

10 The stone for the buildings was obtained from Huayna Picchu. ( )

11 The mystery of the male/female imbalance of bodies in the cemetery has never been satisfactorily explained. ( )

12 The overland hike from Cuzco is not recommended for safety reasons. ( )

13 Machu Picchu was destroyed by earthquake over 100 years ago. ( )

14 The Incas believed Manco was the earthly representative of the Sun God. ( )

15 The paved approach trail could easily be rendered impassable. ( )

16 The Spanish eventually found the last stronghold of Manco Inca. ( )

17 No-one really knows why the settlement at Machu Picchu failed. ( )

THE CAT MUSEUM

EXERCISE 2

READING TEST 6

Kuching is a city of about 350 000 people. It is situated almost on the equator, in the former British colony of Sarawak, which is now part of East Malaysia, in the large island of Borneo. Kuching is a pleasant, safe city. It has a mixture of fine old colonial buildings left over from the time when Sarawak was a colony of Great Britain, as well as some surprising modern constructions. But none are as surprising as the Cat Museum.

The word "kuching" means "cat" in the Malay language and Kuching is known as the "Cat City". It has the only cat museum in the world. That's right, a cat museum! And it's not a small museum either. It is a large modern air-conditioned building, built in native style, with two floors - both devoted to cats.

The Cat Museum is located on the top of a hill called "Bukit Siol" which stands 60 metres above sea level. It is a landmark and has beautiful views of the city and the ocean beyond. The actual floor area of the Cat Museum is 10 359 sq metres. There are four main galleries containing more than 2 000 cat artefacts and memorabilia from all over the world. There are exhibits covering everything from ancient mummified cats from the tombs of Egypt, to the cartoon cats, like Felix, Jerry (of Tom and Jerry) and Garfield. There are exhibits showing photographs of the cats belonging to famous people, to stuffed wildcats from Borneo. Even a wildcat from Australia! Reference to the directory below will give a better idea of the range of wonderful items that can be found inside the museum.

THE CAT MUSEUM DIRECTORY

Gallery A (Ground)

Arched-Back Cats
Cats Fight
Cats In Ancient Egypt
Cats Sleep
Cats At Play

Gallery B (Ground)

Cats In Oriental Art
Cats In Modern Western Art
Cats In Medieval Times
Black Cats
Catnip Tree
Cats and Rats Gallery

Gallery C (1st Floor)

Various Type of Cat Breeds
Five Ages Of Cats
Cat Funerals
Cats In Stamps
Cats In Cards
Cats In Theatre Posters
Caring And Holding
Veterinary Care

Gallery D (1st Floor)

Local Cats
Children's Theatre
Cats As Companions
Garfield's Collection
Wild Cats of Borneo
Children's Corner

The Cat Museum brings together a wide collection of cat-related pictures, paintings, stories, ornaments, statuettes and so on. It also tells the history of the Cat not only in relation to the unusual cats of Kuching with their kinked tails, (the reason why the city got its name), but covers the feline's ancestral role in other cultures. Since its creation in 1988 it has become a meeting place for cat researchers from all over the world. There, cat lovers are able to carry out research on cats, including historical, social and legendary aspects relating to human traditions and beliefs. The Cat

Museum, is a meeting place as well as a seminar and international conference venue for cat lovers' clubs from many countries.

Each year the "Pesta Meow" Festival is held during the school holidays. Organised by the Cat Museum it holds various interesting, competitions mainly to promote the Cat Museum as a tourist attraction in Sarawak. There are competitions in the following ***cat***-egories of cat-related activities and competitions

CAT COMPETITIONS

1 Live Cat Competition and Exhibition
2 Cat Calendar Competition and Exhibition
3 Cat Candid Snap Competition and Exhibition
4 Cat Cartoon Drawing with Funny Dialogue Competition
2 Cat Hunt Competition
5 Cat Voice Imitation Competition
6 Cat Jigsaw Puzzle Competition
7 Cat Essay Writing Competition
8 Cat Creation from Newspaper Competition
9 Cat Kite Making Competition.

There is another 'regular' museum in Kuching, more like the museums that we are used to, but it too has some bizarre exhibits. For instance in one display case near the entrance, there is a gold watch stopped at a quarter to four and a human dental plate. Both items were found in the stomach of a crocodile caught near Kuching. Upstairs there is a chandelier made of shrunken human heads - but then perhaps this is not so unusual because you can see human heads in many of the older longhouses in the forests of Sarawak. Thankfully head hunting in Sarawak was stopped during World War II but you could say that shrunken heads have a long shelf life.

Disregarding the human heads and the contents of the crocodile's stomach too, if that is possible, I would still give my vote to the Cat Museum of Kuching as the most interesting and unusual museum in the world.

Are the following statements True (T) or False (F)?

18 The Cat Museum is not open during the school holidays. ( )
19 The Cat Museum is a good place to view the city and environs. ( )
20 The Cat Museum deals with the cat's role in various cultures through the ages. ( )
21 One section of the Museum deals with cats and postage. ( )
22 The Pesta Meow is held biennially. ( )
23 Each floor contains two galleries. ( )
24 Sarawak has lately become part of Indonesia. ( )
25 Most of the museum's activities are aimed at children. ( )
26 The Cat Museum contains a watch and dental plate found inside a crocodile. ( )
27 There are many examples of Colonial architecture left in Kuching. ( )
28 The Cat Museum's logo features two cats. ( )
29 All true cats of Kuching have one distinguishing feature. ( )

Choose the best answer to complete the following sentences:

30 Many of the Cat Museum's activities are aimed at
- **A** promoting tourism in Kuching.
- **B** encouraging school children to keep cats.
- **C** making people around the world more sympathetic to cats.
- **D** raising money for the city.

31 If I wished to research the role of cats as witches' 'familiars' (companions)I would try
A Gallery A. **B** Gallery B. **C** Gallery C. **D** Gallery D.

32 Sarawak's nearest southern neighbour is
A Borneo. **B** Malaysia. **C** Australia. **D** Indonesia.

33 The author regards the city of Kuching as
A pleasant and secure. **B** hot and unpleasant.
C modern and up-to-date. **D** a place to be avoided at all costs.

34 The Cat Museum has become
- **A** a popular place for weddings in Kuching.
- **B** a popular place for overseas conferences.
- **C** a venue for cat sports.
- **D** the most important cat zoo in the world.

35 A word which could be used to describe the cats of Kuching is
A regrettable. **B** desirable . **C** lovable. **D** distinctive.

Find the word in the passage that means:

36 very strange
37 objects collected that are considered worth remembering.
38 bent
39 belonging to the cat family

Kuching cats come in many shapes, sizes and colours, but they all have peculiar kinked tails.

THE PLAIN OF JARS

EXERCISE 3 READING TEST 6

Our party was a large one, so two small 17-seater propeller planes had to be used to transport us from Vientianne, the capital of Laos, to Phonsavan in the rugged Central Highlands. I held my breath as it seemed that our plane must clip the top of the jagged Annamite mountain chain encircling the Plain of Jars. I need not have worried however for, a breath and a few minutes later, we were dipping down towards the military airfield at Xieng Khuang.

As I looked out the window of I could see the rolling hills of the Plain of Jars that was really a plateau, not a plain. There were a few scattered settlements below, but I could also see strings of whitish bomb craters, some of them quite large made courtesy of the United States during the Vietnam War in the 1960s. (Laotians will proudly tell you that more bombs were dropped on Laos during the War than the total population of the country.) Many of the largest craters were being used as makeshift dams - in Phonsavan later I was to see water containers made out of supplementary fuel tanks jettisoned from American bombers on their long-distance missions. Mixed in with the craters were some other strange scars that, although the right colour, were not the right shape for craters.

The airfield was almost deserted but thankfully Sousath, who was to be our guide, was waiting with a rickety bus to transfer us to Phonsavan. We checked into a simple half-completed building more like a glorified house than a hotel, owned as it turned out, by Sousath. After a quick lunch we set out to find the jars. A dusty bus journey brought us to Ban Ang and we pulled up at an information building, built, according to a sign, with aid funds from Australia. A short distance away, leaning at crazy angles, were the jars that we had come so far to see!

The Plain of Jars' name is derived from the hundreds of ancient stone jars that were discovered in the region by the French in the 19th century. The jars weigh an average of 600 to 1000 kg but some of the largest are estimated to weigh over 5 tonnes. They have been carved from solid stone and are clustered at six places throughout the Plain, although only three sites are available for general tourism. The lichen-covered jars are cylindrical in shape. They swell from a smaller rounded bottom, perhaps a metre in width, to a shoulder section perhaps two metres wide before narrowing down to a metre opening again at the top. Even the smallest jars are big enough for a person to climb into, while a tall person would not be able to see out of the larger ones. All the jars originally had fitted lids but most of these are now broken and lie discarded nearby.

"What in the world were they used for?" questioned one of our party.

Sousath replied in excellent English. "Various theories have been advanced as to the use of the great stone jars; as wine fermenters, for rice or grain storage, even sarcophagi (burial jars), although I think I prefer the wine theory. Similarly it is not known accurately how old the jars are. The earliest record of them is from writings of the Shang Dynasty in China. They tell of their existence at least 3000 years ago, though they may be as much as 4000 years old."

"The First Shang Dynasty sent people here about 3000 years ago and their existence then was noted on the bamboo pages they used for writing," he continued.

After spending a lot of time making Mr Kodak richer, we left the main jar-field and climbed a nearby hill. From the top, the huge stone jars looked like pots thrown out from some giant's kitchen. Looking the other way across from the top of the hill, on the opposing hillside I could see the strange white scars I had noticed from the aeroplane. Of course I had to ask.

"Those white scars are bird traps," Sousath explained. "The villages around here are very poor and the people catch finches and sparrows as an extra food supply and source of protein. But now," warned Sousath, "we must go. The electricity is only switched on in the town for three hours between 6.30 and 9.30, so if you want a shower and a hot meal we will have to get back soon."

That night, after we had washed, some of us settled down in the cramped lounge room to talk while others had an early night. Much excitement developed - I became excited when I realised that Sousath was the person who was a central character that I had read about in a book before coming to Laos.* - Sousath became excited when he realised that he was famous enough to be known about in Australia!

Next day we visited another more isolated field where the jars, though not so many, were in much better condition. The thirty or so jars there were smaller and finer, and some of them still had their lids. Imagine our surprise though when, while we were resting underneath a tree, Sousath informed us that a month before, Australian television personality Ernie Dingo had been at that exact spot with a crew from the Getaway TV show.

On the way back to Phonsavan, Sousath stopped the bus and allowed us to walk through a village that was strung out along the long dusty road. We were followed by hordes of children and were greeted with smiles by their proud parents, some of whom invited us into their homes. As was the case in other parts of Laos, and also Cambodia, many people in the village, including children, were missing arms and legs caused by unexploded mines left over from the Vietnam War. (Cambodia sent a team of amputees to the Sydney 2000 Paralympic Games by the way.)

***Stalking the Elephant Kings, C.Kremmer, published by Allen and Unwin 1997.**

Investigating the first Jar Field

40 What was the question the author just had to ask?

- **A** What were the water tanks used for?
- **B** Why were the jars lids broken?
- **C** Was Sousath the person in the book?
- **D** What were the white scars we could see?

41 Why did Sousath talk to the tourists for an unusually long time ?

- **A** He liked Australians.
- **B** He had relatives in Australia.
- **C** He was impressed that they knew about him.
- **D** He was their guide.

42 Why were there so many maimed people in the village?

- **A** They had been wounded in the war.
- **B** There were very few doctors in the region.
- **C** The bomb craters were extremely dangerous.
- **D** The unexploded bombs and mines kept injuring people.

43 How would you describe the landforms of Laos?

- **A** Partly mountainous with a number of flat plains.
- **B** Extremely mountainous with plateaus and high plains.
- **C** Mainly flat with few hills.
- **D** Very flat and low lying especially along the rivers.

44 Who wrote the book referred to?
A Allen and Unwin B The King of Laos. C S. Sousath. D C. Kremmer.

45 How can we be so sure that the jars are very old?
A They are covered in lichen. B They have been dated by the University.
C They are mentioned in ancient Chinese writings. D It was obvious from their shape.

46 Why was Ernie Dingo at Phonsavan?
A To see the jars. B To film for a television programme.
C To visit his relatives in Laos. D It was such an out-of the-way place.

47 What did the strange white scars turn out to be ?
A Bird traps. B Bomb craters. C Irrigation dams. D Trenches.

48 Laos is landlocked. What does this mean?
A The country has no access to the sea. B The soil is very hard and stony.
C Most villages have a view of the mountains. D None of the preceding.

Find the word in the passage that means:
49 discarded when no longer needed
50 burial jars

THE BEEHIVES OF THE BUNGLE BUNGLES

EXERCISE 1`

READING TEST 7

The rounded domes of the Bungle Bungles

The Bungle Bungles Range is all that is left of an ancient plateau surface. About 360 million years ago, rivers and streams flowing south and east from nearby mountains, washed sand and pebbles out onto a large, low, flat area. As time passed the sandy sediments were pressed together and cemented by silica, iron and other minerals to form sandstone. The sand and pebble grains were only weakly glued together however, so that later, when the whole area was lifted up in one horizontal piece to form a huge plateau, it was easily worn down and eroded. On the western side the heavy rains that fell on the plateau caused rivers to carve deep gorges and steep-sided chasms into the hard rock. But on the eastern side, although the rock was softer, the lighter rainfall formed peculiar round domes like olden-time beehives.

Being soft, the beehive structures would have crumbled away completely except for a strange occurrence. A protective skin made up of orange-coloured silica and black lichen grew on the crumbling domes and walls, giving them a striped appearance. (Silica is a common element in sandstone, while lichen is a tiny plant that lives on rocks and tree trunks.) The strange striped bands of colour on the domes are just the colours produced by the varying mixtures of silica and lichen on the outside of the rock. Underneath the striped skin of the Beehives, the sandstone crumbles so easily that visitors to the area are requested not to touch any part of the rock surfaces. This is a difficult request for people to comply with, because, just like a 'wet-paint' sign hung on a fence, most people want to touch the surface to find out for themselves, in this case, just how crumbly the rock really is. All forms of climbing are banned in the Beehives, mainly for this reason but also because it would be extremely dangerous to climb on the crumbling walls.

The Bungle Bungles Range, about 45 000

hectares in size, now forms part of the larger Purnululu National Park, one of Western Australia's newest National Parks. The Range is roughly U-shaped and is approximately 25 km long and 30 km wide. The famous beehive domes are on the eastern side of the massif (a compact group of mountains), but the western side is interesting too. There, small streams have cut steep sided canyons and gorges into the solid, much harder rock of the western side.

Piccaninny Gorge

Purnululu can be reached from two directions; from the north from Darwin through Kununurra, or from the south through Broome and Derby. The turn-off road leading to the Park from the Great Northern Highway is 250 km south from Kununurra, or alternatively 109 km north from Halls Creek. The great Northern Highway is a sealed road, but then comes the fun! Well maybe it should be '??' because from the Highway it is another 55 km to the Beehives over a track that varies in parts from very rough to impossible. The signs say '4WD VEHICLES ONLY' and they tell the truth!

Once at the Park though, the visitor is pleasantly surprised by the good facilities - whether an unguided camper or, if you are lucky enough, as a guest at the mosquito-proof cabins. The best time to visit Purnululu and the Bungle Bungles is during the dry season, that is, from May to October. Although this is the winter time it is still hot, (maximum temperatures are in the mid 30s) because the Park is at a latitude of $17\frac{1}{2}°$ from the Equator.

The Bungle Bungles is a great place for sight-seeing, photography, camping, nature walks and helicopter and plane rides. One of the best nature walks is in Echidna Chasm. Located 21 km from the Ranger Station, Echidna Chasm is an easy walk once you get there – as long as you don't suffer from claustrophobia. The long Chasm follows the course of a dry creek bed. Its high vertical walls gradually close in on you until you can only just squeeze through to its end, a small circular shaft rising to the surface 200 metres above. No self-respecting echidna would be seen dead inside this narrow chasm.

Piccaninny Gorge is another part of the Bungle Bungles that is worth visiting. 'Piccaninny' is an Aboriginal word meaning 'small child' so the Gorge is *not* well named. It happens to be the largest of all the canyons eating into the side of the massif. On this walk you will see large anthills, some reaching 30 metres up the side of the cliffs. In one part the dry bed of Piccaninny Creek looks as if it has been frozen into ice.

Unlike Piccaninny Gorge, Cathedral Gorge is aptly named. As you walk along it, it gradually narrows down until, just when you think you will not be able to go much further, it suddenly opens out into a huge open cave or amphitheatre over a clear pool. It is a natural cathedral.

If you wish to be lazy or if you wish to have a bit of a thrill, you can take a helicopter ride from the local airstrip. It is guaranteed to make your hair curl! The pilot, within reason, will take you wherever you want to go, including flying right down inside the steep canyons. But don't ask the pilot to do a 'wheelie' unless you have a strong stomach. Many visitors fly in by light, fixed-wing aircraft from Kununurra because their time is precious and to avoid the long trip by road.

Purnululu is an area of tropical savanna grassland with scattered trees. From the distance it has the appearance of a park. On the eastern drier side. there are vast undulating plains of deep red and yellow sand with wattles, grevilleas and leading eventually to the Tanami Desert, one of the driest areas in Australia. Only wallabies and small mammals inhabit the Park, but over 130 species of birds are present, including huge flocks of budgerigars. On occasions Australia's shyest parrot, the nomadic Princess Parrot has been glimpsed along the creeks. Some of the many varieties of wild flowers found in the Park have not been officially named as yet.

1 **The western side of the massif has steep high walls because**
A the sandstone there is softer than in the east. **B** the sandstone there is harder than in the east.
C the rivers are not as large as in the east. **D** the rock faces are smoother as in the east.

2 **A tropical savanna region could be best described as**
A dense monsoon forest. **B** park-like.
C mountainous.
D tiger- striped.

3 **A person who has claustrophobia has a fear of**
A open spaces. **B** spiders.
C confined spaces. **D** falling.

4 **The tiger skin appearance of the beehives is caused by**
A the crumbly nature of the rock.
B the bright sunlight and dry climate.
C the action of the numerous termite mounds.
D alternating bands of silica and lichen.

5 **Overseas tourists fly in to Purnululu so that they can**
A save time. **B** avoid poor access roads.
C save time and avoid poor roads. **D** see the Bungle Bungles from the air.

6 **Rock climbing has been banned in the Park *mainly* because**
A it is dangerous. **B** the beehives are fragile.
C there is no climbing gear available. **D** there are no guides in the remote region.

7 **In contrast to Piccaninny Gorge, Cathedral Gorge**
A has been aptly named. **B** has been poorly named.
C is used by the Flying Doctor Service. **D** has a long, narrow end shaft.

SHIP FROM THAMES

Stay, ship from Thames, with fettered sails
in Sydney Cove this ebb of tide;
your gear untangled from the gales,
imprisoned at your anchor ride.

The portly gentlemen ,who are
the pillars of the land, come down
and greet the Newcomes voyaged far
to make a name in Sydney Town.

The redcoats, too, with shouldered arms,
marshal pale wretches from the hold,
who, cramped in tempests and in calms.
have learned to do as they are told.

Rex Ingamells

EXERCISE 2 READING TEST 7

8 **Another word for 'fettered' could be**
A loose. **B** untied. **C** furled. **D** tattered.

9 **The gentlemen who met the ship were**
A newcomers. **B** energetic. **C** stout. **D** lazy.

10 **The redcoats also**
A had come a long way. **B** left their arms on board.
C were pale and ill. **D** were suffering from seasickness.

11 **The 'wretches'**
A were hard to manage
B had learnt to be obedient.
C were loud and boisterous at reaching shore.
D spent most of their time on deck.

THE STATUE OF LIBERTY

EXERCISE 3

READING TEST 7

In 1875, a young Frenchman named Frederic Auguste Bartholdi was commissioned to build the world's largest statue. The statue was to be of a woman and represent the *Spirit of Liberty*. It was to be given as a present from the people of France to the people of the United States to commemorate the 100th anniversary of the American Declaration of Independence – the time when the Americans gained their freedom or 'liberty' from the British.

Bartholdi was a sculptor, so he knew how to make the statue lifelike, even though it was so large. Building it so that it wouldn't collapse was quite another thing. Bartholdi asked another young Frenchman, Gustave Eiffel, who had some exciting new ideas about using steel for frameworks, to help him construct the huge statue. (Yes, you're right, Eiffel was the man who later built the famous tower in Paris).

The skin of the statue was to be made of copper sheets, but first a wooden frame had to be made. This was covered in plaster, formed to the right shape, so that moulds could be made for each of the skin pieces. The statue was so large that it had to be made in parts - head, arms, chest and so on. Eiffel's contribution was to make the steel skeleton on which to hang the heavy, moulded copper sheets.

The job wasn't easy because the skeleton had to be strong enough to support the great weight, flexible enough to withstand strong wind by bending slightly, and light enough to allow it to be transported all the way to America.

Bartholdi thought that he could finish the statue in time for the anniversary celebrations in 1876, but he soon found out how wrong he was. Only one arm was finished in time, so that was sent off to the United States for 'show and tell' instead. By 1878, two years later, Bartholdi had only finished the head. But this was so impressive that he decided to show it at the World Fair held that year in Paris. The problem was however to find a cart big enough to carry the head. Finally he found one. It took twelve horses to pull the cart carrying the huge head through the narrow streets of Paris and, as you can imagine, it created quite a stir! Some of the houses had to be moved because Bartholdi's studio was in a part of Paris where the streets were narrow.

Four more years passed and the statue was still only completed to the waist. Money for the project had become scarce by that time, so Bartholdi decided to throw a party for the Paris newspaper reporters - he held it on the statue's half-finished knee! This second 'show and tell' held on the knee was very effective, and enough money was raised to complete the work. After eleven long years, Liberty as the statue was now called, was finished.

In June 1886, Liberty was formally presented to the American Ambassador as the representative of the people of the United States of America. Bartholdi led the way up the 168 steps inside the statue to the viewing room behind the eyes. There were two staircases, one for going up and one for coming down, which made things a little easier. This party was a great success too at raising money for Liberty's transport to the United States. This also proved to be a job and a half because the gigantic statue had to be dismantled, sheet-by-sheet and piece-by-piece. Each piece was numbered to make reassembly easier. In all, 214 enormous crates were needed, while the special train, put on to carry Liberty from Paris to the coast, had 70 carriages. The crated Liberty was loaded onto the deck of a French naval boat, Isere.

Now you might think that Bartholdi's troubles were over. You'd be wrong. On the way across the Atlantic, a huge storm blew up and it was thought that Isere would capsize when the weight of the crates affected the centre of gravity of the ship. People waited anxiously in New York because in those days communications were not like they are today. Eventually Isere limped into New York harbour *eleven* days late.

Meanwhile in the United States other problems had arisen. Although Liberty had arrived, there was nowhere to put her! A competition had been held in the United States to design a base for the statue, but work had not started because of lack of funds. The winning design was a classic pedestal or plinth to be made out of sandstone modelled on the bases used for the statues in ancient Egypt.

Luckily for Bartholdi, and for Liberty, Joseph Pulitzer came to the rescue. He was the publisher of a newspaper called the New York World. Running a big campaign in his newspaper he asked the ordinary people of New York to help. He promised that all those who gave money would have their names printed in his newspaper - no matter how small the donation. And help they did. The shop assistants, taxi drivers, school children, labourers, sales people and the like, 124 000 of them, added their nickels and dimes to the building fund. Work restarted and finally Liberty, who had lain on a wharf for 18 months, had a home to go to. The reconstruction of Liberty (remember she was in crates) took two months. Over 600 000 rivets were needed to fasten the copper skin back on the iron framework.

On October 28, 1886 Liberty was in place and ready to be unveiled. The people of New York turned out in force to witness the dedication ceremony. A procession of 200 000 people marched down Broadway, while the harbour was jammed with ships, big and small, all tooting and whistling. The day was officially proclaimed as Bartholdi Day and 600 special guests were ferried out to Bedloe's Island. All the important people were there including President Cleveland and the French Ambassador.

Only two women were included as official guests at the opening ceremony - strange when you consider that Liberty, the statue, was female.

A group of suffragettes (women who fought for women's rights) hired a boat and patrolled the island shouting insults but their noise was lost in the general commotion.

Bartholdi's part of the ceremony was to climb up into the torch and pull a cord releasing the huge French flag which covered Liberty's face. He was supposed to do this after President Cleveland had spoken but he unveiled the face before the President had even reached the platform. No one is quite sure whether this was done deliberately or not, but the people on the boats in New York harbour didn't mind. Not if the din made by thousands of sirens and foghorns was any indication.

While the years since 1886 have been good for Liberty in one way - people came to think of her as the spirit of all that was good and free in America - in other ways the years have been unkind. Pollution, acid rain and salt air, took their toll. Even the great weight of the statue itself began to act upon it. By 1982 parts of the statue were out of shape and corroded, asbestos pads had crumbled away and most of the copper rivets had worked loose (the torch moves over a metre in a strong wind). Liberty had become unsafe and was closed to the public. The task of restoring Liberty was started by the order of President Ronald Reagan. When Bartholdi saw Liberty standing for the first time on top of its impressive pedestal he said. "Thank God it is a success. I believe it will last until eternity'. Liberty, the world's largest statue, is now herself again and looks set to last, if not to eternity, at least another hundred years. (And by the way, Pulitzer kept his promise to publish the names of all those who gave donations.)

The opening ceremony was a long time ago. The years have passed and many millions of migrants, many of them refugees from cruelty or war in their homelands, have been accepted into the USA. For most, their first sight of their new home as they approached the Ellis Island Immigration Centre, has been the Statue of Liberty. For this reason Liberty has a special place in the hearts of many Americans today. The tablet in the left hand of Liberty reads July IV, MDCCLXXXVI, the date on which America declared its independence from Great Britain. The suffragettes would be happy, for today *Liberty* is truly the symbol of Liberty.

12 What was the reason for the building of Liberty?

A To mark the end of the American Civil War.
B To commemorate America's Independence from Great Britain.
C As a memorial to the abolishment of slavery in The United States.
D To commemorate the French Revolution.

13 Why was Liberty's arrival by ship to New York delayed?
- **A** There was nowhere to put her.
- **B** One of the crates was damaged in transit.
- **C** A huge storm blew up in the Atlantic Ocean.
- **D** It took such a long time to reassemble the statue.

14 Why was Eiffel asked to help?
- **A** He had some new ideas about steel.
- **B** He was good at making steel moulds.
- **C** He knew a lot about wooden scaffolding.
- **D** The skeleton needed strengthening.

15 Why was Liberty closed to the public?
- **A** She was no longer safe.
- **B** President Reagan ordered it.
- **C** The pedestal was crumbling.
- **D** The torch had moved a metre.

16 What was Pulitzer's key role in the project?
- **A** He gave much money to build the pedestal.
- **B** He mobilised support from the ordinary people of New York.
- **C** He appealed to the wealthy people of Wall Street.
- **D** He set up the Pulitzer Prize for the 1000 largest donations.

17 Why does Liberty have a special place in the hearts of many Americans?
- **A** Over the years the statue has become the symbol of freedom around the world.
- **B** Many migrants escaping from war and cruelty in Europe passed Liberty on their way to a new free home.
- **C** For many migrants Liberty became the symbol of their newfound freedom.
- **D** All of the above.

IQUITOS: A TOWN WITH CHARACTER

EXERCISE 4 READING TEST 7

You would have to say that Iquitos is a town with character. Everything about it is unusual. To begin with, it is located deep in the Peruvian rainforest and can only be approached by air, or by a long, slow trip up the Amazon River. It was founded in the 1750s as a Jesuit mission and in the late 1800s became a boom town when the world discovered the importance of rubber. Although the population now is over 300 000 the signs of past affluence have just about disappeared.

When we first arrived we were treated to the sight of dozens of decaying aeroplanes littering the single runway. Our feelings of unease were soon dispelled by our cheery guide who welcomed us to his air-conditioned bus (there was no glass in the windows) and took great delight in pointing to the seven kilometres of tarred road leading to the city. It was not only the only tarred highway, but the only highway, full stop!

Our bus eventually deposited us, without undue harm, at a pleasant garden square containing an impressive monument in the centre of town. The square, the Plaza De Armas, (Army Square) was built to commemorate the so-called Pacific War between Brazil, Peru and Bolivia in 1879-83. And talking about arms, armed guards patrolled the public buildings due to unrest over a move by the government to impose a 45% tax on all goods coming to the city by air from outside the region.

As just about everything has to be brought into Iquitos by air, one could understand the locals' concern. On one side of the square stood a church with a clock proudly proclaiming 'Swisse 1910', on another side was the 'Iron House' made of wrought iron designed by Gustave Eiffel (yes you're right, that one) for the Paris Exhibition in 1889. It was transported to Iquitos, piece by piece by the rubber magnate Jules Toth (wrought iron does not rust like ordinary iron). In front of the Iron House was a man selling poor, captured animals from the rainforest, but we ignored all this to get our first sight, up close, of the Amazon River. Although Iquitos is about 2000 km from the sea and the river there is 2 km wide, Iquitos is only 83 m above sea level. Along the waterfront the houses float on rafts.

We were to catch a riverboat, the Delphin, named perhaps after the pink dolphins that are found all along the Amazon. It was owned and operated of all things by Paul Wright, an Australian! By 11 o'clock it had become extremely hot and humid, so we searched for a place where we could be comfortable while having our bouts of sweat enervation. The only place we could find was a café where the seats were saddles, real ones that had been set on posts in the floor. It had open walls to assist in air circulation, and, as we sipped our Seven-Ups, we were able to look at the large Cathedral Church and school across the road. On each section of the roof was a gargoyle and on each gargoyle sat a huge, black vulture. I had endured the heat and marvelled at the Iron House and was impressed by the monument, but I wasn't quite prepared for vultures. That's when I decided that Iquitos was definitely a town with character.

18 What is unusual about the location of Iquitos ?

A It is so far from the sea. **B** It is on the banks of a river.
C There are no roads into it from outside the region. **D** The boat trip was slow.

19 What was special about the air conditioning in the bus?

A It was too cold for it. **B** The driver could not switch it on.
C The humidity fogged up the windows. **D** There wasn't any.

20 What was so special about the highway from the airport?

A It caused the air conditioning to malfunction. **B** It was the only highway.
C It was quicker to go by tramway. **D** It had signs all along it.

21 What were the local residents concerned about?

A The high price of petrol. **B** The high price of goods and services.
C A proposed new tax on goods brought in by air. **D** The GST.

22 What was unusual about the Iron House?

A It hadn't rusted in the hot, wet climate. **B** It was built by Gustave Eiffel.
C It had been brought in piece by piece from overseas. **D** All of the above.

23 What makes the Amazon at River at Iquitos so unusual?

A Although 2000 km from the sea it is still two kilometres wide.
B Although it is 2000 km from the sea it is only 83 metres above sea level.
C The houses along its banks float on rafts.
D All of the preceding.

24 What is unusual about the dolphins of the Amazon?

A They are pink. **B** They live in fresh water.
C They are only found in the Amazon and its tributaries. **D** All of the above.

25 What was unusual about the cafe?

A It was connected to the internet. **B** Its seats were strange.
C It only sold Seven-Up. **D** It was a duty free café.

26 What was unusual about the Delphin?

A It was named after a dolphin. **B** It was a motor boat.
C It was owned and operated by an Australian. **D** It was painted pink.

27 What finally decided the author that Iquitos had character?

A The Swiss clock tower. **B** The iron house. **C** The unusual café. **D** The vultures on the church.

28 What do you think 'signs of past affluence have just about disappeared' means?

A The town has a dilapidated look about it. **B** The town now has a modern look about it .
C Many of the buildings have been destroyed by flood. **D** All of the rich rubber dealers have died.

29 What is the most likely explanation for the large number of out-of-service aeroplanes at the airport?
A Old planes were used for spare parts.
B It was too expensive to get rid of them.
C The aircraft were unreliable.
D The airport wasn't used very often.

From the passage find words that mean:
30 statue of a monster **31** damp or moist **32** prosperity **33** a person with great wealth and power

DEAD HORSE TRAIL

EXERCISE 5

READING TEST 7

On August 17, 1896, George Camack, Tagish Charlie and Skookum Mason found gold on the Klondike, a tributary of the Yukon River. Word spread like wildfire and the world's last great goldrush was on. The was just one small problem, the Yukon Territory was in the remote far north of Canada, one of the coldest regions on Earth. The most popular route to the Klondike was first to the twin towns of Skagway or Dyea, on the coast of Alaska, then over the Rocky Mountains to Lake Bennett. Once in Lake Bennett it was possible to travel down the Yukon to the Klondike, some thousand kilometres away, by boat. But the prospectors had to build these themselves! The trip from Skagway to the goldfields altogether took about 18 months.

Many thousands of prospectors died in their quest for gold, either from cold, starvation, or just plain murder by other prospectors. Travellers over the Chilkoot trail from Dyea were required to carry a ton of supplies, on their backs, up the 'Golden Staircase' over the Chilkoot Pass. More than one trip was needed and a partner was essential to guard the provisions. Those using horses from Skagway were little better off. The horse trail over White Pass became known as the Dead Horse Trail, for obvious reasons.

Digging the Line at Dead Horse in 1889

In May,1898, construction began on a railway over White Pass. Most thought that it couldn't be done, but, working through the endless winter storms, in sub-zero temperatures, up to 2000 men laboured on the line. Crews building the trestle bridges were only worked one-hour shifts before being brought in out of the cold - otherwise frozen fingers were in danger of losing their grip on bridge timbers, and it was long way to the bottom. Against all odds the 110-mile (177 kilometres) line was completed to the town of Whitehorse in July, 1900. At Whitehorse a fleet of stern-wheel steamboats was available to those who could afford to pay for the long trip down the Yukon River. In winter, a horse-drawn sleigh service operated to Dawson City, located on the junction of the Klondike with the Yukon.

Dead Horse Pass today.

When the goldmines of the Yukon finally closed down, so too did the railway. The steam locomotives were phased-out in 1969 although diesel locos lingered on until 1982. In 1988 the line was re-opened as a tourist attraction, and has been a huge success, although now there is a problem keeping the old steam locomotives in service.

From Whitehorse the tourist can travel by bus on the Alaskan Highway to Dawson City, a tourist must, or fly to a number of northern places such as Valdez in Alaska.

The town of Skagway ,which benefits from the attraction of the rail line, is a quaint remnant of the past. With its wide streets and cardboard looking houses it is well worth a visit. There you can get some idea of the roughness of its gold mining past by listening to the story of the duel between Soapy Smith, cardsharp and confidence trickster, and the local vigilante Frank Reid. The duel was fought with pistols on the Skagway wharf and both died as a consequence. It is ironic that they are both buried within sight of each other in the Skagway cemetery that the train passes on its way out of town.

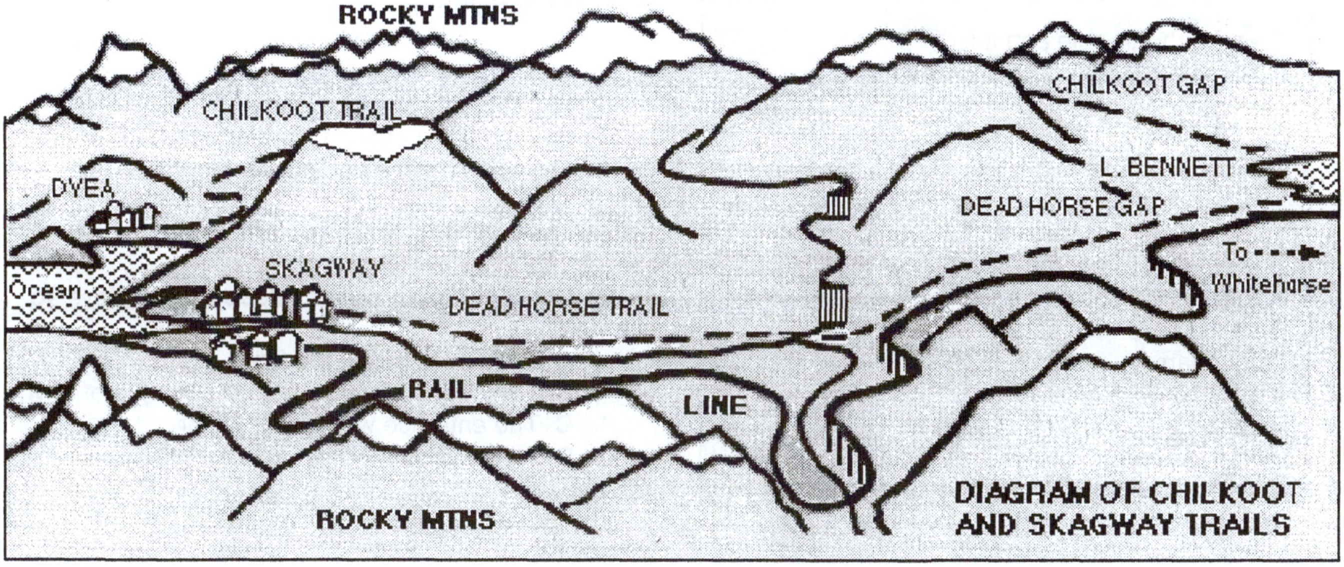

34 Why was it essential to have a partner on the Chilkoot Trail?

- **A** The loneliness was extreme.
- **B** To guard the stores.
- **C** To help build the boat.
- **D** To keep a place in the queue.

35 How do you think the Canadian Mounties responded to the high death rates on the trails?

- **A** By asking the prospectors to carry a gun to protect themselves.
- **B** By requiring the prospectors to carry enough provisions to last out the winter.
- **C** By requiring each prospector to file a travel plan.
- **D** By checking to see that each prospector had a sled or a boat.

36 The large town that developed close to the goldfields was

- **A** Whitehorse.
- **B** Dawson City.
- **C** Skagway.
- **D** Valdez.

37 The problem with the tourist train from Skagway is

- **A** lack of customers.
- **B** the steepness of the rail grades.
- **C** the maintenance of the locomotives.
- **D** the weight of the diesel locomotives on the old track.

38 The main problem facing the workers constructing the rail line over White Pass was

- **A** their murderous crew companions.
- **B** the extreme climate.
- **C** the continual lack of food.
- **D** the steep slopes that they encountered.

From the last paragraph of the story find the word that matches these dictionary definitions.

39 combat between two people with potentially lethal weapons ....

40 charming, old-fashioned quality ....

41 containing humour based on an inner meaning ....

42 a sudden influx of population due to the discovery of gold ....

43 a person who takes the law into his or her own hands ....

OLD MAN PLATYPUS

EXERCISE 6

READING TEST 7

Old Man Platypus

Far from the trouble and toil of town,
Where the reed-beds sweep and shiver.
Look at the fragment of velvet brown –
Old Man Platypus drifting down,
Drifting along the river.

And he plays and dives in the river bends,
In a style that's most elusive;
With few relations and fewer friends.
For Old Man Platypus descends
From a family most exclusive.

He shares his burrow beneath the bank
With his wife and his son and daughter
At the roots of the reeds and the grasses rank;
And the bubbles show where our hero sank
To its entrance under water.

Safe in their burrow below the falls,
They live in a world of wonder,
Where no one visits and no one calls,
They sleep like little brown billiard balls
With their beaks tucked neatly under.

And he talks in a deep unfriendly growl
As he goes on his journey lonely;
For he's no relation to fish or fowl.
Nor to bird nor beast, nor to hornéd owl;
In fact, he's the one and only!

From The Animals Noah Forgot
by A.B.Patterson

From the poem find words that match the following dictionary definitions:

44 hard to find
45 the only one of a kind
46 hard, exhausting work or effort
47 growing in a particularly vigorous way

Choose the best answer to the following:

48 Why were the platypuses' sleeping quarters so safe?
A They were below the falls.
B They were far away from the trouble of town.
C The entrance was under water.
D All the above.

49 Why does Old Man Platypus talk in an unfriendly growl?
A He was forgotten by Noah.
B Other animals annoy him.
C He has few friends and no close relations.
D He has often been hunted for his velvety skin.

50 Why did the platypuses look like billiard balls?
A They were underground.
B They were curled up.
C They didn't want to be recognised.
D They were cold.

THE IGUACU FALLS

EXERCISE 1

READING TEST 8

We were very lucky. Because it was a fine, clear day and there was a large party of us from the NSW Geographical Society on board, the plane flew low in a circular pattern. Below us the Parana River, spreading widely across a flat plateau, plunged abruptly over a line of cliffs to form the Iguacu Falls. The sight was spectacular; a wide plume of spray spiralled upwards like smoke almost to the height of our plane.

Lying on the boundary between Brazil and Argentina in central South America, and draining a huge area of Brazil, the Iguacu Falls are the widest in the world and, during the wet season, the most spectacular. On a front of 2.5 km the Parana River drops 80 metres to the land below, where the extra energy from the falling water has cut and channelled it into a narrow, swift-flowing gorge. The gorge at one point comes directly under the 'wings' of the waterfall forming into a maelstrom of turbulent water, appropriately called 'The Devil's Throat'.

Down to the left under the plane and almost on the edge of Falls on the Argentinean side, was the imposing Hotel Das Caratas, (Hotel of the Cataracts), where we were to spend the next two nights. Plainly visible was the hotel tower built so that sightseers could gain an overall view of the Falls (less than a kilometre away) through the curtaining spray.

By the time we had landed, collected our luggage and travelled by coach to the hotel it was getting quite late, but there was still time to explore the majestic old hotel. We had seen signs advertising the corresponding hotel on the Brazilian side, but we could not imagine that it would be better than the one we were in. The antique furniture, glittering chandeliers, old world charm and the wonderful meal that followed, set the mood for the coming day.

Our guide had told us to expect a hot day so we made an early start to view the Falls. He did not mention anything about humidity and we were soon to find out just how hot and humid it would be. The path to the Falls slowly descends the gorge towards the Falls base about two kilometres away. Every hundred metres or so, viewing points have been cut to clear the luxuriant vegetation as you descend, and you are treated with fascinating, constantly-changing views of the Falls on the Brazilian side.

Now you would think that travelling downhill on a graded bitumen path, with frequent stops, would be easy, but it wasn't. Let me explain. As time passed (because of the frequent stops to view) it became hotter and as we came closer to the falls proper, it became more and more humid. By the time we reached the bottom of the gorge under the falls we were soaked with perspiration. Water was literally running off us. But it was worth the discomfort. A few metres away a huge wall of water was cascading down into a deep plunge pool. We were reduced to sign language, as there was no way that you could talk over the deafening roar of the water. The narrow and extremely dangerous Devil's Throat was a kilometre away, hidden behind the mist generated by the Falls.

"You should have been here last week," our Guide said. " The temperature was 38 °. It is only about 32 ° today."

Thankfully there was a lift to carry us back to the top. Here a viewing platform overlooked the plateau area. The remains of a hundred-metre walkout on the Brazilian side,even on the flat area, testified to the force of water during the wet season. of the previous year.

That afternoon some of our party decided to go on a helicopter flight over the Falls, but three of my friends and I decided to take a safer option. The Hotel had been advertising trips by boat up to the Devil's Throat. So off we went. They forgot to mention that the Zodiac was made of plastic and had an outboard motor.

To describe the trip as bumpy, hazardous, dangerous, foolhardy, but exciting, would not even begin the process. We bumped, swung, wallowed, careered, surged and zoomed up the gorge. The noise was thunderous and the spectacle of the crashing water was mind numbing. We hung onto our safety ropes for dear life; our cameras got wet and so did we. But once again it was worth it, just for the relief of getting back onto dry, firm land if nothing else. If you get a chance to view the Iguacu Falls, please don't miss it. Be brave! Oh, and be careful of those nasty, friendly little animals called coatis that will jump all over you looking for bread and put muddy footprints all over your clothes.

Approaching the Devil's Throat.

1 Why was the first sight of the Falls so spectacular?

A The day was clear.
B There was a visible plume of spray.
C The pilot was particularly co-operative.
D All the preceding.

2 Why was the channel below the falls so narrow?

A The Devil's Throat was narrow.
B The rock below the falls was softer.
C The walkway had been washed away during the wet season.
D The extra energy generated by the falling water had cut a narrow channel.

3 Why is it necessary to be cautious with the coatis?

A They have a nasty bite.
B They will jump all over you with their muddy paws.
C They are an endangered species.
D They take up too much of your time.

4 The Zodiac was

A an almanac of star signs.
B the name of the guide.
C a type of engine.
D a kind of boat.

5 What made the tourists most uncomfortable at the lower viewing levels?

A The water vapour in the air.
B The roar of the falls.
C The advertising signs that were everywhere.
D A sudden drop in temperature.

Are the following statements True (T) or False (F) ?

6 There had been heavy rain the previous year. ( )
7 There was rivalry between the Brazilian and Argentinean hotels. ( )
8 It was impossible to see the falls from the Hotel Das Caratas. ( )

From the passage find words that mean:

9 turbulent whirlpool
10 to move clumsily, as if in mud

ULURU AND KATA TJUTA

EXERCISE 2

READING TEST 8

Uluru, or to give it its English name, Ayers Rock, is the best-known tourist attraction in the whole of Australia. Every year many thousands of overseas visitors make the pilgrimage to see, and perhaps climb, the huge rock that rises abruptly from the flat surrounding desert plains. Uluru is a monolith or single stone, the biggest in the world. Its sheer size, with its extraordinary colouring that changes from orange-to-red-to-purple at sunrise and sunset, make it one of the great geographical wonders of the world. About 50 kilometres west of Uluru lie the strange domes of Kata Tjuta (also known as the Olgas). The two formations, Kata Tjuta and Uluru, are linked underground, being opposite ends of the same geological formation. In the case of Uluru, the sandstone of which it is made has been able to resist erosion because it is extremely hard and free of cracks. At the Kata Tjuta end, the sandstone is softer and has weathered into a set of spectacular domes even steeper and more spectacular than Uluru.

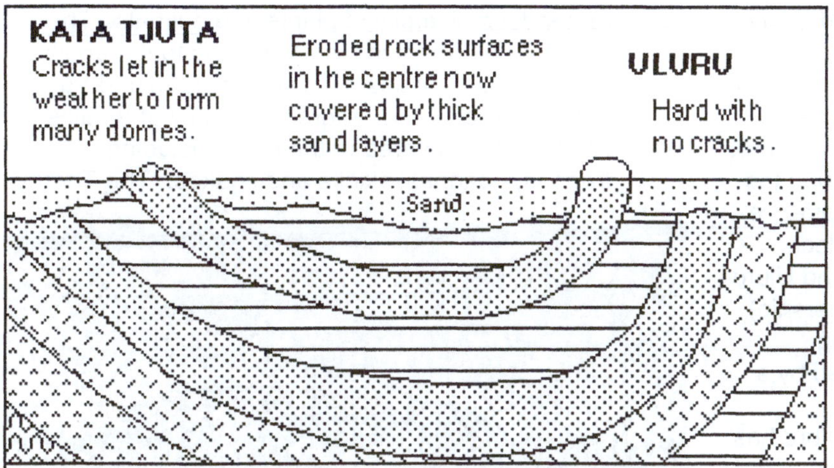

THE FORMATION OF ULURU AND KATA TJUTA
The rock strata of Uluru is made of very hard sandstone laid down about 600 million years ago. About 300 million years later this Strata and those nearby were folded and twisted into their present positions.

Although it is hard, the surface of Uluru is uneven. From the distance it looks smooth, but up close the surface is pitted with caves and waterholes. The rainwater that runs off the sides of Uluru after infrequent rains has created a narrow, fertile area around its base. Many unique animals and birds live in this special environment.

Through the ages, Aboriginal peoples regularly visited the colossal rock searching for food and water. They marvelled at its great size and they gave mystical qualities to it until it became part of their Creation Time or Dreamtime. They named it Uluru and they made up stories to explain the many irregularities of its surface. Its caves became a treasure house of paintings done in red and yellow ochre, charcoal and white pipeclay, recording the events of their culture and history.

Each tribe had its own particular area and its own set of beliefs that were handed down through the ages by word of mouth. The Pitjanjatjara people for example believe that the red colouring on the surface of the rock was caused by blood streaming from the nose of a wounded warrior who died there in the Dreamtime. They believe too that Uluru was originally a low flat sand hill with a waterhole in the centre that was occupied permanently by an Aboriginal tribe because food was always plentiful there. The women of the tribe made bread from grass seeds gathered on the plain while the men hunted kangaroos, wallabies and emus. The men particularly liked to lie in the shade at the base of the sand hill after hunting. At the time of the creation of the rock, the Pitjanjatjara believe that the sand hill people were turned into the

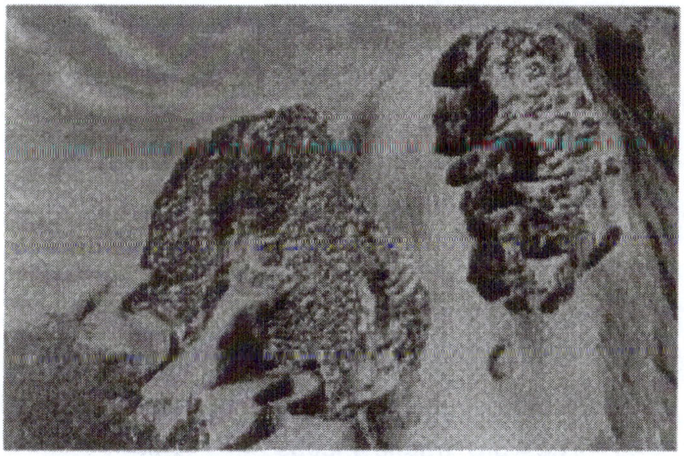

The pitted surface of one part of Uluru.

boulders seen lying at the foot of the cliffs today, while the women became large rocks in one of the side gorges. A coolamon (carrying dish) became a tall slab of rock at the head of the largest gorge and their baking fire became a rock waterhole. They believe that the tufts of grass that grow in the area are all that is left of the women's hair.

The Australian explorer Ernest Giles was dazzled by the colours and strange shapes of the formations at Kata Tjuta. He wrote that some were like "enormous pink haystacks leaning against one another" while others were like "the backs of monstrous pink elephants." The Aborigines, seeing the 36 domes, called the formation 'Kata Tjuta' meaning 'many heads'. Like the markings on Uluru, each dome has its collection of stories. In 1950 the Australian Government recognised the importance of Uluru and Kata Tjuta to the Anangu, the local Aboriginal peoples of Uluru. The area around Uluru was declared a National Park and title (ownership) was transferred to the local tribes. A leasing arrangement allows the Park to be controlled by a Board of Management that has a majority of Anangu representatives on it. Since then Uluru has become a major tourist destination with close to a million visitors each year. Tourist development is strictly controlled to ensure that the traditional way of life of the Anangu can be maintained while they gain a substantial income from rental and entrance fees and the sale of craftwork.

Yulara is the name of a modern, luxury tourist resort that has been built to accommodate the many tourists that visit Uluru and Kata Tjuta. It is located about 450 km south-west of Alice Springs, 7km from the foot of Uluru and about 50 km from Kata Tjuta. It is a large development providing hotels, motels, swimming pools and camping facilities. By providing a variety of accommodation ranging from cheap to expensive, the tourists can be kept in one area thus keeping damage of the fragile desert ecosystem to a minimum. Although the hotel/motel is modern and could perhaps be said to be out of step with the fragile beauty of the surrounding desert, it is not intrusive.

The climb of Uluru is potentially dangerous and should not be attempted by people with a medical condition. Nearly 40 people have died while climbing. High winds, high temperatures and steep, crumbly surfaces contribute to heart attacks and falls. Because of the often-dangerous conditions the Park Rangers have published a number of safety rules that should be followed.

Uluru National Park is part of the larger desert region of Central Australia and so many people expect the desert area surrounding Uluru and Kata Tjuta to be lifeless and barren. This is far from the truth, and the 'desert' is able to sustain a tremendous diversity of plants and animals. The plant life has adapted over the years to the aridity and over 400 species of flowers, shrubs and trees have been recorded. A great diversity of reptiles is also found in the area of the Park, including dragons, goannas, skinks and snakes. The Thorny Devil is often seen sunning itself along tracks and roadsides. Dingoes are common and many small mammals are present including several species of hopping mouse. The birds of Uluru are also adapted to living in dry conditions. These include white-backed swallows, budgerigars, pink cockatoos and singing honeyeaters. In the past 80 years a number of feral (introduced) animals including the rabbit, fox, cat, house mouse and camel have become established in the Park and unfortunately these pose a serious threat to many of the indigenous (native) animals.

Uluru from Yulara Resort 7km distant.

The following questions refer to words found in the passage .

11 The word 'fragile' means

A rare. **B** dry. **C** unique. **D** easily damaged.

12 The word 'traditional' means
A handed down. B controlled. C substantial. D modern.

13 The word that means the *opposite* of 'feral' is
A threatened. B native. C common. D introduced.

14 The word 'abruptly' means
A suspiciously. B flatly. D gradually. D steeply.

Choose the best answer to complete the following .

15 The Yulara complex is not intrusive because
A it blends in with the surrounding desert.
B it cannot be seen from the top of the Rock.
C only top grade materials have been used.
D it is out of step with the ecosystem.

The Valley of the Winds, Kata Tjuta

16 Many unique plants survive near the base of Uluru because of
A run-off from the rock surfaces.
B its pitted surfaces.
C the many waterholes on Uluru.
D the care of the Park Rangers.

17 Uluru's colour changes are due to
A the iron stains in the rock.
B the reflections from the carpet of wildflowers.
C the season of the year.
D the angle of the Sun's rays.

18 The climb to the top of Uluru is potentially dangerous because of
A the high winds often encountered.
B the high temperatures often experienced.
C the steepness of the trail in places.
D All of the preceding.

Are the following statements True (T) or False (F) ?

19 Legends from the Dreamtime explain the pitted surface of the rock. ( )
20 Uluru is a twisted and folded volcanic rock. ( )
21 The Park is controlled by the National Parks and Wildlife Service. ( )
22 Kata Tjuta has more domes because the rock there is harder. ( )
23 The common house mouse is classed as a feral animal. ( )
24 Uluru is surrounded by barren and lifeless desert. ( )
25 The two outcrops of Uluru and Kata Tjuta are of the same geological structure. ( )
26 The Pitjanjatjara peoples now control the Park. ( )
27 A large range of facilities is available in nearby Alice Springs. ( )
28 The early explorer, Ernest Giles, described the domes of Kata Tjuta in detail. ( )

THE STONE FOREST OF LUNAN

EXERCISE 3

READING TEST 8

Most people know what stalactites and stalagmites are. You know, those needles of rock found in caves made by the action of rainwater on layers of limestone rock. Cracks in the rock allow the acidic rainwater to seep in dissolving the hard rock. The process is very slow, taking millions of years. Sometimes, when the beds of limestone are not very thick, instead of caves, so-called

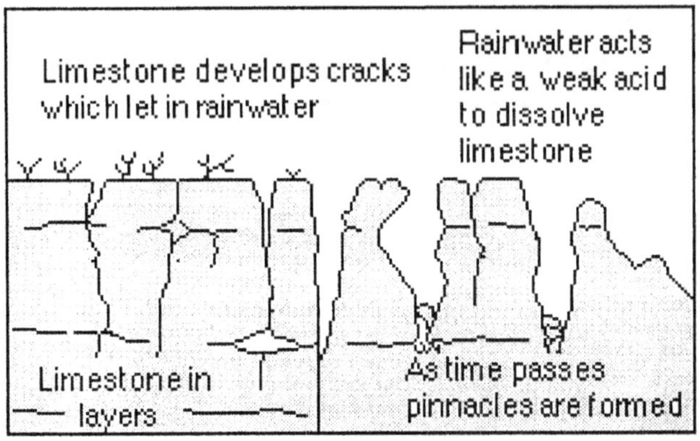

'forests' of sharp rock pinnacles are formed.

The Stone Forest of Lunan in China was formed in this way. It covers a vast area of over 160,000 hectares some 120 kilometres southeast of Kunming.

The pinnacles of stone are too tall to see over, some up to 15 metres high, and there is a myriad of paths between them. The paths twist and turn on themselves and although each pinnacle has its own distorted and unique shape, after a while they all look the same. Once inside a stone forest the visitor loses all sense of direction, and, for that reason a strict rule of the Lunan Forest is that a guide must accompany all visitors. It might only take a few minutes to become lost but it can take many hours to be found! It is not a bad thing to have a guide though because on the edge of the Stone Forest is a Sani village. The guides from this village dress in brightly-coloured ethnic costume (the Sani are one of the twenty-three minority ethnic groups of China).

As you enter the Lunan Stone Forest you are confronted by a huge sign in Chinese characters stating the, rather obvious, 'Stone Forest'. A large pinnacle has had its side smoothed to accommodate this awful graffiti. But you soon forget this. According to historical records the Stone forest has been one of the most famous scenic spots in China going back to the time of the Emperors of the Ming Dynasty (1368-1644 AD). And rightly so because it is spectacular.

Each of the strange peaked formations has been named after the object that it looks like. So there are crocodiles and elephants, demons and lovers, mothers and daughters, mushrooms and farmers sowing rice - the strange shapes stir the memories of the visitors and add to the appeal of the limestone Forest.

Inside the Forest one unforgettable sight that bursts upon the tourist is the "Sword Peak Pond". Its jade-coloured water is so clear that one can see to the bottom 5 metres down. Leaning against the red railing by the pond, one can enjoy the peculiar sight of the countless stone peaks, shimmering in reverse in the water, while goldfish leisurely assume a thousand different shapes in the deep pool.

In the evening, after spending the day exploring the stone forest you will no doubt be entertained in the only hotel by the people from the village. The Sani people are very good at singing and dancing, especially the young people.

The Sword Peak Pond

While the boys play drums and a kind of three-stringed guitar, the girls clap their hands enthusiastically and dance the strong, rhythmic, traditional dances of the Sani. Some slower dances tell about village fairy tales and legends of the stones while other more energetic dances show aspects of everyday village life - sowing, planting and reaping rice. But the seats in the hall are very hard!

Choose the best answer to complete the following sentences:

29 The stone pinnacles are
A a last stage in the erosion process.
B the first stage in the erosion process.
C the result of earth movements.
D None of the above.

30 The rainwater
A contains small quantities of acid.
B dissolves the limestone.
C takes a long time to affect the limestone.
D All of the above.

31 Guides are necessary because
A the Sani depend on the money received from guiding.
B strangers can get lost easily.
C the visitors like to see the colourful costumes.
D the stone is hard if you fall.

32 The Stone Forest of Lunan
A contains many first class hotels.
B houses the Sani villages.
C is the source for many of the Sani legends.
D contains many large waterfalls.

33 The painted sign on one of the large pinnacles
A although not pretty, serves a useful purpose.
B has been put there to help English-speaking tourists.
C looks just like huge Chinese graffiti.
D advertises the nearby hotel.

34 The Stone Forest must be spectacular because
A the water is so clear.
B the goldfish and carp are so beautiful.
C it has been visited by Chinese Emperors.
D guides must accompany all tourists.

35 Part of the charm of the Stone Forest comes about when
A the villagers dance for the tourists.
B the strange shapes jog people's memories.
C you realise how old it is.
D you can rest after so many hours of walking.

36 It is easy to lose your sense of direction in the stone forest because
A you can't see very far.
B many of the stones look alike.
C the paths twist and turn.
D All of the above.

Find words in the passage that mean:

37 charm

38 racial

39 individual, one of a kind

40 rock with sharp, pointed top

"HORAS!" FROM SAMOSIR

EXERCISE 4 READING TEST 8

Sami was all of five years old and his eyes were as round as saucers. Very carefully for one of such great age, he peered around the edge of the huge circular pole that formed one support for the large, raised house of the village Headman. Above him, on a kind of platform, the musicians had begun to play and the procession from the side of the large open square had just started. In pairs, arranged in order of importance, the dancers of the village slowly wound their way in and formed a large circle around a central stake to which was tied a large, and rather sad and bewildered, buffalo. On the farthest side, opposite to Sami, stood a group of tourists armed to the teeth with cameras, for this was a special ceremony that they had paid a lot of money to witness. Still in pairs, as each dancer passed the tourist group they shouted, "Horas!" which is the traditional greeting of the Bataks of Samosir Island.

Samosir Island is an island in an island, for it is located in the middle of Lake Toba, the largest lake in South-east Asia that is itself located in the large Island of Sumatra.

People say that the loudest noise in recorded history was when the Island of Krakatau exploded in 1883, but the explosion that formed Lake Toba is thought to have been the largest explosion to have occurred since the arrival of the human race on the planet. Lake Toba, a volcanic crater lake, is 100 km long, 50 km wide and 150 metres deep, so you can only imagine the noise. When the explosion that formed Lake Toba occurred, a portion of crater wall of the volcano collapsed into the Lake to form Samosir Island.

Samosir is quite large, being about 30 km in length. It is the isolated home of a number of tribal groups, collectively called the Bataks. whose history goes back to Megalithic (Stone Age) times.

The once fierce and cannibalistic Bataks have been "Christianised" for only about 100 years and they retain many of their old customs and beliefs. One of which, in a modified way, Sami was witnessing.

* * * * * *

As the circular procession of dancers progressed their circle became, very slowly, smaller and smaller. At the same time the chanting and the music performed on flutes, drums and peculiar stringed instruments became more and more pronounced and insistent. As the dancers seemed to become more and more mesmerised the number of camera clicks intensified.

* * * * * *

The stone walls that used to protect the Batak villages still stand today, and there are other Stone Age remnants; above-the-ground coffins smeared with the blood of enemies killed in battle, and stone chairs and seats arranged in circles where torture and sacrificial killings were carried out. Being made of stone they have survived through the ages.

The distinctive Batak houses have lasted too. They are built on thick, stilt-like poles with thatched roofs shaped like the curved horns of a buffalo. As in many other parts of Indonesia, the houses and barns are put together without nails or screws. Many are over 200 years old, although the thatch has to be replaced every 80 years or so.

The Batak people are good singers and dancers and will call out "Horas!" when they see you, ('horas' means "Hullo, I'm glad to see you.") especially if you are a tourist come to spend money to see the ceremony and buy their handicrafts. In fact, many of the villages around the shore of the

Island have made a business out of catering to the tourists. You even have to pay to hire a canoe and boatman to take you to the village.

* * * * * *

Now you will remember that I told you before that the Bataks were once cannibals. When enemies were captured they were tied to a stake (the same stake still standing in the centre of the square today) and of course you can imagine what happened to them there. Well maybe you can't, but that was what Sami was witnessing, except that the 'enemy' was a buffalo. Just as the procession, moving in ever-dwindling circles, reached the unfortunate buffalo to kill it, a great shout went up and Sami was grabbed roughly by the shoulder. Sami's heart almost stopped but his legs didn't because he jumped half a metre in the air.

* * * * * *

Lake Toba is a great place to swim. It is near the equator, but is about 800 metres above sea level and being so deep it remains at 27° Celsius all year round. There is a small submarine ledge, but once past that, about 10 metres, you are on your own because the bottom drops away almost vertically. The water is very refreshing, but mind you, it is a long way to go for a swim. A plane to Bali or Djakarta then a plane to Padang in Sumatra, overland to the lake's edge, then a boat to Samosir Island where the only tourist accommodation is. Did I tell you about the rats in the ceiling of the hotel? No that's another story.

* * * * * *

Now where was I? Oh yes, it was Sami's father who had grabbed him. He had spotted him from the balcony above, but being a loving father (and having done the same thing when he was Sami's age) he just told him that he had no right to be there and shooed him back off to his mother.

An above-ground Megalithic stone sarcophagus on Samosir Island.

And in case you are really worried, the buffalo wasn't killed, it was just a show put on for the tourists – buffalos are too valuable, I thought you would have known that!.

Choose the best answer to complete the following sentences:

41 Lake Toba was formed as a result of
- **A** the collapse of the crater wall.
- **B** tidal waves approaching South-east Asia.
- **C** massive volcanic activity.
- **D** the arrival of a large meteorite.

42 The villages were fortified in ancient times
- **A** by the use of large moats filled from the Lake.
- **B** using coils of sharpened bamboo stakes.
- **C** with sturdy stone walls.
- **D** with an extensive system of warriors in canoes.

43 A word that could be used to describe the conversion of the Bataks to Christianity is
- **A** 'recent'.
- **B** 'incredible'.
- **C** 'necessary'.
- **D** 'continuous'.

44 A possible reason for the survival of the Batak customs to the present is
- **A** their healthy diet.
- **B** the remoteness of their homeland.
- **C** their conversion to Christianity.
- **D** their use of original materials for building.

45 Why did Sami nearly have a heart attack?
A His father grabbed him.
B He didn't see his father coming up behind him.
C The shout from the dancers surprised him.
D The shout and his father's arrival frightened him.

46 The traditional greeting of one Batak to another is
A by playing music on old-fashioned instruments. **B** by staging a mock battle.
C by shouting a friendly hullo. **D** to be constantly on the alert.

47 A word that could be used to describe the camera-holding tourists is
A 'insistent'. **B** 'mesmerised' . **C** 'enthusiastic'. **D** 'disinterested'.

48 The relics of the Megalithic Age have lasted because
A they were made of thick, seasoned wood . **B** they were made of stone.
C they were in constant use. **D** the thatch was regularly replaced.

49 Sumatra is part of which nation?
A Australia. **B** Indonesia. **C** China. **D** Malaysia.

50 A word that could be used to describe Sami's father is
A 'doting'. **B** 'unforgiving '. **C** 'selfish'. **D** 'grumpy'.

51 Why don't the tourists see the full, original version of the ceremony?
A It involves human sacrifice. **B** It is too difficult to organise.
C The Government frowns on such activities.
D The buffalos are too valuable.

52 Probably the value of having the tourists visiting Samosir Island is
A it provides employment for the Islanders.
B it keeps old customs and traditions alive.
C it brings the people into contact with the outside world in a gentle way.
D All of the above.

53 We can tell that Sami's father intended to give Sami a fright because
A he came up behind Sami. B he grabbed Sami roughly.
C he left his post in the balcony. D All of the preceding.

From the passage find words that match the following dictionary definitions:

54 a stone or marble coffin

55 decreasing, little by little

56 fascinated or hypnotised

57 a symbolic offering made to a god

58 a series of people coming after each other.

59 underwater

60 observing an important event

61 confused

THE DIGGERS

EXERCISE 5

READING TEST 8

Weary Willie, the wombat king,
Said he was champion excavator;
But the Bristler said "You ain't no such thing;
You couldn't dig up a new pertater!"
So a match was made on their mining skill –
Bristling Billy and Weary Will.

Both of the creatures were stout as steel,
With knife-like claws that could dig for ever.
The wombat dug with greater zeal,
But he hadn't the style or the action clever
Of Bristling Billy, who looked a winner
Till he struck some ants, and he stopped for dinner.

Down where the ants hid their young
Underground in a secret tunnel,
Scooping them up with his sticky tongue
Into his mouth that was like a funnel:
"Why should I dig for your wagers scanty,"
Said he, "When I'm feeling so full and ant-y?"

A kangaroo who had lost his cash
Was wild at this most absurd come-uppance.
"Now listen you poor ant-eating trash,
I'd give you a kick in the ribs for twopence!"
"Well, when I'm finished with this here diet,"
Said Bristling Billy, "You come and try it."

Bristling Billy the porcupine,
A person that nobody likes,
Wanders away on his lonely line,
Rattles his fearful spikes.
Says he, "There's none of you long-haired squibs
Is game to give me a kick in the ribs."

Choose the best answer to the following:

62 The match was to determine
- **A** who was the stronger.
- **B** who was the king of the wombats.
- **C** who had the sharper claws.
- **D** who was the better digger.

63 Why did Bristling Billy stop?
- **A** He found some ants.
- **B** His tongue was sticky.
- **C** The wombat had greater zeal.
- **D** The wombat had claws of steel.

64 What were the 'wagers' involved?
- **A** The twopence that the kangaroo lost.
- **B** The right to be king of the diggers.
- **C** A kind of potato.
- **D** Bets made between other animals.

65 Why was the Kangaroo upset?
- **A** He felt 'antsy'.
- **B** He had bet on the porcupine.
- **C** Someone should have told him not to worry.
- **D** You can't please everyone.

66 Why wasn't anyone game to kick Billy?
- **A** His body spikes were formidable.
- **B** They didn't have the courage.
- **C** Nobody expected him to win.
- **D** They all had long hair.

67 Wombat was the most keen to win but what did he lack that Bristling Billy had?
- **A** A better digging style.
- **B** A better digging action.
- **C** Both A and C.
- **D** None of the above

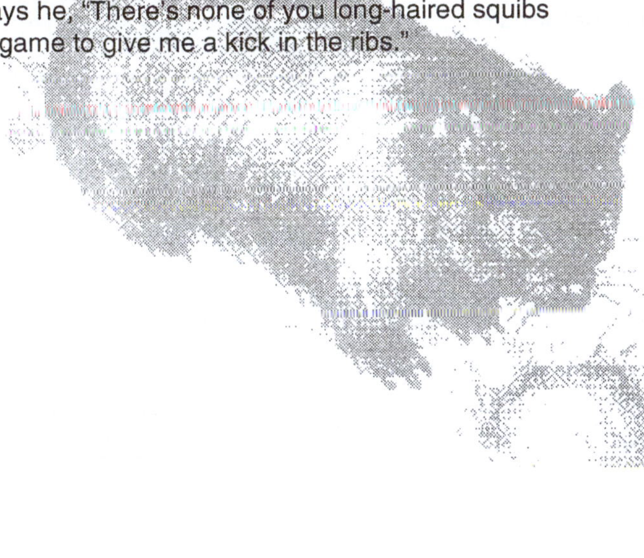

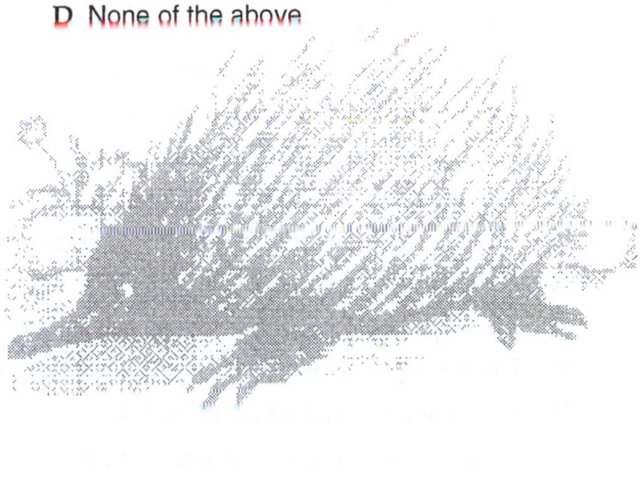

REVISION READING TEST - Part B

The words asked for in this test have all been used in the comprehension exercises in Part B of this book. How many of them can you recall? Choices for the first exercise are given in the box.

Definitions.

1	____________	respect and allegiance to a ruler
2	____________	large round or oval building without a roof
3	____________	kind of wooden flooring with many small pieces
4	____________	something remaining from the past when the rest has decayed
5	____________	high ranking class of people
6	____________	light volcanic rock
7	____________	kind of Asian temple
8	____________	very strange
9	____________	showed deep sorrow
10	____________	thrown away
11	____________	belonging to the cat family
12	____________	day living, as opposed to nocturnal
13	____________	air-filled, as in tyres
14	____________	wooden frame for carrying a coffin
15	____________	somebody seeking safety in a foreign country

Choices
pagoda diurnal refugee
mourned parquetry bier
homage pneumatic jettisoned
amphitheatre nobility pumice
bizarre feline relic

Choose which word *best* defines each of the following

16 **effigy** : statue, plant, role, masonry. ____________
17 **abode** : menacing, vault, alternative, dwelling. ____________
18 **restored** : made, imagined, assembled, refurbished. ____________
19 **indigenous** : feral, barren, native, fragile. ____________
20 **elusive** : secretive, co-operative, intelligent, simple. ____________
21 **extravagant** : thrifty, wasteful, cautious, kind. ____________
22 **ritual** : ceremony, belief, culture, signal. ____________
23 **quest** : search, hope, disappointment, story. ____________
24 **whim** : goal, certainty, fancy, temple. ____________
25 **persecution** : embarrassment, harassment, envy, indifference. ____________

Can you remember the word that fits each of these definitions?

26 Having very high and steep cliffs. p____________
27 A room or apartment where an artist works. s____________
28 A rolled up parchment or paper document. s____________
29 A series of wars carried out by a king or a general. c____________
30 The sinking of land due to added weight or perhaps too much water. s____________
31 The area where gladiators fought. a____________
32 Striving for superiority with somebody for something. a____________
33 Destroyed by chemical action, as in rusting. c____________
34 An animal not indigenous to an area is said to be this. f____________
35 Drawn or designed by scratching on a hard surface. e____________
36 Completely absorbed as if hynotised. m____________
37 Completely confused and unable to think clearly. b____________
38 To risk money on the outcome of a game or event. w____________

ANSWERS. Part A

Reading Test 1

Exercise 1 Large Paintings and Larger Artists Page 2 1 B 2 D 3 D 4 B 5 A 6 B 7 C
2 Large Holes from Small Diggers Page 3 8 B 9 C 10 D 11 B 12 B 13 D
3 Glacier Page 4 14 B 15 D 16 B 17 B 18 B 19 A 20 D 21 C
4 Grizzly Page 5 22 D 23 D 24 A 25 D 26 B 27 B 28 A
5 Big Isn't Necessarily Better Page 6 29 B 30 B 31 A 32 D 33 B 34 A 35 B 36 C 37 D 38 A 39 B
6 The Wind in a Frolic Page 7 40 A 41 C 42 D 43 B 44 C
7 Plan Ahead Page 8 45 D 46 D 47 C 48 A 49 C 50 A

Reading Test 2

Exercise 1 Pandora's Box Page 9 1 B 2 D 3 D 4 C 5 D
2 Buying a House Page 10 6 C 7 B 8 A 9 B 10 C 11 D
3 Old Shellover Page 10 12 D 13 D 14 A
4 The Climate of Mt Isa Page 11 15 C 16 C 17 A 18 B 19 C
5 Tractor Page 11 20 B 21 D 22 C
6 The Rifle Bird Page 12 23 C 24 C 25 A
7 Believe It Or Not – The Nose Page12 26 C 27 D 28 D
8 Murder most Foul Page 13 29 C 30 D 31 A 32 C 33 D 34 B 35 B
9 Land Grant 1 Page 14 36 C 37 D 38 B 39 D 40 B 41 B 42 C 44 A
10 Believe It Or Not - The Tongue Page15 45 A 46 D
11 Temperature Page 16 47 B 48 C 49 D 50 D

Reading Test 3

Exercise 1 Norfolk Island Page 17 1 A 2 C 3 A 4 B 5 C 6 A 7 D
2 William James Farrer Page 18 8 A 9 C 10 D 11 C 12 B 13 A 14 D 15 D
3 The Bandicoot Page19 16 B, E, and F
4 My Country Page 20 17 A 18 B 19 D 20 D 21 A 22 B 23 D
5 Storms of Fury Page 21 24 A 25 B 26 B 27 C
6 Pinchgut Page 22 28 A 29 C 30 A 31 C 32 C 33 A 34 B
7 Coat of Arms Page 23 35 A 36 B 37 A
8 The Gulf Stream Page 24 38 C 39 D 40 B 41 D 42 B 43 B
9 The Gopher or Ground Squirrel Page 25 44 A 45 B 46 C 47 D 48 A 49 D 50 A

Reading Test 4

Exercise 1 Chicken, Alaska Page 26 1 A 2 B 3 B 4 D 5 B 6 C 7 C
2 Quicksand Page 27 8 B 9 C 10 B 11 D
3 Rainfall in Australia Page 28 12 A 13 C 14 D 15 B 16 A 17 B
4 The Rime of the Ancient Mariner Page 29 18 C 19 A 20 B 21 D 22 B
5 Waratah Page 30 23 B 24 A 25 D 26 B 27 D 28 C 29 B 30 A
6 Wind Mining Page 31 31 D 32 B 33 C 34 D
7 The Sinking of the Quetta Page 32 35 D 36 D 37 B 38 C 39 D 40 D 41 C 42 A
43 a pinnacle B allegations C impending D orderly (fashion)
8 The Golden Apples of the Hesperides Page 34 44 B 45 C 46 A 47 C 48 B 49 A 50 D

Reading Test 5

Exercise 1 Ready, Aim Fire! Page 35 1 B 2 D 3 C 4 C 5 A
2 James Bond 007 Page 36 6 B 7 D 8 B 9 A 10 B 11 D 12 D
3 Believe It Or Not – Saliva Page 37 13 C 14 D 15 C 16 D 17 B
4 Ash Wednesday Page 38 18 B 19 B 20 D 21B 22 D 23 A 24 B 25 C 26 B
5 The Gods Must Be Angry Page 39 27 B 28 B 29 C

6 **The Teams Page 40** 30 C 31 B 32 B 33 D 34 D 35 A 36 A 37 C 38 B 39 D 40 B
7 **The Boll Weevil Page 41** 41 B 42 D 43 C
8 **Danger Lurks Page 42** 44 B 45 C 46 B 47 A 48 A 49 D 50 B

Reading Test 6
Exercise 1 The Lava Tubes of Undara Page 43 1 B 2 D 3 B 4 D 5 B
2 **The Wreck of the Sirius Page 44** 6 B 7 C 8 C 9 B 10 D
3 **Home Baked Bread Page 45** 11 D 12 D 13 B 14 B 15 C
4 **Matthew Flinders Page 46** 16 C 17 B 18 A 19 C 20 A 21 C 22 D 23 A
5 **Believe It Or Not - Muscles Page 47** 24 A 25 A 26 C
6 **Hot Air Page 48** 27 D 28 D 29 A 30 C 31D 32 B 33 C
7 **The Hammock Page 49** 34 D 35 B 36 C 37 A
8 **Bombaderry Creek Page 50** 38 A 39 B 40 B 41 D 42 A 43 C 44 B 45 D
9 **Andy's Gone With Cattle Page 51** 46 B 47 B 48 D 49 C 50 D

Reading Test 7
Exercise 1 Bloody Bridge Page 52 1 C 2 C 3 C 4 D 5 C 6 A 7 A 8 C
2 **Peculiar Pikas Page 53** 8 D 9 C 10 D 11 A 12 C 13 C 14 B
3 **H.M.S. Bellerophon Page 54** 15 D 16 A 17 B 18 D 19 C 20 C 21 B
4 **Floating and Painful Page 55** 22 B 23 D 24 D 25 A 26 B
5 **Lighthouses Page 56** 27 D 28 B 29 B 30 C 31 C 32 B 33 A a flurry of construction
33 B Hardly a reliable guide 34 B
6 **Andy's Return Page 57** 35 D 36 B 37 B 38 C
7 **Department Directory Page 58** 39 A 40 B 41 C 42 D 43 A 44 D 45 A
8 **Coral Page 59** 46 B 47 A 48 D 49 B 50 C

REVISION VOCABULARY TEST

1 moraine 2 plight 3 mitigate 4 pristine 5 oblivious
6 presumptuous 7 inference 8 vermin 9 dissipate 10 unkempt
11 journal 12 meticulous 13 reclusive 14 shortened 15 appropriate
16 unyielding 17 myth 18 robust 19 imminent 20 infamous 21 chew
22 renew 23 earlier 24 surroundings 25 moisture 26 susceptible 27 cultivable 28 unused
29 fierce 30 detachment

RESULTS

Reading Test 1 Score

Reading Test 2 Score

Reading Test 3 Score

Reading Test 4 Score

Reading Test 5 Score

Reading Test 6 Score

Reading Test 7 Score

Vocabulary Revision Score ________

TOTAL **Out of 380**

ANSWERS - PART B

Reading Test 1

Exercise 1 The Great Wall of China Page 62 1 C 2 A 3 C 4 A 5 D 6 D 7 C 8 B 9 D 10 B 11 B 12 C 13 bastion 14 hero 15 peasant 16 cauldron 17 ramp 18 numb

2 Mysterious Moai Page 64 19 C 20 B 21 D 22 B 23 B 24 A 25 D 26 A 27 T 28 F 29 T 30 F 31 F 32 T 33 T 34 T 35 F 36 F 37 T 38 F 39 F 41 missionaries 42 sad or sorry 42 warfare 43 excess 44 diseases 45 domination 46 advanced 47 immune 48 archaeologist 49 vacantly 50 pedestal

Reading Test 2

Exercise 1 The World's Greatest Explosion Page 67 1 B 2 A 3 C 4 D 5 A 6 B 7 A 8 B 9 C 10 C 11 B 12 caldera 13 ejected 14 pumice 15 inclination 16 submarine 17 anak 18 shelter 19 nauseated 20 cone 21 colonise

2 Mulu National Park Page 69 22 C 23 B 24 D 25 D 26 C 27 C 28 A

3 The Stone jumpers of Nias Page 71 29 As a preparation for headhunting forays on other villages. 30 Only a small part was unpaved and the jumper had to twist as he jumped then land in a small square of soft earth. 31 In front of the King's house. 32 Two in eighteen months. 33 Bamboo spikes were placed on top of the stone pyramid. 34 B 35 D 36 A 37 B 38 C 39 B 40 D 41 relentless 42 veritable 43 basking 44 etched 45 culminating in 46 aspiring 47 unifying 48 hazardous

4 Captain Arthur Phillip And The Birds Page 73 49 C 50 B

Reading Test 3

Exercise 1 The Ruined Temple of Ta Prohm Page 74 1 B 2 B 3 A 4 D 5 B 6 A 7 C 8 A 9 A 10 D

2 The World's Largest Stone Building Page 76 11 C 12 D 13 D 14 A 15 C 16 B 17 B 18 A 19 D 20 B 21 B 22 C 23 emanating (from) 24 abode 25 homage 26 demons 27 gallery 28 vandals

3 The Colosseum Page 78 29 T 30 T 31 T 32 F 33 T 34 F 35 T 36 F 37 F 38 T 39 T 40 F 41 T 42 F 43 T 44 exterminated 45 arena 46 pamphlet 47 canopy 48 audience 49 fashionable 50 amphitheatre

Reading Test 4

Exercise 1 Flying Stone Geese Page 81 1 D 2 C 3 D 4 C 5 A 6 D 7 A 8 D 9 B 10 C 11 scriptures 12 focus 13 plinth 14 intricate 15 enshrine 16 relics

2 Interment in Toraja Page 83 17 D 18 D 19 A 20 D 21 C 22 A 23 B 24 C 25 D 26 B 27 A 28 D 29 effigy 30 extravagant 31 bier 32 vie (with)

3 The Leaning Tower of Pisa Page 86 33 C 34 B 35 B 36 D 37 C 38 C 39 D 40 D 41 C 42 D 43 B 44 B 45 A and E 46 stabilise 47 perpendicular 48 subsidence 49 foundations 50 persecution

Reading Test 5

Exercise 1 The Dragons of Komodo Page 89 1 D 2 D 3 C 4 A 5 T 6 T 7 F 8 F 9 T 10 T 11 F 12 T 13 F 14 F 15 F 16 F 17 T 18 T 19 F 20 F

2 Another Opera House Page 91 21 D 22 B 23 C 24 B 25 D 26 B 27 gilded 28 mosaic 29 chandelier 30 upholstery 31 depicting 32 restored

3 The Taj Mahal Page 93 33 C 34 D 35 D 36 A 37 B 38 D 39 B 40 A 41 C 42 F 43 F 44 T 45 F 46 T 47 mourned 48 fanatical 49 campaign 50 mausoleum.

Reading Test 6

Exercise 1 Lost City of the Incas Page 95 1 D 2 B 3 A 4 C 5 B 6 D 7 F 8 F 9 T 10 F 11 T 12 T 13 F 14 T 15 T 16 F 17 T

2 The Cat Museum Page 98 18 F 19 T 20 T 21 T 22 F 23 T 24 F 25 F 26 F 27 T 28 T 29 T 30 A 31 B 32 D 33 A 34 B 35 D 36 bizarre 37 memorabilia 38 kinked 39 feline

3 The Plain of Jars Page 101 40 D 41 C 42 D 43 B 44 D 45 C 46 B 47 A 48 A 49 jettisoned 50 sarcophagi

Reading Test 7

Exercise 1 The Beehives of the Bungle Bungles Page 103 1 B 2 B 3 C 4 D 5 C 6 B 7 A

2 Ship From Thames Page 103 8 C 9 C 10 A 11 B

3 The Statue of Liberty Page 106 12 B 13 C 14 A 15 A 16 B 17 D

4 Iquitos: A Town With Character Page 108 18 C 19 D 20 B 21 C 22 D 23 D 24 D 25 B 26 C 27 D 28 A 29 A 30 gargoyle 31 humid 32 affluence 33 magnate

5 Dead Horse Trail Page 110 34 B 35 B 36 B 37 C 38 B 39 duel 40 quaint 41 ironic 42 goldrush 43 vigilante

6 Old Man Platypus Page 112 44 elusive 45 exclusive 46 toil 47 rank 48 D 49 C 50 B

Reading Test 8

Exercise 1 The Iguacu Falls Page 113 1D 2 D 3 B 4 D 5 A 6 T 7 T 8 F 9 maelstrom 10 wallow

2 Uluru and Kata Tjuta Page115 11D 12 A 13 B 14 D 15 A 16 A 17 D 18 D 19 T 20 F 21 F 22 F 23 T 24 F 25 T 26 F 27 F 28 T

3 The Stone Forest of Lunan Page 118 29 A 30 D 31 B 32 C 33 C 34C 35 B 36 D 37 appeal 38 ethnic 39 unique 40 pinnacle

4 "Horas!" from Samosir Page 120 41 C 42 C 43 A 44 B 45 D 46 C 47 C 48 B 49 B 50 A 51 A 52 D 53 D 54 sarcophagus 55 dwindling 56 mesmerised 57 sacrificial 58 procession 59 submarine 60 witnessing 61 bewildered

5 The Diggers Page 123 62 D 63 A 64 D 65 B 66 A 67 C

Revision Vocabulary Test Part B Page 123

1 homage 2 amphitheatre 3 parquetry 4 relic 5 nobility 6 pumice 7 pagoda 8 bizarre 9 mourned 10 jettisoned 11 feline 12 diurnal 13 pneumatic 14 bier 15 refugee 16 statue 17 dwelling 18 refurbished 19 native 20 secretive 21 wasteful 22 ceremony 23 search 24 fancy 25 harassment 26 precipitous 27 studio 28 scroll 29 campaign 30 subsidence 31 arena 32 aspiring 33 corroded 34 feral 35 etched 36 mesmerised 37 bewildered 38 wager

RESULTS - Part B

Reading Test 1	Score
Reading Test 2	Score
Reading Test 3	Score
Reading Test 4	Score
Reading Test 5	Score
Reading Test 6	Score
Reading Test 7	Score
Vocabulary Revision	Score ________

TOTAL **Out of 455**